I0772320

COLLECTED PAPERS ON SOUTH ASIA

INDIAN RELIGION

CENTRE OF SOUTH ASIAN STUDIES
SCHOOL OF ORIENTAL AND AFRICAN STUDIES
UNIVERSITY OF LONDON

COLLECTED PAPERS ON SOUTH ASIA

1. RULE, PROTEST, IDENTITY: Aspects of Modern South Asia
Edited by Peter Robb and David Taylor

2. POLITICAL IDENTITY IN SOUTH ASIA
Edited by David Taylor and Malcolm Yapp

3. THE CITY IN SOUTH ASIA
Edited by Kenneth Ballhatchet and John Harrison

4. BUDDHIST STUDIES
Edited by Philip Denwood and Alexander Piatigorsky

5. RURAL SOUTH ASIA
Edited by Peter Robb

6. RURAL INDIA
Edited by Peter Robb

7. INDIAN RELIGION
Edited by Richard Burghart and Andrey Cantlie
(co-published with St. Martin's Press, New York)

BL
2003
I53
1985

IRVINE VALLEY COLLEGE LIBRARY
[redacted]

16055

COLLECTED PAPERS ON SOUTH ASIA NO. 7

DISCARD

INDIAN RELIGION

Edited by
RICHARD BURGHART and AUDREY CANTLIE

CURZON PRESS: *London*
ST. MARTIN'S PRESS: *New York*

First published 1985 in the United Kingdom by
Curzon Press Ltd., 42 Gray's Inn Road, London WC1
ISBN 0 7007 0168 0

First published 1985 in the United States of America by
St. Martin's Press Inc., 175 Fifth Avenue, New York, NY 10010
ISBN 0 312 41400 5

All rights reserved

© Centre of South Asian Studies, SOAS, 1985

Library of Congress Cataloging in Publication Data

Main entry under title:

Indian Religion.
Includes bibliographies.
1. India — Religious life and customs — Addresses, essays, lectures. I. Burghart, Richard. II. Cantlie, Audrey.
BL2003.153 1985 306'.6'0954 84-15115
ISBN 0-312-41400-5

Printed in Hungary

CONTENTS

Contributors

Editors' Preface

1 *Introduction: theoretical approaches in the anthropology of South Asia*
RICHARD BURGHART

2 *The Concept of Nirvana in Village Buddhism*
MARTIN SOUTHWOLD

3 *The Aghori Ascetics of Benares*
JONATHAN P. PARRY

4 *The Indian Renouncer: structure and transformation in a Lingayat community*
N. J. BRADFORD

5 *Initiation and Consecration: priestly rituals in a South Indian temple*
C. J. FULLER

6 *Vaishnava Reform Sects in Assam*
AUDREY CANTLIE

7 *Lordship and Caste in Hindu Discourse*
RONALD INDEN

8 *Paradigms of Body Symbolism: an analysis of selected themes in Hindu culture*
VEENA DAS

9 *Some Phenomenological Obsevations on the Study of Indian Religion*
A. PIATIGORSKY

CONTRIBUTORS

N. J. BRADFORD
Lecturer in Sociology, University of Aberdeen

RICHARD BURGHART
Lecturer in Asian Anthropology, School of Oriental and African Studies, University of London

AUDREY CANTLIE
Lecturer in Sociology, School of Oriental and African Studies, University of London

VEENA DAS
Lecturer in Sociology, University of Delhi

C. J. FULLER
Lecturer in Anthropology, London School of Economics and Political Science, University of London

RONALD INDEN
Associate Professor of History, University of Chicago

JONATHAN P. PARRY
Lecturer in Anthropology, London School of Economics and Political Science, University of London

A. PIATIGORSKY
Lecturer in the Ancient History of South Asia, School of Oriental and African Studies, University of London

MARTIN SOUTHWOLD
Lecturer in Social Anthropology, University of Manchester

EDITORS' PREFACE

This book is an essay in self-awareness: its purpose is to assist social anthropologists working in the field of South Asian studies to know what they are about. The idea of the project was conceived when a group of social anthropologists engaged on conceptual problems in South Asia decided to collaborate with Alexander Piatigorsky, a philosopher and indologist, in a work designed to serve as a practical demonstration of the interdependence of anthropological and indological studies. The contribution of the anthropologists was to consist of individual papers on their current research; on these Dr. Piatigorsky was to provide a commentary. The specific task of the commentator was to relate ancient knowledge to contemporary field material by placing the contributions in a different and more general context in which their assumptions and conceptual apparatus would be made explicit. All the contributions in one way or other relate to religion: hence the title of the volume. Although there are a number of religious traditions in South Asia, the title assumes that Vedic Brahmanism, Buddhism, Jainism and Hinduism, together with the various traditions that developed within them, are not only historically but also conceptually related so that it is possible to identify the specific characteristics of Indian religions taken as a whole. (Islam does not find a place here because although Islam, like Christianity, has millions of adherents in the subcontinent where it has taken on a local colour, it is to be understood as a religion of South Asia rather than a specifically Indian religion.)[1]

The major problem, in our view, of a Western anthropologist—and perhaps also of a South Asian anthropologist—engaged in the study of Indian religion is to find an apposite explanatory framework through which to filter his field material. The anthropological experience itself does not constitute, except in an indirect way, the content of anthropological communication. The experiences of the individual become available to him as thoughts: a thought is thus the prototypical symbol in that it represents the thing thought of but is not it. The original experience, until transformed into a thought, i.e. into material capable of being consciously known, is unavailable to the individual for purposes of communication even with himself, and *a fortiori* to anyone else. What the individual thinks his experience to be is, however, in some degree communicable, chiefly through language, symbols and other concepts in which thoughts are organized into various configurations. As these are generally specific to a given culture, it has been questioned whether many of the concepts which we take for granted in our everyday life can be universalized and assumed for other cultures. There are, for example, no specifically Indian terms which seem to correspond to our notions of 'hierarchy', 'equality', 'religion', 'god', 'monotheism', 'polytheism', 'individual', 'myth', 'sacrifice', 'faith', or 'belief'. The question, 'Do you believe in Vishnu?', makes no sense in the Indian context: it cannot be put. Conversely, there are no English equivalents of *dharma*, *ṛta*, *karma*, *bhakti*, *yajña*, *ātma*, *puruṣa*, *nirvāṇa*, *guru*, *dān*, *dakṣiṇa* and so forth. Further, the distinctions, as we conceive them, between subjective and objective and between mind and matter are differently construed in Indian thought. The problem, therefore, of analysing Indian religions is not simply a matter of translating specific alien concepts, but of comprehending the matrix of which these concepts are a highly selected expression.

Some anthropologists, of course, are more open than others to the education of living among peoples of a different culture which, in its catalytic effect, constitutes the unique anthropological experience, enabling the participant both to think new thoughts and—a point often made—to attain a conscious knowledge of his own cultural models by comparison with what they are not. In his paper on the meaning of *nirvāṇa* among Sinhalese villagers Southwold tells us that his foreknowledge of Buddhism proved a handicap in understanding his material in the field, the significance of which he first dismissed by assimilating it to the categories he had brought with him: later he attempted to understand the meaning of the concept in his own way, searching for parallels in his experience by which he could find his way to understanding his informants. The capacity for re-education is, however, limited. The method associated with the anthropologist in the field is that of participant-observation. Of this probably about ten per cent is participation and some ninety per cent observation. Most anthropological work is necessarily done from the standpoint of the outside observer and the data communicated through models, occasionally through native models in those cases where the religious tradition has developed its own theories by becoming aware of itself as an object, but more often through meta-models external to the culture described. Parry, for example, in analysing the practices of the Aghoris, uses an explanatory framework which he takes from Eliade and not from the religious philosophy of the Aghoris. In other words, the anthropologist does not talk his data, he only talks about it and sometimes he alone realizes how radical is the transformation. The loss in fidelity, however, is to be set against the fact that it is only when viewed as an object, whether from within or outside the culture, that a religious tradition passes from the unreflecting state of subjective experience to be represented, at least in some of its aspects, in describable form. It is precisely the inability of the outside observer to participate, except in a very limited way, in the religious situation he is studying that makes it for him an object of thought which, although it ceases thereby to be what it is, is refracted through the language and models of another culture to emerge as material capable of being known.

As the anthropologist of necessity communicates his raw material through the language and cultural categories of his own society, the success of his effort at communication depends on understanding not only the categories of his informants but also the nature of his own categories in order to establish a bridge between the two. The specific contribution of this volume is that the concepts used by individual anthropologists in their analysis are made explicit from a phenomenological point of view and discussed in relation to Indian concepts as these emerge from an indological study of textual material. The introduction by Richard Burghart provides an outline of the successive theoretical approaches that have guided social anthropology in South Asia since its inception and assesses both the current direction of interests and the wider indological problems which these involve. There are seven ethnographic papers. The first of these, by Martin Southwold, explores the problem of how Nirvana is understood by village Buddhists. There follow two papers related to asceticism. Parry presents his dramatic material on the Aghori ascetics of Benares, and Bradford analyses the reasons for the rising influence of the ascetic *guru* as compared with the hereditary *guru* among contemporary Lingayats. Two further papers are concerned in different ways with tradition. Fuller discusses the gap between written text and current practice in the initiation ritual of the temple priests in the Minakshi Temple at Madurai, and Cantlie outlines the emergence of 'reform' movements in the Vaishnava religious tradition of Assam. The last two papers relate specifically to categorization and symbolism: Inden's to the category of lordship and Das's to the symbolism of the body. We hope that each of the papers will command interest in its own right. The intention of the commentary is to set the anthropological data of the papers together with the anthropological analysis of the data within the wider perspective of a phenomenological approach to Indian religion. Whether we have succeeded in our endeavour must be left to the judgment of the reader.

NOTE

1 The term 'South Asia' has come into use to fill the vacuum caused by the partition of India into two and eventually, with Bangladesh, into three political territories and indicates a cultural field embracing the Indian sub-continent including Nepal together with the neighbouring island of Sri Lanka. Anthropologists working in this field are no longer styled 'Indianist' but 'South Asianist'. The term 'Indian' is used here, not in its political sense as relating to the state of India, but in its cultural sense as denoting an institution which has its roots and development in Indian soil and is specifically 'Indian' in character. As such, the institution of caste in Pakistan and Sri Lanka is 'Indian', while Islam and Christianity, although present in India, are not.

INTRODUCTION: THEORETICAL APPROACHES IN THE ANTHROPOLOGY OF SOUTH ASIA

Richard Burghart

The contributions to this volume on Indian religion illustrate a variety of theoretical approaches, ranging in sources from early Buddhist texts to recent field observations and comprising a number of topics pertaining to both caste and sect as well as groups such as the Lingayats whose religious life seems to confound these very categories. The purpose of this brief methodological introduction is not to summarize the content of these individual contributions but to clarify our understanding of the theoretical context in which their content is fixed. One way of coming to understand this context is to use the past as a source of variation in the relation between the theoretical postulates of anthropology and our object of study in South Asia. The purpose of this introduction, therefore, is not to narrate the continuities of influence within an academic discipline but rather to use the past in order to understand the present significance which field-workers attach to Indian religion.

The interest shown by social anthropologists in the complex civilizations of South Asia is relatively recent. Throughout the late eighteenth and nineteenth centuries both missionary societies as well as Company (and later Imperial) administration provided an institutional context in which research was carried out on Indian civilization. This research was not necessarily disinterested in aim: caste surveys were conducted with a view to the administration of the realm and Sanskrit studies were financed, in part, to facilitate the conversion of Hindus by translating the sacred texts of Christianity into the language of Brahmans (Monier-Williams 1899: ix). Yet such research, in spite of its ephemeral motivation, was of lasting scholarly value and found its way into western sociological theory through the writings of Maine, Marx, Durkheim, and Weber. Given the importance of this research for sociologists, it is interesting to note that the social anthropology of

South Asia emerged outside this area of interest. Instead of investigating Indian civilization, the early field-working anthropologists, such as Rivers, Seligman, and Radcliffe-Brown, travelled to remote regions of British India where they carried out research on the so-called 'primitive' peoples of the subcontinent.[1]

One reason for the lack of social anthropological interest in the complex civilizations of South Asia lay with the fact that the founders of the discipline envisaged anthropology to be a natural science of society. Social anthropology, of course, was not an experimental science; nevertheless the founders tried to approximate anthropology to the experimental sciences by transforming the field situation into a laboratory in which the natural laws of society might be discovered.[2] Their field laboratory was too unwieldy to allow the artificial production of observable natural data, but the early ethnographers did attempt to control their observations of social behaviour by applying certain methods of the natural sciences to their field work. Rivers (1908: 65) devised his genealogical method on Murray Island in the Torres Straits in order to test and control for 'real parentage' as a factor in his experiments on perception. It was only some weeks later on Mabuiag and Badu Islands that he realized the sociological significance of his method, and he began to collect data on both real and putative parentage. Upon his return from the Torres Straits Rivers perfected the genealogical method as a means of delineating the social organization of a people with 'low culture' and subsequently demonstrated its usefulness among the Todas (1906: 461–71). Malinowski's (1922: 7–8) use of the method of participant-observation, in which the ethnographer lived among the people rather than at the administrative centre, was seen as a means of controlling for the ethnographer's presence as a laboratory condition. It was thought that after living among a people for a certain period, the ethnographer would cease to be a disturbing element in the society at which time the natives would revert to their normal social intercourse. From that time onward the ethnographer could assume that his field observations comprised naturally occurring phenomena. Another means of controlling the production of data in the anthropological laboratory lay in the choice of field site. The experimental scientist simplifies the production of natural data in his experiment in order to test only one variable factor at a time. The early ethnographers were unable to produce natural behavioural data under artificial conditions, but they thought that they could control the number of variable factors by concentrating their research on isolated primitive peoples. 'Simple' or 'elementary' societies were thought to be the historical, genetic, or logical basis of 'complex' societies and hence among preliterate peoples possessing only a rudimentary technology and living in isolated, self-contained communities (the early social anthropologists had a predeliction for islands) the natural laws of society would be more readily observable and discoverable. In this regard research in British India was no exception. The early field-workers avoided the complex historical civilizations of South Asia in which lived at that time three hundred million Hindu, Muslim, Buddhist, Christian, Jain, Parsi, and Jewish people comprising roughly 97 per cent of the total population of the subcontinent (*Census of India*, 1911: 1; 1; 141). Instead, Rivers (1906: 473) in the first decade of this century carried out field-work among the Todas (total population 905) who lived atop the Nilgiri plateau, Radcliffe-Brown (1922: 16) studied the Andamanese (total population 625) who were isolated on Great Andaman Island, and Seligman (1922: vii, 35) in his search for the 'pure' hunting and gathering Veddas of the jungles of Ceylon (not the accessible coastal and village Veddas who had been 'degenerated' by Tamil fishermen and Sinhalese cultivators) found only four families and heard of two more.

The theoretical work of these early ethnographers has been neglected for some time, but their research methods were perpetuated within the discipline when social anthropological interest shifted in the 1940s from the tribal peoples of British India to the Hindu, Muslim, and Buddhist peoples.[3] Radcliffe-Brown's (1940: 5) 'convenient locality of a suitable size' in which a universe of social relations might be perceived in synchronic terms became the 'village study' of social anthropology in the 1940s and 1950s.[4] The Indian village was thought to be a community differentiated according to caste, stratified by unequal access to productive resources, and internally divided by factions, yet it was still a solidary unit whose form was thought to have remained unchanged over the centuries. Even though these field-workers believed (as their predecessors in tribal India and Melanesia had believed before them) that this pristine traditional way of life had recently been engulfed (Srinivas 1960: 20–21) or was about to be engulfed (Gough 1955: 51) by the politico-economic forces of the outside world, nonetheless for the present the village could be thought of theoretically as a system, as an island in an ocean of similar islands which was so vast that the solitary ethnographer could never encompass the entire society from within his own village in the manner of the early field-workers, such as Rivers whose genealogical records included the personal name of nearly every Toda, living as well as remembered dead. Nonetheless village India was in some sense *the* India. In 1950 there were 560,000 villages in India (Srinivas 1960: 19) in which roughly 80 per cent of the population derived its livelihood (*Census of India 1951*: 1(II–C), 2, 26). Hence field-workers no longer sought a laboratory in which the conditions were simple; instead they sought a laboratory which was representative of the other potential laboratories. Social anthropologists turned from the 'simple society' to the 'typical village'; and once the typicality of the data became apparent (the '*jajmani* system', the 'dominant caste', etc.), anthropologists began to entertain the possibility of considering variations in the data between villages in an experimental mode (Mayer 1960: xiii).[5]

Throughout the 1950s village India was the object of field investigations in the course of which empirical generalizations were refined and regional variations demonstrated. In the course of these investigations, however, a few social anthropologists began to question whether the totality of social relations in South Asian society could be adequately described by means of a synchronic account of village social behaviour. These particular critics of the village study approach did not seek to controvert the idea that villages exist as a unit of study, but instead called into question the adequacy of such studies as comments on the universe of social relations in Hindu society. Criticism focused especially on the fact that the village did not comprise a bounded universe of social relations. Recognition of this problem emerged in the course of village-based studies on the caste and kin relationships which linked the villages of a region (Mayer 1960). Such regional networks of social relations, however, did not necessarily exhaust the universe of meaning of its inhabitants; instead an encompassing presence was seen to lie rather amorphously in the great tradition which transcended the little traditions of village society. The great tradition was conceived in a unitary manner, identified with Sanskritic beliefs and practices, and located in the centres of South Asian civilizations. The little traditions were various, identified with rural beliefs and practices, and located in village society. Civilization in South Asia was a process whereby great traditional beliefs and practices were parochialized in the formation of little traditions and the little traditional beliefs and practices were universalized in the formation of the great tradition. This process could be observed at the village level in certain rituals and religious festivals. The bounded Hindu universe became something called civilization; the village was now reduced to a 'half-world' (Marriott 1955).[6]

Although some social anthropologists began to turn to Indian civilization as their object of study, their necessarily local field base and the agreement that behavioural observations constitute the data of social anthropology served to confine the investigator to his village. The ethnographic programme of the 1960s became increasingly constrained by the research methods and assumptions which had been established by the founders of social anthropology among the tribal peoples of the subcontinent at the turn of the century and subsequently developed in the 1930s by anthropologists working in Africa and Melanesia. This research programme, which had guided field investigations in village India, began to change, however, with anthropological recourse to indological and historical materials.

Recourse to indological materials in the anthropological investigation of Indian civilization was advocated from the late 1950s by Dumont. For Dumont the Brahmanical model of society compiled in written form two millenia ago and the ethnographic data on village India collected in the 1940s and 1950s reveal the presence at the ideological level of the value of purity which transcends the regional and historical differences of Indian civilization. It is at this ideological level that caste appears as a system whose form is governed by the oppositional structure of purity/impurity. For Dumont, the caste system is the most fundamental and most specifically Hindu institution of Hindu society. This fundamentality is evident in the way in which the value of ritual purity encompasses the value of politico-economic power. By virtue of this encompassment Dumont was led to consider the institution of caste rather than the locality of the 'typical village' as the universe of social relations in South Asia. In controverting the village as the valid unit of study, Dumont and Pocock (1957:25 et seq.) postulated the 'sociological reality' of Indian civilization. Moreover, in opposition to those who theorized that Indian civilization was constituted of two strands—a great tradition and a little tradition—Dumont (1957b: 40) claimed instead that there was a unity of Indian civilization—that Indian villagers had 'not two traditions but simply one which is their life'. Because of Dumont's theory of the oppositional structure of caste and because of his intellectual debt to Lévi-Strauss (Dumont 1957:14; 1966:59–63), Dumont's approach has often been characterized as 'structuralist'. His understanding of caste, however, entails the subordination of a concept of structure to that of system (1966:51–59), and in his commitment to the cultural context of this system Dumont appears to be more a Weberian sociologist than a Lévi-Straussian structuralist, the Weberian nature of Dumont's project becoming even more apparent with the publication of *Homo Aequalis* as the companion piece of *Homo Hierarchicus*.[7] In sum, Dumont (1957:7) urged that the anthropological investigation of Indian civilization situate itself at the confluence of sociology and indology yet it was because of Weber that the different waters mingled and became one. His theory of Hindu society was generally valid because of the unity and continuity of the values of Indian civilization. The unity and continuity of Indian civilization became at once an empirical claim as well as the theoretical assumption which made empirical generalization possible.

During the late 1960s and 1970s a somewhat different, but related trend became apparent in anthropology. Certain social anthropologists as well as anthropologically-minded historians began to combine their field observations with documentary materials in order to analyse particular aspects of village and regional social relations in terms of processes. In the light of this temporal extension of the field situation anthropologists began to call into question the adequacy of those descriptions of village social relations which had been cast in terms of a synchronic system. This synchronic system, constructed in terms of rule-conscious behaviour and couched in the fiction of the ethnographic present, had placed the anthropologist in either one of two untenable positions with respect to time. Either the system failed to account for the behaviour which did not have a customary rule-like character according to native testimony so that such behaviour appeared to be senseless from both the native's point of view as well as the ethnographer's generalized view of the system. This senseless element was often called social change, its source lay perforce outside the system, and village society was seen to be vulnerable to such external forces (Gough 1955). Or the anthropologist situated the synchronic system in a 'prehistory' of events after which certain changes occurred—often for the worse—e.g. caste duties were being neglected or the joint family was 'breaking down' (Bailey 1957).[8] Resort to documentary materials from the modern period enabled anthropologists and historians to view Hindu society as a diachronic process involving relations of inclusion and exclusion whereby a social group establishes its position and identity *vis-à-vis* other equivalent social groups. Of particular importance were those studies (Pocock 1972; Conlon 1977; Leonard 1978; etc.) which, following the programme of Dumont and Pocock, shifted their object of study from caste as a system of apparently fixed relations between entities in a locality to the study of a specific caste unit composed of local descent groups which by means of various strategies and in the context of certain rules perpetuated an idea of itself in a region.[9] In sum, the programme of Dumont and Pocock left social anthropologists with a concept of structure and of process and with the assumption of the ideological unity of Indian civilization. By virtue of this assumption the explanations of Hindu society in terms of these two concepts were thought to be generally valid.

The issues involved in the commitment of social anthropology to the goals of the natural sciences were, in part, resolved, and, in part, set aside by the end of the 1960s as culture rather than society came to be seen as the object of anthropological study and as linguistics and philosophy came to exert as pervasive an influence upon social anthropology as the experimental sciences had done fifty years earlier. Moreover, the recognition of the verbal nature of behavioural observations meant that indigenous textual material became a legitimate part of one's own field data. Although Dumont is not a culturologist in this modern sense (his value of purity, for example, is not an emic category), still his analysis of social behaviour in terms of a culturally specific value provided continuity between the followers of Dumont and recent investigators of culture. Anthropological recourse to textual material did not lead to the abandonment of field observations; rather those anthropologists who were especially interested in general theories of Hindu, Buddhist, or Islamic society shifted the locus of their fieldwork from the village to the centres of civilization in South Asia. In the last decade field research has been carried out in the pilgrimage centres, temple complexes, and political capitals of South Asia, or, if in a village, then with a specific occupational category of priests or with the local members of an ascetic sect. Examples of this trend may be readily found in both recent and current research on the subcontinent, but it would be appropriate here to limit the illustrations to the contributors to this volume. Parry has worked among the funeral priests and Aghori ascetics of Benares; Fuller with the Brahman priests at Minakshi temple in Madurai; and Burghart among the Ramanandi ascetics at their pilgrimage centre of Janakpur in the eastern Tarai of Nepal. Bradford and Cantlie have worked in villages, but have investigated sectarian movements in a village context, Bradford with the Lingayats and Cantlie with the Shankaradeva sect in Assam. Das and Inden have investigated Indian religion and politics (these terms not necessarily describing separate semantic domains), basing their research on the literature compiled by sectarian Brahmans and Buddhist monks. Only Southwold stands somewhat outside this trend yet even here his work on village Buddhism is conscious of this dimension, for in his contribution to this volume he attempts to understand village Buddhism on its own terms devoid of its external evaluation from the contemporary urban centres of Sri Lanka.

This brief methodological introduction is not a history of social anthropological research in South Asia; rather it is a purview of the relation between the assumptions of the explainable and the presence to be explained in anthropology. From the 'simple society' to the 'typical village' to the 'unity of civilization' social anthropologists have reconstituted the object of study out of their own theoretical presuppositions concerning the generalizability of their data and then imputed an empirical reality to their possibilities of knowledge. The risks which one runs in making this connection are enormous yet they are not necessarily obvious until one steps outside the confines of any one specific connection. The most recent connection, and in that sense the most significant one, concerns the assumption of the unity and continuity of Indian civilization. In spite of and in addition to the fact that

Indian civilization is the purported object of anthropological investigation, it is also an object of interpretation by those people whose communicability provides our material for study. As a topic of native discourse Indian civilization exists as an object in relation to interpreting subjects. By treating this subject-object relation as our basic generalizable assumption (rather than generalizing the object pole into our purported anthropological object of study), one may arrive at a view of society as an arena of interpretation in which certain civilizational values or patterns of social relations are thought to constitute the most fundamental value or structure of the civilization and thereby serve within the arena as an internal representation of the unity and continuity of the total arena. If the anthropologist, as an external observer, recognizes that such values or structures are representations of civilization from within the arena rather than constituting the civilization itself then one can shift the analysis from the locality or the institution as being the totality of social relations to the arena of interpretation. Having made this shift, then 'society' itself can no longer be identified with the arena but instead may be seen as a certain interpretation of events in the arena. One might surmise here that such a systematic conception of events as 'society' is especially articulated by those persons who mobilize other people for action.[10] In other words, such persons as Brahmans, ascetics, and kings were also the persons who objectified the arena and produced, quite literally, 'universes' of social relations in which they situated themselves at or near the zenith. Having objectified the arena, or part of it, as 'society', these persons construed their objectivity as divine autonomy (i.e., *their* methodological situation) and saw themselves as gods in relation to the rest of mankind. It is no coincidence, therefore, that much of the current research on South Asia has focused on the topic of religion.

By objectifying the arena, these native interpretations provide social scientists (who are also objectifiers of the arena) with a variety of ready-made schemes of the social universe. One may take such schemes as ideological statements but to take any one such scheme, in the manner of Dumont, as being the most fundamental one is to commit oneself to the assumption of the unity of the civilization at this ideological level. In this commitment one attributes to the scheme a givenness which it does not, in fact, possess. Moreover, one takes the main problem of interpretation to be the translation of concepts between cultures. If, however, one takes the scheme as being simply one scheme among various others whose ideological fundamentality does not become an anthropological assumption, then a variety of schemes may in a given context serve as a means of construing events and the anthropological problem then becomes the relation between such schemes and how the terms of one scheme might be rendered into the terms of another. The problem becomes one of 'translation' within a culture and in order to investigate this problem one must adopt an intra-cultural view. This view, arrived at by generalizing the subject-object relation, focuses the analysis at a level which is intermediary between the individual and the civilization, namely the specific roles which articulate an ideology or certain schools or traditions of interpretation with their subjectively partial but objectively total view of this arena.[11]

Admittedly these methodological preoccupations may not be shared by all anthropologists working in South Asia, and the contributors to this volume may not necessarily see the intra-cultural view as being either the reason or the consequence of their research; yet if one is willing to grant that the topics of anthropological discourse are also topics of native discourse then it is imperative that the relationship between our knowledge and the object of our study be clarified. Such methodological preoccupations concerned the founders of social anthropology working among the tribal peoples of South Asia some eighty years ago. To be sure, their efforts—such as Rivers' and Radcliffe-Brown's division of chapters in *The Todas* and *The Andaman Islanders* into those of facts and those of theory—seem naive in the light of contemporary epistemological awareness, yet such a concern would benefit those field-workers who have abandoned experimental procedures for interpretive ones. In this regard the meta-philosophical procedures discussed and applied by Dr. Alexander Piatigorsky in the afterword of this book will be of particular interest to anthropologists working in South Asia today.

NOTES

I am grateful for the comments of Adrian Mayer, Audrey Cantlie, Mark Hobart, and James Urry on an earlier draft of this essay. Also I would like to record my debt to Alexander Piatigorsky and Friedhelm Hardy for many stimulating discussions on Indian religion.

1 In 1891 Risley, having completed an ethnographic and racial survey of the castes and tribes of Bengal, tried to coax British anthropologists out of their proverbial armchairs and into the field, even though recognizing that 'the prospect of such an ordeal would perhaps thin the ranks of the votaries of a new science' (p.238). It was not until one decade later, however, that field-workers travelled to British India in order to collect material on social organization. When they eventually arrived, they investigated the 'primitive' people and not the caste groups in which Risley was particularly interested.

2 Some of the means by which this transformation took place were, of course, purely rhetorical.

3 My purpose in investigating the past is to become aware of differences in the relation between our theoretical postulates and our object of study, not to recount continuities of individual influence among anthropologists. I ignore, therefore, the fact that the methods of the founders of social anthropology were transmitted to field-workers in village India by a different generation of scholars, such as Firth, Evans-Pritchard, Fortes, and Nadel, who had worked in Melanesia and sub-Saharan Africa.

4 Radcliffe-Brown, however, did not identify the convenient locality with a bounded total social system; rather the locality was the base from which one can 'study the structural system as it appears in and from that region.. . .' In the same article Radcliffe-Brown (1940:5) queried whether 'a Chinese village [is] a society, or is it merely a fragment of the Republic of China?' Unfortunately he did not address himself at all to this question except to reiterate that a locality may be thought of as a system of social structure.

5 Admittedly the village study approach has a more complex history than my brief presentation indicates. During the nineteenth century British administrators conceived of Indian villagers as living in 'village communities' which were stable enduring settlements isolated from the political upheavals of the outside world. This administrative vision of rural India was particularly taken up by Maine and Marx in their evolutionist theories of civilization. It is difficult to assess, however, whether the Indian 'village community' of the nineteenth-century sociologist was the progenitor of the 'village study' of the twentieth-century social anthropologist. My own impression is that this influence was minimal, for from the 1930s an increasing number of anthropologists in both London (Malinowski and Firth) and Chicago (Radcliffe-Brown, Redfield, etc.) became interested in peasant studies. Research on peasant villages, or 'little communities',

was carried out in Mexico, Ireland, Japan, and China. The early investigations of village India—led by Radcliffe-Brown's student Srinivas and by Redfield's students at Chicago—seem to have been part of this general trend in social anthropology and not an outcome of a specific regional interest in the Indian subcontinent.

6 This approach to the relation between civilization, tradition, and locality had been developed by Redfield with reference to Mexican peasant society and subsequently applied to the South Asian context. The centres of Indian civilization identified with the great tradition would presumably be analysed also as 'half-worlds'. Marriott, however, did not follow up this possibility, nor did Vidyarthi (1961) who to my knowledge was the only member of the Chicago school at this time to study a centre rather than a regional outpost of civilization.

7 In this respect it is interesting to compare Lévi-Strauss' universalist structuralist approach to caste (1962:144–177) in relation to totemism with Dumont's culturally specific structuralist approach to caste. The influence of Weber upon Dumont is even more direct in the conception of the complex opposition between the man-in-the-world and the individual-outside-the-world, which according to Dumont's own account (1966:235, n.92a) is an overlapping of three elementary oppositions: Weber's worldly/other-worldly and Dumont's Brahman/renouncer and interdependence of caste/individual. Elsewhere Dumont (1960:47) suggests that Brahman and renouncer may be seen as two different 'ideal types'.

8 Kessinger's *Vilyatpur 1848–1968* is an especially valuable comment on the inadequacy of the assumption that the Indian village ever was, or is, a synchronic system.

9 To be sure, as early as the 1950s anthropologists had claimed to be investigating social processes and a number of terms, such as Sanskritization, westernization, and modernization had either been coined or adopted to that effect. But in spite of such claims these so-called processes had merely been described with reference to checklists of salient characteristics rather than analysed diachronically and understood internally in terms of the rules and strategies which governed their operation.

10 In this connection one might say that 'morally aware and responsible persons' or the value of friendship might serve as an interpretation of an orderly course of events which does not entail a concept of a social system. Although such an interpretation might be found anywhere in the arena, the interpretations which are systematic might be perpetrated more by the mobilizers of people rather than by the mobilized. Dumont has occasionally been criticized for presenting only the Brahman's view of Indian society. Such critics suggest that one might expect a different view of the social system from untouchables. There is not yet any evidence, however, which would prove that untouchables, as untouchables, have produced any other systematic scheme of social relations except for inversions of the Brahmanical scheme. Instead it would appear more likely that untouchables talk about the personal qualities of individuals than about society as a totality (Freeman 1979) so that the criticisms of Dumont may be correct but not the consequent expectation.

11 Abstract arguments without empirical content run the risk of being in-

comprehensible. I have tried to work out this approach elsewhere (1978, 1983). I have benefited in this regard from a reading of an unpublished paper by Friedhelm Hardy on lovesickness among the Tamils.

REFERENCES

Bailey, F. G. 1957 *Caste and the economic frontier*. Manchester: Univ. Press.

Burghart, R. 1978 Hierarchical models of the Hindu social system. *Man* (N. S.) 13, 519–36.

—— 1983 Renunciation in the religious traditions of South Asia. *Man* (N.S.) 18, 635–53.

Census of India 1911 1913 Compiled by E. A. Gait. Vol. 1. Calcutta: Superintendent of Government Printing.

Census of India 1951 1954 Economic Tables, vol. I, Part II-C. Delhi: Manager of Publications.

Conlon, F. F. 1977 *A caste in a changing world: the Chitrapur Saraswat Brahmans 1700–1935*. Berkeley: Univ. of California Press.

Dumont, L. 1957 For a sociology of India. *Contributions to Indian Sociology* 1, 7–22.

—— 1960 World renunciation in Indian religion. *Contributions to Indian Sociology* 4, 33–62.

—— 1966 *Homo hierarchicus*. Paris: Gallimard.

—— 1977 *Homo aequalis*. Paris: Gallimard.

Dumont, L. & Pocock, D. 1957 Village studies. *Contributions to Indian Sociology* 1, 23–41.

Freeman, J. M. 1979 *Untouchable: an Indian life history*. London: Allen & Unwin.

Gough, E. K. 1955 The social structure of a Tanjore village. In McKim Marriott (ed.) *Village India: studies in the little community*. Chicago: Univ. Press.

Hardy, F. 1983 From the 'illness of love' to social hermeneutics. *Contributions to South Asian Studies*, 3.

Kessinger, T. G. 1974 *Vilyatpur: 1848–1968*. Berkeley: Univ. of California Press.

Leonard, K. I. 1978 *Social history of an Indian caste: the Kayasths of Hyderabad* Berkeley: Univ. of California Press.

Lévi-Strauss, C. 1962 *La pensée sauvage*. Paris. Plon.

Malinowski, B. 1922 *Argonauts of the western Pacific*. London: Routledge & Kegan Paul.

Marriott, McKim 1955 Little communities in an indigenous civilization. In McKim Marriott (ed.) *Village India: studies in the little community*. Chicago: Univ. Press.

Mayer, A. C. 1960 *Caste and kinship in central India*. Berkeley: Univ. of California Press.

Monier-Williams, M. 1899 *A Sanskrit-English dictionary*. Oxford: Clarendon Press.

Pocock, D. 1972 *Kanbi and Patidar*. Oxford: Clarendon Press.

Radcliffe-Brown, A. R. 1922 *The Andaman islanders*. Cambridge: Univ. Press.
—— 1940 On social structure. *Journal of the Royal Anthropological Institute* 70, 1–12.
Risley, H.H. 1891 The study of ethnology in India. *Journal of the Anthropological Institute* 20, 235–263.
Rivers, W. H. R. 1906 *The Todas*. London: Macmillan.
—— 1908 Genealogies. In *Sociology, magic, and religion of the eastern islands*. Reports of the Cambridge Anthropological Expedition to the Torres Straits, vol. 6. Cambridge: Univ. Press.
Seligman, C. G. 1911 *The Veddas*. Cambridge: Univ. Press.
Srinivas, M. N. 1960 The social structure of a Mysore village. In M. N. Srinivas (ed.) *India's villages*. Bombay: Asia Publishing House.
Vidyarthi, L. P. 1961 *The sacred complex in Hindu Gaya*. Bombay: Asia Publishing House.

THE CONCEPT OF NIRVANA IN VILLAGE BUDDHISM

Martin Southwold

I

The term 'village Buddhism', and its Sinhala equivalent *gamē Buddhāgama*[1], are regularly used by Sinhalese to refer to the form of Buddhism, both practice and belief, that they find a feature of the culture of village people (*gamē minissu*). Village people are the ordinary people of the countryside who constitute the vast majority of the population. In these phrases, as in most others in which it occurs, the term *gamē* (literally, 'of the village') refers primarily to a distinctive sub-culture and its bearers. The fact that these bearers do normally live in settlements which we may term villages is not strictly to the point. Some of those who are village people live in fact in towns; and some of those who live in villages are not village people.

Use of the word *gamē* carries an implied contrast with those who are not *gamē minissu*, namely members of the élite who term themselves middle-class and are distinguished chiefly by the ability to speak English. The word thus has hierarchical connotations; it is evaluative and, when used by middle-class people, commonly opprobrious. It is in line with this bias that when middle-class people speak of village Buddhism, they normally convey disdain: 'it is a corruption of Buddhism', 'not true Buddhism', 'sheer Mahayana', 'not Buddhism at all', they will say. Several of my middle-class friends told me, with real concern, that I was making a grave mistake in studying village Buddhism, and begged me at least to find out what true Buddhism is: referring me, for this purpose, to texts with which I had been familiar long before I thought of studying Buddhism as an anthropologist. 'True Buddhism' is, of course, middle-class Buddhism: which is identical with what Gombrich (1971:56n.), following Bechert (1966:34–108), has termed 'Buddhist modernism'. I agree with Gombrich (1971: 45–46) in his reasons for dissenting from the view that Buddhist modernism is true Buddhism, and village Buddhism a corruption thereof: and I have others.

Both village Buddhism and middle-class Buddhism (Buddhist modernism) are forms of what Leach (1968) has termed 'practical religion'. Both are real elements within Sinhalese culture and are attached to real elements of Sinhalese society; neither can be fully understood without reference to its interaction on the ground with the other. Analytically, both together must be distinguished from what Leach would call 'philosophical Buddhism'. But this distinction is hard to maintain in practice. Middle-class Buddhists identify their doctrine with philosophical Buddhism; when one hears it said that Buddhism is really a philosphy (*darśanaya*) but the common people have made it a religion, one knows what one is dealing with. Empirically, I doubt if the distinction is a real one. If, by 'philosophical Buddhism', one refers to what Western scholars have made of Buddhism, then this is at least, as Gombrich shows, highly cognate with Buddhist modernism.

This produces serious difficulties for the student: anyone who comes, as I did, to the study of village Buddhism with foreknowledge of Buddhism is implicitly committed to the assumption that village Buddhism is at least a distortion of Buddhism. I had supposed that my familiarity with Buddhist thought, acquired from a one-time non-professional addiction, would be an asset to my study. In some ways it was. To my informants I was very evidently, in their terms, a serious student; and I was able, even with Buddhist clergy, to sustain discussion as abstruse as they wished, and even to tease them with doctrinal riddles, which they enjoyed as much as I. But it was all too easy; when familiar concepts came up and were spoken of in doctrinally sound terms, I assumed that the speaker had the concept that I had. I rarely probed further, as I should have been obliged to do if I had known nothing of concepts beyond what I heard my informants say. I was, in effect, in the position of an anthropologist working in his own culture: everything was too familiar, so that I could not recognize problems, too easily putting my data into categories I had brought with me.

I did most of my study of village Buddhism in a village I call Polgama, in Kurunegala District in western Sri Lanka, about sixty miles north-by-east of Colombo, and thirty miles north-west of Kandy. Kurunegala District is part of the Up-country, the former Kandyan Kingdom, though, because of relative isolation from

Kandy, it had, and to some extent still has, a somewhat distinctive sub-culture.

I chose this village on the grounds that Kurunegala District should be less atypical than the areas near Kandy, or in Southern Province, where other studies have been made.[2] What I saw of religion in Polgama, however, seemed to fall far short of what I had read, and was often told, was the normal standard of Buddhist religious life. Ritual and religious gatherings were notably infrequent and, for the most part, poorly attended, and it seemed that religion was a matter of slight concern in the lives of most villagers. More or less obliquely, people in neighbouring villages and even in Polgama itself conveyed a similar judgement, and they laid the blame at the door of the village priest (see note 3 for my usage of the terms 'priest' and 'monk').[3]

The Rev. Silaratana—as I call him—had the reputation of being a politician rather than a man of religion, who interpreted his vocation largely in terms of social service, and had not only been active in the early 1950s in the founding of S. W. R. D., Bandaranaike's Sri Lanka Freedom Party,[4] but had served for many years as President of the Polgama Rural Development Society. The numerous allegations against him included embezzlement and sexual misconduct, and his leadership in ritual activities, fitful at the best of times, was generally understood to be motivated only by a desire for self-glorification. Given the common understanding that Buddhist religious life is focused on and inspired by the local representatives of the Sangha (clergy), it seemed to me that I had found a village where religious life was notably shrivelled because of the disreputable character of its priest. This judgement was supported by people who knew Silaratana, and by people to whom I spoke of my observations in the village.

On the other hand a number of Sinhalese with wide knowledge, mainly government administrators, have told me that my findings are very typical of their own experience, at least in Up-country areas.[5] If they are right, it would seem that Sinhalese Buddhism is rather widely in a sorry state, as has indeed often enough been reported throughout its history of more than two millennia. But I have my doubts, and not only for the reason just implied. It is commonplace to be told that Buddhist priests, in particular and in general, are bad, not to say arrant rogues: so commonplace that I was emboldened to include a question on this in our survey questionnaire. In reply to the question, 'Are Buddhist priests (*hāmuduruvō*) mostly good?', 37 per cent of Buddhist respondents said 'mostly bad', several of them offering us greater statistical precision with '75 per cent . . .', '90 per cent. . .', '98 per cent of them are bad' (as was also often said in more spontaneous remarks). In my own judgement nearly all the clergy I knew were good and earnest men, and conscientious clerics—and the only exception had been condemned and virtually excommunicated by his colleagues in the Sangha. It seems clear to me that Sinhalese disparage their clergy in order to sustain their virtually unattainable ideal of clerical conduct, and that they have to maintain this exaggerated ideal because the clergy, the Sangha, are one of the Three Jewels of the Buddhist sacred.[6] Hostility towards the village priest, which was prominent in each of the four nearby villages which I know well enough to form a judgement, is also a product of the resentment and envy that Sinhalese villagers seem to feel towards anyone with any claim to leadership in the village (cf. Robinson 1975). Disparagement of Silaratana was, in part at least, a response to his actual merits as an effective and forceful leader in village affairs.

I conclude that my impression that Silaratana and his village were quite atypical of village Buddhism was the result of comparing realities with an ideal pattern which is, I guess, rarely if ever realized. To the extent that I can separate out the probable realities of life in other villages from the pervasive idealization colouring what is said or written about them, village Buddhism in Polgama seems to me typical enough: at least it falls squarely within the common range of variation in what Gombrich (1971: 21) aptly calls 'this amazingly diverse island'.

The data I draw upon were obtained in the course of interviews and of conversations more or less casual and informal, both in Polgama and in other villages within cycling range; I also draw on a few sermons I tape-recorded and had translated. Much of the information was collected by my wife, and we both worked with Sinhalese research assistants. Only in Polgama were we able to conduct a thorough village survey using a questionnaire. It was applied to 50 per cent of the households—in effect to every second household as we found them along the roads and paths—and the questions were usually asked of the household head, but in some cases of his wife. Of the seventy households thus selected, six were non-Buddhist, and in three others some of the questions about Buddhism were not asked.

II

The word 'Nirvana'—by which I render the Sinhala *nivān* and Pali *nibbana*—is rarely heard outside of distinctively religious contexts; which is natural enough, given Ling's (1973:235) identification of the concept with 'the sacred' in Pali Buddhism. I heard it frequently since my inquiries commonly constituted a religious context. Clergy often, and lay persons less often, told me that they aimed and hoped to attain Nirvana. This is virtually a cliché: notices announcing a death, which are distributed before funerals, invariably close with the words 'May he attain blissful Nirvana!' (*Nivan säpa läbēvā!*) where we would write *Requiescat in pace* (with I think just the same sense).[7] It is therefore all the more striking how often the word Nirvana was not used where it might have been expected.

I asked all the priests and novices I interviewed why they had decided to enter the Sangha (clergy). Only one answered directly that his motive was to attain Nirvana. I was so struck by this that I asked several priests about it, and they all discounted such a motive; as one said, with a laugh, 'What could a boy possibly know about Nirvana? Why, it is only just beginning to make sense to me now.' They did, as I have remarked, often express at some other point in the interview an aspiration to attain Nirvana; but they did not, without pressure, enlarge on this, nor show any marked yearning. The priest just quoted said, on another occasion, 'For people like us who haven't developed, Nirvana doesn't mean anything, but for one who has reached at least *sovan* [an advanced stage of spiritual development][8] Nirvana is a very precious state.' Another priest—Dhammatilaka—told me on one occasion that attaining Nirvana must be very gradual; it takes about a million years (through many births). This is a standard view among both clergy and laity—many say it will not be possible to attain before the time of the next Buddha, Maitri, in the distant future (cf. Gombrich 1971:290). Dhammatilaka added that Lord Buddha himself had had to progress through thousands of births to achieve Buddhahood—another standard view. On another occasion, he remarked to my wife that he was not in a hurry to achieve Nirvana. Silaratana said, in a sermon, that Lord Buddha could have entered Nirvana thousands of births before he did—but he preferred to go on until he could achieve Buddhahood and help everyone. This is the clearest evidence I have of the truth of the statement that I heard from several middle-class Buddhists (and also from Dhammatilaka) that there is a lot of Mahayana in Sinhalese village Buddhism.[9] It was certainly an attempt by Silaratana to legitimize his own, unusual but far from rare, interpretation of his vocation in terms of social service to the villagers. On another occasion he told me that it will take a very long time for *granthadhura* priests such as himself to attain Nirvana. On the other hand, matters are no better with *vidarśanādhura* monks: they are selfish and do not help people, and if it had been left to them Buddhism would have died out. They endure much hardship and still they do not achieve Nirvana. It seems rather plain that Silaratana had little interest in attaining Nirvana.

A similar picture emerges from the statements of lay persons. In reply to the question 'why are you a Buddhist?' which was asked on the village survey, 82 per cent of respondents said it was because they had been brought up as Buddhists, because of tradition, because everyone else is a Buddhist: none said it was in order to attain Nirvana. When asked what benefits they expected to receive from engaging in Buddhist worship (*pūjā*), 31 per cent replied 'Nirvana', 32 per cent 'Merit' (*pin*), and 29 per cent 'A better next birth'. (There was some overlap: 5 per cent mentioned both Nirvana and Merit, 6 per cent both Merit and next birth.) At first sight these might appear to represent different views; but the structure of concepts is such that they may also be three different ways of saying the same thing. Since nearly everyone accepts that Nirvana is unattainable before the remote period when Maitri cames, the way to it must be by continuous improvement through many births. By doing good deeds one earns Merit, and the more Merit one has the better one's next birth; i.e. one's talents, condition of life, etc. (As we shall see, however, it is doubtful whether by a better next birth people always understand one further along the path to Nirvana.) Of the respondents, 18 per cent said they expected benefits, e.g. freedom from diseases and troubles, in this life. This seems contrary to the usual view that Buddhism is for benefits in the next birth, whereas other things (including propitiation of the gods) are for benefits in this life. There is in fact good scriptural warrant for it—though not, I think, for the claim of one respondent that 'Lord Buddha will make sure that we have enough food to eat if we worship him'.

Although people do quite frequently use and imply the term Nirvana in religious contexts, it is much harder to determine what concept, if any, they have of it. When asked—and sometimes spontaneously—both clergy and laity will say 'Nirvana is no rebirth, no suffering (*duka*)'. If one presses them further, laymen say that the ending of rebirth (which they understand as extinction) is good because life is suffering. If asked to specify the suffering (*duka*), they regularly mention death, disease, poverty, oppression. This is a sound, if crude, account of Buddhist doctrine; as we shall see, the Pāli *dukkha* by which the Buddha characterized life means a great deal more than these obvious sufferings (cf. Obeyesekere 1968:19). I normally found it impossible to get beyond this. I had the strong impression that people were merely repeating by rote formulae which they must have heard many times in sermons and in schools; that they were not accustomed to think about the formulae, and were disconcerted by being asked to do so.

Several clergy, and a few laymen, characterized Nirvana more positively by the word *säpa* (pleasurable, in well-being). A priest told me that Nirvana is 'permanent *suwaya*', which word my assistant rendered as 'comfort'. It also carries the idea of 'cure, healing', thus retaining the original sense, or imagery, of Nirvana as 'a recovery of health' (Ling 1973:112; cf. Smart 1964:33). It would be typical of the preservation of archaisms in Sri Lankan English if the word comfort still had the sense in which Cranmer could write of 'the Holy Ghost, the Comforter'. Those of my informants who said that they expected as a benefit from Buddhist worship freedom from diseases in this life were at least figuratively right.

A *sil mǟniyō*—a woman who has undertaken the precepts and way of life of a member of the Sangha (cf. Gombrich 1971:57)—seems to convey this in the following excerpt from a conversation I had with her. She uses not the word *suwaya* but more common *säpa* which seems to have a similar range of meaning.

MS (anthropologist): What is Nirvana?

SM (*sil māniyō*): *Dāna* (donations), *sīla* (morality), *bhāvanā* (meditation), and *pin karavanā* (Merit-making)—one must do for many *kalpa* (aeons) to get Nirvana. Nirvana is no birth.

MS: Why is that good?

SM: Birth (i.e. life) is *duka*.

MS: But it is not *all duka*?

SM: It is *duka*. Birth is suffering because you cannot be healthy all the time, you lose teeth, get grey hair, and then death.

MS: If Nirvana is no birth, then isn't it no *säpa* either?

SM: It is *säpa*. Nirvana has nothing tangible, but it is *säpa* as Lord Buddha said. I can't say what kind of *säpa*.

As we saw, a few people when asked what benefits they expected from Buddhist worship mentioned benefits in this life. One said he expected *sahanaya* (relief, allayment, mitigation, refreshment, ease, comfort—Carter 1924:669.) Clergy often remark in their teaching that a good Buddhist can expect benefits here and now. In a sermon, a Nayaka[10] priest said that a good Buddhist 'will become a good, disciplined, calm person who will respect teachers, parents, and the Three Refuges [Buddha, Dhamma, Sangha]. By living according to the teachings of the Buddha he will become a good, lucky person, and that type of person can have comforts in the other world as well as in this world. It is this person who collects *pin* (Merit) who will be able to attain Nirvana.'

Laymen, however, do not often speak in this way; on the contrary they regularly stress that Buddhism will benefit them in the future, the next birth, and that when they want help in this life they must apply to the gods. Ames (1966:37) refers to 'Robert Knox's famous dictum that the Sinhalese have "Budu for the soul and the gods for this world" '. Atypically, Knox did not in fact express himself so pithily; what he actually wrote was, referring to religious festivals: 'Now of these there are two sorts, some belonging to their Gods that govern the Earth, and all things referring to this life; and some belonging to the Buddou, whose province is to take care of the Soul and future well-being of men' (Knox 1958:148). But my informants frequently did—except that, as good Buddhists, they did not actually refer to a 'soul'. The word *ātmaya*, which Carter (1924:12) renders as 'spirit, soul; self', has the former sense only for Christians; when used by a Buddhist it refers to a future birth (life), primarily the next. One of the most intelligent of the villagers I interviewed—a man who, unusually, both meditates and studies Dhamma (religious) books—explained the word in this sense; though, as will be evident, I failed to understand what he was saying:

Appuhamy: When I am meditating I am fighting with the *ātmaya*. *Ātmaya* and mind (*hita*) are competitors, and mind must win.

MS: What is *ātmaya?*

A: By *ātmaya* I mean the next birth. If you are doing wrong, troubles come to the body (*śarīra*) and after death these go to the *ātmaya*.

MS: What happens after death?

A: The body is destroyed and what is left of the person is the *ātmaya*. If a person does good, his life now is good and his *ātmaya* is also good. This is my own idea.

MS: What is *ātmaya* like?

A: In English 'noun' is the name of a person, place, thing, etc., and Pāli *atta* is the same.

MS: Why did Lord Buddha teach *anatta* [doctrine of no soul]?

A: He meant that people must finish this *ātmaya*. The end of *anātmaya* is Nirvana.

MS: I can't understand that.

A: I'm sorry, I can't explain it. Before a person gets Nirvana he must find *anātmaya*. *Anātmaya* means there is no more *ātmaya*.

MS: Is it difficult to get Nirvana?

A: It is not difficult to get Nirvana if one works at it. An intelligent person can achieve it in this life. But it depends on one's achievement in previous births. I don't think I will get Nirvana in this life as I am rooting out only two faults (*akusala*)—I never drink and I never eat meat. In future births I will get to master other faults.

Appuhamy was not a typical villager; he was highly intelligent, well-informed, and a man of his own mind. If his view of Nirvana as attainable now, and his practice of meditation as a layman, resembled positions typical of middle-class Buddhists, his estimate of jungle-dwelling monks could not have been more different. On another occasion, when we were not talking about religion at all, he suddenly interjected:

A: I think the monks in *āraññа* [monasteries or hermitages ideally far from human habitation] are off their heads (*pissu*)! Maybe I'm crazy myself just for having visited to take a look. Cutting themselves off from people in the jungles, indeed!

MS: But isn't meditating and training the mind good?

A: How do I know what they really get up to in the night? I reckon those monks are just inventing methods to get their meals provided. It is we people who sweat and look after children who should really get Nirvana.

Few villagers, I think, would be able explicitly to relate the concept of *ātmaya* to the Buddha's doctrine of *anatta*—if only because they mostly do not read Dhamma books—, and clergy, who are surely taught the doctrine, do not seem to use it in their teaching. But to suppose that this understanding is implicit makes better sense of what they did say than did my own assumption that when they spoke of future births as *ātma* they were using the concept of a soul (*ātman*) in ignorance of the Buddha's teaching. In fact that concept would not be available to persons reared in a Buddhist culture, unless they had, as few do, discussed religion with Christians or Tamil Hindus. Thus the commonplace definition of Nirvana as 'no *duka* (suffering), no *ātmaya* (rebirth)' may render the Buddha's teaching more exactly than I supposed.

III

I frequently found the word *āgama* a useful key for unlocking views about Buddhism, among laymen as well as clerics. It is a Sanskrit loan-word, originally introduced by Christians (Malalgoda 1972) to mean 'religion'. It is now, as Gombrich (1971: 58) says, fully naturalized in Sinhala, and commonly used by Buddhists. They use it to refer to any and all of the principal religions they know of—Buddhism, Christianity, Hinduism, and Islam—and to religion generally and Buddhism specifically. Referentially, 'it translates religion very well' (Gombrich loc. cit.); but its signification is notably different. Where we tend to define 'religion' in relation to gods or godlike beings, Sinhalese Buddhists say 'Gods are nothing to do with *āgama*' (cf. Gombrich 1971: 46, 176).

Two clerics told me that the word *āgama* means: '*ā* for *ātmaya*+*ga* for *gälavima* (salvation)+*ma* for *mārga* (path)'; and my assistant told me that this is commonly taught in Buddhist Sunday Schools. As etymology this is nonsense (the Sanskrit word means 'tradition, sacred tradition, sacred text'—Gombrich 1971:58); but as folk-etymology it reveals how Buddhists construe the concept as 'a path to salvation [or better, 'getting free'—Carter 1924:210] from the round of existence'. This is a thoroughly orthodox description of the Buddha's doctrine; and it expresses what Buddhists see as definitive of all *āgama*.

Though I had this explicitly only from two clerics, it seems to be implicit in what most people said. When I asked them 'What is an *āgama*?', most people replied that an *āgama* is concerned with *lōkōttara* matters, and not *laukika* matters as the cult of the gods is. Both these words are derived from *lōkaya*, meaning a world. *Laukika* means wordly, in almost exactly the sense of the English word. For *lōkōttara* Carter (1924:55) gives 'pre-eminent in the world, the opposite of *laukika*'. The latter of these two senses is the one in question, and it is well defined contrastively, for everyone knows *laukika* matters by experience, whereas the *lōkōttara*, being fully manifest only in the state of Nirvana, can be conceived only as radically different from familiar experience. The contrast between *lōkōttara* and *laukika* resembles—with important qualifications—Durkheim's (1912, 1915) contrast between sacred and profane (cf. Southwold 1968: 363).

When I asked informants what the *lōkōttara* was, they sometimes referred to Buddhism or its major symbols—Buddha, Dhamma, Sangha, or sometimes said it was the opposite of *laukika*, or, as was most often the case among men, said the *lōkōttara* was concerned with the next birth and the *laukika* with one's present existence.

Referring to the terms *laukika* and *lōkōttara* Gombrich writes:

> . . . these terms are pure Sanskrit, and purely learned; I have never heard them used in conversation, and to most villagers they are not even intelligible. The sacred-profane dichotomy is not conceptualized by ordinary Sinhalese—which is far from saying that he does not know what is religion and what is not (1971:58).

Evidently these terms which I, like Ames (1964b), found freely used, are not everywhere standard elements in village Buddhism. But a similar contrast is made by the terms *melova* (this world) and *paralova* (other world, future state). We thus have here a pair of non-Sanskritic terms which appear to make a contrast similar to that between *laukika* and *lōkōttara.* I heard them used in the sense that *melova* is one's current life, and *paralova* a future existence, especially the next birth, e.g. 'We must always remember there is the *paralova.* We are reborn in another birth after living in this world'.

We must conclude, then, that a contrast between what is 'this-worldly' and what is 'other-worldly' is central to village Buddhism, whether it is expressed in the Elu terms *melova/paralova* or the Sanskritic terms *laukika/lōkōttara.* I agree with Gombrich that this is not precisely Durkheim's contrast between profane and sacred (see Southwold 1978: note 7); but I think it is the basic religious contrast that Durkheim's conceptualization distorted. Just as Christians do, Buddhists figure the contrast as that between life here-and-now and the life to come; they do not, however, often figure it as a spatial contrast—Christian Earth contrasted with Heaven—although the use of roots meaning 'a world' might suggest that to us.

It is understandable that the *lōkōttara* or *paralova* should be particularly identified with the next birth. Since by common consent, among village Buddhists at least, no one is going to attain Nirvana until the time of the next Buddha, Maitri, in the far future, Nirvana cannot be an immediate goal of striving; it will be reached only along a way leading through many births, and one must aim at progress by stages. Thus the immediate aim is that one's next birth be better. The meritorious acts which eventually bring Nirvana more immediately bring a next birth which is that much better. In this scheme of things Merit, a better next birth, and Nirvana, are not really distinct goals, but are integrated, wherever the immediate stress may be placed. Thus the Nayaka in his sermon said:

> . . . careful and pious listening to *bana* (preaching) helps one to achieve Nirvana, and have better life in other births, and Merit . . . ; and a person who does Meritorious acts gets comforts in *divyalōka* (heavens) and at the end he can attain Nirvana too. By living according to the teachings of the Buddha a person becomes a good, lucky person, and that type of person can have comforts in the other world as well as in this world. It is this person who collects merit who will be able to attain Nirvana. As people who are following the teachings of Buddha we must treat resentment (*krōdhaya*) as a thing which bring suffering (*duka*), and turning the blood bad gives pain to the mind. That is in this world (*melova*). When you think about *paralova* it brings low births and Nirvana gets further away.

But the immediate stress is usually neither on benefits in this life nor on Nirvana, but on a better next birth; not on the present nor the far future, but the near future. A next birth will be better, strictly speaking, if it takes one futher along the way to Nirvana; but the good Karma, the Merit, which brings such spiritual advance brings also comforts of a more worldly kind: health, wealth, power, high status. With sufficient Merit one is reborn not merely as a fortunate human in the world of men, but even as a god in one of the worlds of gods (*divyalōka*) i.e. heavens. It seems evident that most people are in fact aiming at such comforts.

In everyday conversation people frequently speak of *karma* (*karumaya*), and of their hopes for their next birth; this often, though by no means only, comes up when attention is drawn to some good deed or course of conduct. They say they hope to be born healthy, rich powerful, of high status—or at least not unhealthy, poor, oppressed, or lowly. Rather less readily—doubtless to avoid the appearance of presumption—people will say they hope to be reborn in one of the heavens, if not in the next birth at any rate fairly soon. As we have seen, these aspirations are not inconsistent with the Nirvana quest; on the other hand, they are not wholly consistent with it. People do speak of gods attaining Nirvana in their *divyalōka*. This is not strictly in accordance with Buddhist doctrine, which teaches that only humans can attain Nirvana; some people at least are aware of this, since if I raised the point they would correct themselves and say the god as such will not attain Nirvana, but will do so having been born as a person. They are more aware that a being, having attained godhood, is not very likely to progress futher towards Nirvana since he will forget that life is *duka*. Similarly they will concede that those who are reborn as rich and fortunate humans are less likely to think about *duka* and hence actively to strive for Nirvana.

In speaking of a better next birth people hardly ever speak of this as life in the Sangha. That no one unequivocally expresses an aspiration to be reborn as a cleric must certainly be related to the low esteem in which clergy are actually held. On the other hand, people would readily concede that the life of the cleric affords far better opportunities than the life of the layman for making progress towards Nirvana; it is much easier for a cleric to avoid faults (*akusala*) and he has far more opportunity for meditation (*bhāvanāva*). The lack of aspiration for rebirth as a cleric certainly suggests that the wish to attain Nirvana is less than impetuous. This is illustrated by the following conversation with Banda, a small but ambitious shopkeeper.

MS:	You said that life is *duka:* what does that mean?
Banda:	We have many births, each one with sickness. There is no freedom, always troubles.
MS:	But there are also pleasant things in life?
Banda:	True, life is between suffering and enjoyment. According to *āgama* if you earn Merit you are reborn in the heavens (*divyalōka*).
MS:	Or attain Nirvana?
Banda:	Some people want to achieve Nirvana. In Nirvana there is no *duka*.
MS:	Is there bliss (*säpa*) all the time, in Nirvana?
Banda:	There is nothing, it is like . . . [I missed this].
MS:	If you do good in this life, you can be reborn in a good condition?
Banda:	Yes, but you never know. Perhaps you have done wrong, and then you get a bad birth.
MS:	Yes, there is that risk. But then there is a risk in opening a shop, and you have taken this risk. So why are you not prepared to take this other risk, and hope for many future births instead of wanting them to cease? [He hedged and wriggled for some time, evidently distressed at the thought that it was rebirth he wanted, not its cessation. Eventually he confessed:]
Banda:	Really, I would like to go to heavens (*divyalōka*), but others don't like this and would prefer to go to Nirvana. I still have no wish to achieve Nirvana. Perhaps in future I may choose it.

Banda was not a typical village Buddhist; on the contrary he showed various clear signs of preferring middle-class Buddhism. This is probably why he equated Nirvana so uncompromisingly with extinction, nothing.[11] Typical village Buddhists will readily volunteer that Nirvana is blissful (*säpa*), and certainly would not reject my leading question as Banda did. Nevertheless village Buddhists do regard Nirvana as extinction in at least two ways: it is the extinction of *ātmaya*, so no rebirth follows; and it is the extinction of desire or craving (*taṇhā*), which produces *ātmaya*. They do not appear to be seeking such extinctions, but rather happiness in the worlds of men and the gods.

This is of course logical. Only Nirvana ends *ātmaya*; since Nirvana will not be attained before the time of Maitri, one has the certain prospect of many *ātma*; because one does more wrong than one readily recognizes, these are likely to be worse than the life one has now unless one exerts oneself to get good *karma*; such exertion is motivated by desire for a better rebirth; *desire* for a better *rebirth* is doubly inconsistent with Nirvana; hence heavens are the best that can be expected. It would seem that I drove Banda to confess the logical conclusion of a position to which villagers in general are implicitly committed. All this dissolves of course if one removes the premise that Nirvana is attainable only in the remote future. One then asks why this premise is in fact accepted. The remoteness of Nirvana renders it effectively irrelevant as a goal of striving; should we not suppose that it came to be seen as remote *because* it was not a goal of striving? The remoteness of Nirvana from one's actual concerns and aspirations becomes figured as a temporal remoteness, so that the latter serves to legitimize the former.

IV

My observations led me to conclude that village Buddhists are not really seeking Nirvana, do not really want it; and hence that their religion differs in its aim from original, authentic Buddhism, whether this be identified as the teaching of the Buddha, or more cautiously, as the doctrine of the scriptures. This is the conclusion of most writers who have studied village Buddhism. Spiro (1971), for example, in his study of Burmese Buddhism, makes much of it, especially in his Chapter Three; indeed it is central to his analysis. He adds (p.77): 'The Burmese, of course, are not the only *Theravada* Buddhists for whom a pleasurable rebirth is preferable to nirvana. All our evidence indicates that this preference obtains throughout the *Theravada* world'. He cites in support writers on nineteenth century Thailand, and on Burma fifty years, and nearly a thousand years, ago.

Students of Sinhalese Buddhism have stated the same conclusion; among them Gombrich has expressed it with striking clarity and force. I shall quote his words, which express my own conclusion far better than I could (Gombrich 1971:16–17).

> My second example is one of changing aims. It was the aim of the Buddha to attain *nirvāṇa*, a mystical release from normal states of consciousness; it is attained in life, and someone who has attained it is not reborn: he escapes from the wheel of rebirth, to which all creatures are tied. Rebirth the Buddha considered misery; the peace of *nirvāṇa* was the only good worth having. But most Sinhalese villagers do not want *nirvāṇa*—yet. They are like St. Augustine who prayed, 'Make me chaste and continent, O Lord—but not yet'.[12] They say they want to be born in heaven; some of them would even like to be reborn in a favourable station on earth. They fear, as their Teacher did not, the extinction of sensation, and want to go on feeling. Moreover, though they will probably utter the impeccably orthodox sentiment that life is suffering, most of them plainly do believe—and say so when they are not speaking in a religious context—that people with wealth and power are happy. This shifting of an aim, from *nirvāṇa* to heaven or even to earth, is thus explicable in terms of higher-level changing aim—wish to go on living, and a changed belief—that rich people, or at least gods, are happy.

In the light of data such as I have presented this conclusion indeed seems unavoidable. But it does raise a rather large difficulty. Right aim is the second step of the Buddha's Noble Eightfold Path; and that aim, we know, was Nirvana. But this account seems to show us that village Buddhists do not have that right aim. What sort of path can it be that is not even aiming in the right direction? What sort of Buddhism can there be when Nirvana is not wanted, is merely a term to which people pay lip-service? As Ling (1973: 235) remarks, 'Whatever is venerated for its "sacred" character is in Buddhism that which has a very close or special relationship to *nibbana*. . .' But according to our observations, this sacred is effectively a dead letter in village Buddhism. And we know from our own history what happens when the sacred—for us, God—becomes dead.

But Buddhism is not dead. It is one of Gombrich's (1971:40, 56) principal conclusions that the Buddhism which he observed in Kandyan villages was surprisingly orthodox: 'Religious doctrines and practices seem to have changed very little over the last 1,500 years . . . The Sinhalese Buddhist villager today may have a religion quite like the Buddhist villager nearly 2,500 years ago'. The alleged change of aim would seem to be no recent phenomenon. Moreover village Buddhism has always been virtually the whole of Buddhism—at least the trunk without which royal courts and monasteries would soon have shrivelled (as they did throughout India). In Sri Lanka, it would seem that the Buddhism which has survived, and with rare exceptions flourished, for 1,500 if not nearly 2,500 years, has hardly been Buddhism at all, for it has been dead at its nirvanic core. Such a change of aim is explicable—and both Gombrich and Spiro explain it in broadly similar psychological terms. But it leaves inexplicable the raw historical fact: and the fact, observable today, that a religion fundamentally oriented to Nirvana is a living religion.

The consensual conclusion, though it seems so obviously right, begins to crumble if we examine it critically. The analogy with St. Augustine's insincere prayer for chastity, though it seems so striking—it struck both Gombrich and Spiro (1971:79) independently—is not really just. St. Augustine prayed for chastity, which he might have had at once, to be deferred, showing thereby that he did not wholly want it. But in aspiring to Nirvana only in the remote future village Buddhists are not seeking the deferment of what they might have now: they take it as a fact that Nirvana is not attainable now, unlike middle-class Buddhists who hold that Nirvana can (and therefore should) be attained now. It is not at all obvious that the middle-class view is authentic and the village view inauthentic Buddhism. Despite the confidence of Gombrich and so many other writers, we do not really know what the Buddha thought and taught. We have only the scriptures to go on; and these, as Gombrich (1971:40, 45; 1972:491–2), has made plain, support the position of village Buddhists as well as that of middle-class Buddhists. In defence of their view that it is no longer possible to attain Nirvana, village Buddhists regularly cite the prophecy attributed to the Buddha that the spiritual capacities of mankind would steadily decline after his death. And several of my informants seemed to be implying that if Nirvana is indeed attainable now, it is odd that no one shows clear signs of having attained it.

The more one examines the contrary contentions of middle-class Buddhists (and most Western scholars) and village Buddhists, the more evident it becomes that the differences between them are attributable to two major factors. On the one hand, different modes of social experience and aspiration, related to different class situations; on the other, different modes of thought and action, interpretation and evaluation. It is these latter I wish to consider, since they affect not only our analysis but our very perception of the data.

V

Differences so basic cannot be accurately conveyed by simple labels; for an initial outline of what I shall argue I must have recourse to excessively crude terms. Briefly, and crudely, we—western scholars and middle-class Sinhalese—are positivists, but villagers are religious. We have selected from the scriptures passages which can be interpreted in line with our positivist preconceptions; from these we have constructed a positivist doctrine that we call 'Buddhism', and a positivist—if inescapably mystical—Teacher whom we identify with the unknowable historical Buddha. From this standpoint we look at village Buddhism and find it defective. All religions appear defective when analysed on positivist assumptions; that is why anthropologists try to analyse them on other assumptions which make better sense of them, and putatively are closer to the modes of thought which actually generate them. But this rather obvious advance has hardly occurred in the study of Buddhism, because we have trapped ourselves in the positivism we have projected as authentic Buddhism—a projection which is manifested, for example, in the assumption that original Buddhism was not religious (see, for example, Ling 1973: 34, 120 and *passim*). I shall argue that to analyse village Buddhism as specifically religious is to make better sense of it not only as a human phenomenon but also as authentically Buddhist. We shall then see that village Buddhists do care about Nirvana, do believe in it, but in a way which eludes our ordinary analysis.

It is common among anthropologists to make a distinction between technical action and ritual or magico-religious action; or better, following Leach (1968:13) between these not as *types* but as *aspects* of action. An act is technical to the extent that its object is to alter the state of the world, the empirical objective environment of the actor, the act being chosen rationally (though not always correctly) as an efficacious means to that end. I shall use the term 'instrumental' (cf. Beattie 1966:63 and n. 4), rather than 'technical', for this sense. Ritual acts have—for us, not necessarily for the actors—a non-instrumental aspect: they are not simply, if at all, serving as means to alter the state of the world, but have other functions, commonly indicated by describing them as 'symbolic' or 'expressive'. If we view such acts simply as instrumental they appear irrational, to an extent that makes it unlikely that sane and sensitive people would persist in them; but such people not only persist, they regard such acts as of great value. Hence, we infer, they must have some rationale other than the instrumental.

If we are to say how religious action should be analysed, we need another ideal-type concept, to be contrasted with that of instrumental action. That of non-instrumental action is too much of a residual category: it covers too much to bring out what needs to be understood of religious behaviour specifically. The concepts of 'symbolic' or 'expressive' action, which we frequently use, are better, despite being somewhat vague and ambiguous. They have the advantage of bringing out the important similarities between religious behaviour and artistic creation and expression; and the corresponding disadvantage that they cannot show in what religion is distinctively different from art. We should seek an analytic concept, an ideal type, which will make clear what is crucial in religious action, what fundamentally distinguishes it from action which can appropriately be analysed as instrumental.

To speak simply of instrumental action is too limiting; for such action is but an aspect of a system of thought and action, of assumptions and interpretations, evaluations and orientations. It is the system as a whole that we should consider. I shall refer to it as 'instrumentalism', and to one who thinks and acts within its framework as an 'instrumentalist'; these are of course ideal types.

The instrumentalist—in common with the non-instrumentalist—assumes that there are two distinct but connected domains of reality: the inner domain of experience and the outer domain of objective physical reality. He assumes that his various inner states of experience are determined, wholly or largely, by various states of the outer objective reality; hence his actions are directed at bringing about those states of outer reality which he knows, or believes, determine the more gratifying inner states of experience. When I spoke earlier, and crudely, of 'positivists', I meant those who assume that instrumentalism is the only rational strategy for action and understanding: thought and action are either instrumentalist or senseless, or at least irrational. If it is actually the case that religious thought and action, or some of it, are generated by an alternative, non-instrumental, rationale, such an assumption will normally make this alternative rationale appear more or less senseless. This will be so either by definition, in the case when that rationale is recognized; or, in the case when the thought and action are analysed as if they followed an instrumentalist rationale, because they will be found to be more or less arbitrary. I suggest that we have misunderstood village Buddhism because we have tacitly made that assumption.

Indeed this assumption is more than tacit in Gombrich's work, for he is admirably explicit about his methodology. 'It may seem paradoxical', he writes, 'that the social study of religion should concentrate on the rational, but Popper, the begetter of what he calls the "rationality principle", has shown that there is no other way' (1971:12). The rationality principle, I suggest, is tailored to the analysis of instrumental action, and it is, or may be, quite inappropriate for analysing non-instrumental behaviour. Some of the assumptions involved when we apply it to religious actions are shown by Gombrich (1971:15) when he writes:

> A religious action is based on a belief about facts and directed to certain aims. Either the belief or the aims may change. What does not change is the relation between these two: that the action based on the beliefs and directed to the aims follows the rationality principle. If it does not it is not amenable to systematic study.

He had earlier justified the application of the rationality principle to the sociology of religion by reference to Jarvie (1964), summarizing an example from that book. 'If we see a man in an agricultural community oppressed by a drought enter a special building (called, maybe, a church), get on his knees, fold his hands and start muttering, we may assume that he is insane, in which case we can offer no further testable explanation of his conduct, or that he thinks his actions may bring rain. And if that is what he thinks, we must assume that he thinks some entity is capable of giving him rain, and that that entity, which begins to look rather human in its emotions, will be placated by his suppliant posture and humble gesture, and listen to his words' (Gombrich 1971:12, referring to Jarvie 1964: 111–14).

It is of course true that people who perform rites are sometimes quite as naive as their interpreters take them to be; and it is more widely true that people offer instrumental rationalizations for their ritual acts when they are unable, or unwilling, to formulate a profounder rationale. But it is simply wrong to say that a man performing rain ritual either thinks it will bring rain or is else insane. Lienhardt (1961:280) remarks that Dinka rain rituals are performed when, as the Dinka well know, the rainy season is approaching, and comments '. . . their human symbolic action moves with the rhythm of the natural world around them, re-creating that rhythm in moral terms and not merely attempting to *coerce* it to conformity with human desires'; a comment the force of which can be fully appreciated only when it is read in its context, the chapter entitled 'The control of experience: symbolic action'. In a similar vein, and more explicitly directed against instrumentalist interpretation, we might consider Winch's (1970:106) sensitive remarks on Zande agricultural magic:

> [MacIntyre can see in Zande magic] only a (misguided) technique for producing consumer goods. But a Zande's crops are not just potential objects of consumption: the life he lives, his relations with his fellows, his chances for acting decently or doing evil, may all spring from his relation to his crops. Magical rites constitute a form of expression in which these possibilities and dangers may be contemplated and reflected on—and perhaps also thereby transformed and deepened.

VI

Whether all magico-religious thought and action, inasmuch as it is non-instrumental, has one and the same underlying rationale I cannot say. But in Buddhism clearly, and in some other religious systems clearly enough, I see a rationale, a system of thought and action, alternative to instrumentalism. It seems evident to me why, within this system, thought and action should tend to be symbolic and expressive, and should have other of those characteristics of religion which make it more or less refractory to instrumentalist analysis. For this reason I think it may be basic to much that is religious. But at least it is basic to Buddhism.

In this alternative system of thought and action—which again we must treat as an ideal type, since no man lives by this alone—it is not taken for granted that states of experience are determined by states of outer objective reality, and can be bettered only by changing them. On the contrary, it is posited that states of experience are shaped, and their quality as gratifying attributed, by the experiencing subject, the self. It is not denied that the bases of experience are given by states of outer reality; but it is stressed that what chiefly matters is what man makes of them, the constructions he puts upon them. Hence in this system the strategy for ameliorating experience is by changing the self, rather than by changing the states of outer objective reality. In Buddhism it is fundamental, and quite explicit, that one's fate is determined by one's states of mind; this is clearly grasped and stated even by apparently unsophisticated village Buddhists. In other religious systems, as Lienhardt (1961:149–156) has so brilliantly argued for the Dinka, what we in our secular idiom—together with Buddhists—think of as states of mind are rather imaged as Powers and spirits acting upon the experiencing self. This is indeed a notable difference of idiom, which has led us to suppose that the Buddhist system of thought and action is quite different from those we readily identify as religious. I argue that behind the difference of idiom there is a more fundamental similarity: Buddhism, like the religion of the Dinka (and perhaps like the religions of other peoples) manifests a strategy for the control of experience (Lienhardt's phrase) through the constructions one puts upon what is given. Even Buddhism, with its strongly psychological idiom, does not suppose that one's states of mind are merely an intellectual matter: one does not ameliorate experience merely by discarding intellectual errors, adopting a sounder theory, important as this is. As one thinks, so one does; but just as importantly, as one does, so one thinks. Experience is ameliorated by construing it better, by changing one's mind, but the change of mind that is effective goes far beyond a change of opinion, of theory, of belief; instead it is a more thorough and radical change of personality. In this sense the strategy is one of changing the self, not merely the intellect.

This strategy is part of a system of thought and action, analytically alternative to instrumentalism, though in actual life complementary to it. It would be useful to have a term to label and designate it; but I have failed to find one which is really satisfactory. The concept of an amelioration of life through a radical change of mind and of personality resembles the Biblical concept which in English versions is translated as 'repentance':

> Thus though the Greek word *metanoein* is often used for 'repent', in its New Testament usage it implies much more than a mere 'change of mind', it involves a whole reorientation of the personality, a 'conversion' (Richardson 1950:192, under 'Repent').

It is unfortunate that in modern English 'to repent' means especially 'to feel regret, sorrow, or contrition for (some fault, misconduct, sin, or other offence)' (Shorter Oxford English Dictionary); this was accessory, not central, to the Biblical concept and is hardly to be detected at all in the corresponding Buddhist concept. (That the Biblical term has become so trivialized, and has not been replaced by another, is doubtless a measure of how alien the concept is to our—instrumentalist—cast of thought.) For want of a better term, I have decided to give the system of thought and action I have defined the label 'repentalism'. I have made clear what I mean by it; I must ask the reader to free his mind as far as possible from any connotations of regret or contrition, sin or offence.

In this sense, Buddhism is a 'repental' system: that is, it resembles that ideal type to such an extent that it cannot really be understood except on that model and will certainly be misunderstood if we try to analyse it as an instrumentalist system. Buddhist doctrine proposes a new self, claimed to be better than that which is normal to man, and a way by which this new self may be realized. Buddhism is more explicitly and radically repental than other religions. A theistic religion may appear on analysis to be concerned with the control of inner experience—as in Lienhardt's analysis of Dinka religion; but to the actors themselves, as we have seen, it is concerned with the control of Powers and spirits, imagined denizens of the outer domain of objective reality. Thus the account that the Dinka themselves, like other theists, give of their religion fits the instrumentalist schema. This is perhaps because instrumentalism seems natural to human common sense, whereas explicit repentalism is a product of analytical reflection. It is significant that Gombrich (1971:8–9) argues, in the face of clear evidence to the contrary, that the real ('affective') beliefs of Buddhists are theistic (cf. my comments in Southwold 1978: 366–7).

What in other religions are taken to be spiritual beings in the domain of objective reality are regarded in Buddhist theory as 'projections of human psychological forces' (Ortner 1978:99); and as Ortner also remarks, with particular reference to Sherpa demons, 'The point has filtered down into popular consciousness, albeit not fully understood' (loc. cit.). Indeed Buddhist theory tends to reduce far more of what others see as objective reality to projections of the mind. For Buddhist thought, of most schools at least, outer reality exists—but it only exists, it does not objectively have the shape that we perceive in it. For the outer existent is a formless flux of point-instants (*kṣaṇa*), linked only by causation.[13] What it gives to us in experience is equally formless, and it becomes a world, acquires shape, only from the ideas we bring to it. If the world appears to be given to us, this is only because the ideas by which we shape it appear given. But they are not given, they are constructed, by us, and we can replace them by other ideas, shaping thereby another world. Thus, where I said earlier that the object of Buddhist repentalism is to realize a new self, we could equally well say that it is to realize a new world—to see reality in a different form. I do not claim that village Buddhists express themselves in such philosophically abstruse terms, to me any rate; but I do say that 'the point has filtered down into popular consciousness'. This is why the distinction between the state of everyday unreformed man, and that which Buddhism presents as the goal to be attained, is figured by the terms *laukika/lōk-ōttara, melova/paralova.* Probably ordinary Buddhists, like the adherents of other religions, see the other-worldly (*lōkōttara, paralova*) less as something to be increasingly realized, made real for themselves, as they make progress on their repental way than as something already entirely real which they must try to recognize more adequately. But this makes little practical difference. That they often identify the other-worldly with their next birth is a cruder simplification; but again it makes less difference than we usually suppose.

A repentalist system, then, proposes to ameliorate experience by realizing a new self—a new man, as Burridge (1960:247–8) puts it—and a new world: which are new construals and constructions of inner and outer reality. If a man recognizes that the new construal is better—pragmatically 'truer'—than the old construal of everyday worldly common sense, he might reasonably concentrate on realizing it in himself. But this seems to be contrary to the spirit of actual repental systems; the new man cannot be cultivated alone for his nature is rooted in fellowship, community. '. . . the Dinka quite explicitly state that *individual* action in religious contexts is ineffective' (Lienhardt 1961:246).[14] In Buddhism the notion of a purely individual salvation makes no sense, since salvation, Nirvana, is constituted by realization of the truth of *anatta*, the unreality of the individual self. Despite the deviation of middle-class Buddhists, and many Western scholars, this has always been the understanding of most clergy (and almost certainly of most laymen also). Referring directly to Sinhalese Buddhism of the Anuradhapura Period (third century B.C. to tenth century A.D.), but obliquely no doubt to that of the present day, Rahula (1956:193), himself a learned cleric, writes:

> One class of monks devoted themselves only to meditation, with the sole purpose of saving themselves, without taking any interest in the welfare of the people. The other . . . [clearly much the larger and more highly esteemed—op. cit. 160] seems to have taken an interest in the welfare of the people—both spiritual and material—in addition to their own salvation. This attitude seems to be healthier than the first one, and is in keeping with the spirit of the Master.

In accordance with both the example and the precept of the Buddha of tradition, to realize the Dhamma has normally been held to entail teaching it, sharing it, also.

The fact that repental 'truth' must be shared, whether in collective ritual or by teaching, produces problems. To invite men to adopt a new consciousness, a new man, a new world, is to ask them to forsake the old and familiar; but this is normally a long and difficult process. The natural man knows this world—knows it by acquaintance and lives by it; why should he change, and extinguish the world he lives in? He may be told of the other world, and told that it is better; but why should be believe (credit) this? How can he credit it, when his experience tells him nothing of it?

Men normally cannot be won to a repental system by argument alone, because discursive thought and its concepts lack the power to turn a man round, to convert him. The ideas by which the repentalist reshapes experience are normally not so much concepts, of the kind which constitute discursive thought, as symbols. But a symbol is not here to be understood as it appears to instrumentalist thought, namely as a sign which stands for some element of the outer world. Rather, we should join Sperber (1975:33) in following 'the metaphorical expression that the Ndembu use to designate symbols: the world *chijikijilu* which means a 'landmark'. A landmark is not a sign but an index which serves cognitively to organize our experience of space. This Ndembu metaphor seems much more apposite and subtle to me than the Western metaphor which compares symbols to words.' I shall call such a symbol a 'Mark'. As a landmark 'serves cognitively to organize our experience of space', a Mark serves to organize and shape our experience, our inner domain.

This is why symbols, and symbolic expression, are so important in repental systems, in religions. Both symbols of the major kind, which I have called Marks, and those of lesser kinds which we may term images, figures, and metaphors, have more power to move men than have the concepts of discursive thought; and they serve too to bridge over, or merely to paper over, the gaps and implausibilities of logical demonstration. It is by Marks that worlds are changed; as this world is real—dominates natural man—because he cleaves to his natural Mark, so the other world becomes real to him to the extent that he cleaves to its Mark—which in Buddhism is Nirvana. To cleave to a Mark is what we normally express by the term 'believe in' (and the comparable Sinhala terms, such as *visvāsa karanavā*, *adahanavā*, have the same sense; (cf. Gombrich 1971:58–60). Inasmuch as a Mark, or its corollaries, is expressed in statements, propositions, the repentalist 'believes' them. But this is notably different from instrumentalist belief: thus Wittgenstein (1966:59): 'Also, there is this extraordinary use of the word "believe". One talks of believing and at the same time one doesn't use "believe" as one does ordinarily'. And Pears, (1971:174 quoted in Gudmunsen 1977:102), summarizing Wittgenstein's view, writes:

> A religious tenet is not a factual hypothesis, but something which affects our thoughts and actions in a different way. This sort of view of religion fits very naturally into his later philosophy: the meaning of a religious proposition is not a function of what would have to be the case if it were true, but a function of the difference that it makes to the lives of those who maintain it.

Belief, and beliefs of this kind, are regularly misunderstood by the instrumentalist. This is why we have misapprehended the place and the role of the concept of Nirvana in village Buddhism.

VII

To believe in, to cleave to a Mark is necessary but not sufficient to realize the other world, replacing the seeming reality of this everyday world. A Mark is like a beacon (another sense of the Ndembu word '*chijikijilu*'—Turner 1969:15) lighting the destination, showing the direction of the way. But however bright the beacon, it cannot convince us that the destination is where we want to be. Even with the aid of symbolic expression, the basic impasse remains: we cannot be sure enough that the other world is better than this until we get there, but we are not sufficiently motivated to get there until we are more convinced.

Hence another device, very characteristic of repental systems generally, and especially clear in Buddhism. Everyone knows that, broadly, as a man thinks (or really believes) so he does; it is also true, though less familiar, that as a man does, so he thinks.[15] Buddhists regularly stress the importance of acting well so as to bring about better states of mind. Village Buddhists (as also the middle-class) frequently make offerings, of flowers, lamps, words of devotion, food and drink, to Lord Buddha: which seems odd when they all firmly assert that Lord Buddha does not exist. Gombrich (1971: 8–9, 139–43) concludes from this that they really ('affectively') believe that Lord Buddha does exist—a reasonable interpretation, on instrumentalist assumptions. But the people themselves—at least the more articulate of them—explain that they do this for the effect on their state of mind. To give gifts arouses the feeling of gratitude; and it is healthy to feel gratitude to Lord Buddha, for this enhances our appreciation of the teaching he gave us, and hence our commitment to it. Thus they echo Durkheim's statement about rites generally, that their 'true justification . . . does not lie in the apparent ends which they pursue [e.g. influencing the gods], but rather in the invisible influence which they exercise over the mind and in the way in which they affect our level of consciousness' (Durkheim 1912:514; 1915:360 —I have used Lukes's translation of the sentence— 1973:473–4).

This is certainly the major function of ritual in repental systems generally (cf. Geertz 1966:28–9; 1968:100). At first sight the point appears not very relevant for the analysis of Buddhism, in which ritual, in the sense of rites and ceremonies, is notably unimportant. In village Buddhism ritual performances are infrequent and spare (in both senses), in comparison with other religions; and people readily volunteer that ritual is quite unnecessary for Buddhists. This accords with the view of the scriptural Buddha, who clearly had little time for ritual, though he was too tolerant actually to condemn it (cf. Ling 1973:106, 151–2). But if we see rather little ritual in Buddhism, this is because we do not know where to look: what is functionally ritual has an unfamiliar form. In his Rock Edict IX, the Emperor Asoka referred to various ceremonies—rites of passage and curative rites—and stated:

> It is right that ceremonies be performed. But this kind bears little fruit. The ceremony of Dharma (*Dharma-mangala*), on the contrary, is very fruitful. It consists in proper treatment of slaves and servants, reverence to teachers, restraint of violence toward living creatures, and liberality to priests and ascetics. These and like actions are called the ceremonies of Dharma (Nikam and McKeon 1978:46).

In Buddhism, then, it is primarily ethical conduct which has the function that Geertz (1968:100) attributes to ritual ceremonies:

> For the overwhelming majority of the religious in any population . . . engagement in some form of ritualized traffic with sacred symbols is the major mechanism by means of which they come not only to encounter a world view but actually to adopt it, to internalize it as part of their personality.

Ethical conduct is esteemed for its instrumental effects, the practical benefits it brings to those to whom it is directed. But much more it is esteemed, and urged, for the sake of its repental effects on the state of mind. Primarily for its effects on the state of mind of the doer; but significantly also, in view of the necessarily communal character of Buddhism (see above), for its effects on the minds of those towards whom it is done. Thus Asoka again, in his Pillar Edict VII:

> King Priyadarsi [Asoka] says:
>
> I have ordered banyan trees to be planted along the roads to give shade to men and animals. I have ordered mango groves to be planted. I have ordered wells to be dug every [half-mile] and I have ordered rest houses built. I have had many watering stations built for the convenience of men and animals.
>
> These are trifling comforts. For the people have received various facilities from previous kings as well as from me. But I have done what I have primarily in order that the people may follow the path of Dharma with faith and devotion (Nikam and McKeon 1978: 64–5).

This is similar to the rationale that Silaratana gave for his own deviation to social service, and his political involvement; though I never heard him, nor any other village Buddhist, refer to Asoka in this connection.

Village Buddhists lay great stress on the ethical aspects of Buddhism: to the point, sometimes, of defining an *āgama* as an ethical system with ornaments. 'The most frequent religious act of Buddhists', Gombrich writes, 'is the recitation of a few lines in Pali. Many Buddhists recite them daily in private; their recitation begins, and often punctuates every public religious occasion' —and, I would add, many that we should not perceive as religious. Gombrich gives the full text, with translation. In summary, the lines are: a salutation to the Buddha; the Three Refuges, whereby a man cleaves to the Buddha, the Dhamma, and the Sangha; and the Five Precepts, whereby he undertakes to abstain from five kinds of Fault. Gombrich (1971: 64–65) comments:

> A person who takes the Three Refuges and Five Precepts is thereby a Buddhist layman. There is no ceremony for conversion to Buddhism beyond the recital of these lines, so anyone who says these words and means them can rightly call himself a Buddhist. To go so far and then to keep the precepts is considered sufficient for great religious progress.

I comment further that these lines are comparable to the Lord's Prayer and the Creeds in Christianity, both in their typical occasions of utterance and in their functions, for in Buddhism ethical Precepts take the place of affirmations of belief.

I remember asking people, in the early days of my research, just what Buddhism is all about. I was struck by the reply I received from several people: 'Not killing animals' which seemed to me, at the time, naive. In fact it is not. The First of the Five Precepts is that to abstain from taking life; since Buddhists suppose that abstention from taking human life is enjoined by all religions, they see the injunction to abstain from taking animal life subsumed in the First Precept, as distinctive of Buddhist ethics. 'Not killing animals' thus expresses synecdochically the basis of Buddhist ethics: hence the basis of Buddhism as villagers commonly see it. It seems a far cry from this simple phrase to the elaborate subtleties of Buddhist doctrine.

Villagers do in fact earnestly try to observe the First Precept. Though they will kill living creatures when they must, they do so with evident reluctance. I was often impressed by the care people took to avoid killing where I should not have hesitated to kill; and when I killed insects and other vermin, as I regularly did, I sometimes noticed the evident, though unvoiced, distress of Sinhalese who were present. I was so impressed that eventually when I moved to kill an insect, shame prevented me. This apparently trivial abstention had an astonishing effect on my consciousness:

at once I felt affection for the insect whose life I had spared, delight in its being, and a powerful sense of community, harmony, and peace.

It is unlikely that not killing animals has such an astonishing effect on Sinhalese villagers: one is not astonished by an everyday familiar experience. But I do suggest that through following the First and the other Precepts they experience the same kind of transformation of consciousness—less dramatically than I, but more pervasively. This is certainly what Buddhist analysis would predict. And if their experience resembles mine at all, I can see how the concept of Nirvana makes sense to them. The sense of harmony and peace that took me when I spared an insect is not Nirvana: but if I understand the concept rightly, it is unmistakably nirvanic. Through ethical action, I suggest, Buddhists get openings and glimpses enough to assure them that Nirvana is no mere dream, but is rather the perfection of what they already know at their best.

Why then are village Buddhists—in contrast with middle-class Buddhists and the jungle-dwelling meditating monks they extol—apparently so little concerned to attain Nirvana, to the point of denying that it could be attained in the foreseeable future? Precisely, I suggest, because they do know what they are talking about. Because they know the nirvanic, a little but genuinely, they are able to gauge how far off must be its perfection. A man who imagines he might attain Nirvana in short measure must have either a remarkably high estimate of himself, or a remarkably low estimate of Nirvana. It is out of reverence, not unconcern, that villagers see Nirvana as far off. When Dhammatilaka remarked 'I am not in a hurry to attain Nirvana' (see above), he was showing not flippancy but understanding. To be in a hurry to attain Nirvana is in practice to seek it selfishly; to recognize as village clergy—most clergy—do that enlightenment must be shared, one must travel in convoy, is to know there can be no haste. Indeed, not to be in a hurry at all is so unmistakable a characteristic of nirvanic experience, that to be in a hurry to attain is as odd and self-contradictory as to desire Nirvana: both would suggest that one does not know what one is talking about.

It is instrumentalism—and here, perhaps 'positivism' is not too crude a term—that leads us to imagine that Nirvana is a condition a man might easily grab for himself, and then to remark that village Buddhists are not really interested in that. Indeed they are not; in their religion Nirvana is a *chijikijilu*, a Mark and a beacon, which guides men in their progress towards perfection. They place it rightly far off in the future, in a time out of this time, when Maitri, the next Buddha, comes. And hence it is not by defalcation, but by a proper estimate of the task before them, that they concern themselves with the immediate future, with bettering themselves and others in this life, figuring the other-worldly as the next birth. Their concern with *karma* and rebirth is not, as Spiro (1971, especially Chapter 3) maintains, a deviation from normative canonical Buddhism (what he takes as such is neither normative nor uniquely canonical): on the contrary, it is a faithful application of what the Dhamma is about. People would tell me that they will not kill an animal, even an insect, because it might be the reincarnation of a deceased kinsman, or because they might themselves be reborn in that form. This is not, as it may appear, and did appear to me, a mere childish fancy: it is rather a kind of myth which serves as a charter for the First Precept, which is, I have suggested, a key to Buddhism as a system of life. More basically, the doctrine of Rebirth is a symbolic transformation of the central Buddhist doctrine of *anatta*, rendering it more vivid and readily apprehensible: the *anatta* doctrine of the synchronic indistinction, continuity, and community of all living beings is translated into a statement of their diachronic transmutability and potential identity. The effect in life is the same. Village Buddhism is no corruption; rather, in the words with which Gombrich concluded his book:[16]

'*Vox populi*, *vox Buddhae*'.

NOTES

I am indebted to the Social Science Research Council for a Research Grant (no. HR 2969/1) which supported the research on which this paper is based; to the University of Manchester for much assistance, not least the grant of a sabbatical year during part of which this paper was written; and to my Sinhalese assistants, informants, and friends. I am grateful too to Professors Richard Gombrich and Rodney Needham, and Drs. Richard Burghart, Audrey Cantlie and Chris. Fuller for their helpful criticisms of an earlier version of this paper.

1 In writing Sinhala words I have followed the convention of Gombrich (1971:xiii-xiv): that is, I have transliterated the Sinhalese orthography. This closely represents the sounds of actual speech; the principal exception is that the termination-*aya* is actually pronounced as *ē*.

2 In particular, Gombrich (1971) and Ames (1964a, 1964b, 1966). Other published ethnographic studies, some of which refer to other areas, tell us little about village Buddhism, but Ryan (1958), which describes a village not far from Colombo, is an exception.

3 I use the term 'priest' where most writers on Buddhism have preferred the term 'monk'. Unfortunately there is much more at issue here than a mere matter of terminological convention. Use of the term 'monk' insidiously conveys a distorted and perhaps idealized view of the actual place of most of the clergy in Buddhist societies (cf. Ling 1973:123). There was nothing in the least monastic about any of the clerics I refer to as 'priests'. The word 'priest'—which is that most commonly used by English-speaking Sinhalese—has perhaps been avoided because it is thought to connote a ritual intermediary between man and the sacred (cf. Ling 1973:255 n.2). Though I do not intend it, this connotation is not entirely inapt. I have used the word 'priest' because the role and status of village Buddhist clergy seem to me highly comparable with those of priests in rural Catholicism (see, for example, Christian 1972). In other ways also I have drawn more freely than is usual on the terminology of the Christian Church to designate elements in practical Buddhism (e.g. in using the terms 'ecclesiastical', 'parishioners'). I have done so deliberately because I find it more illuminating to overstress than to understress the similarities between practical Buddhism and practical Christianity.

My usage enables me to use the term 'monk' specifically to refer to those members of the Buddhist clergy who actually are monastic—who have withdrawn from close involvement with lay society to live the contemplative life in monasteries or hermitages. As Gombrich (1971:269–70) remarks, following Rahula (1956:158 ff.), for nearly two millennia Buddhist clergy in Sri Lanka have recognized a distinction between two vocations. One of these, called *granthadhura*, is in practice that of teaching the Doctrine (*dhamma*) to the laity; the other, called *vidarśanādhura*, is that of engaging in meditation (mind-training) with minimal involvement with laymen. Originally, and in the usage of my informants, the distinction largely corresponds with another: *granthadhura* clergy are *grāmavāsin*, that is, dwelling in village or town, and *vidarśanādhura* clergy are usually *āraññavāsin* or *vanavāsin*, meaning jungle-dwelling (Rahula 1956:196, 197 n.1). I should add, however, that Gombrich (1971:270) correctly notes another usage in which the terms *grāmavāsin* and *āraññavāsin* are quite nominal, reflecting no real difference in modes of life. In my experience, clergy who live in villages—those I call 'village priests'—see themselves as priests, ministers, pastors, teachers, often explicitly identifying themselves with the *granthadhura* vocation; and both they and many of their parishioners, so far from seeing this as second-best to the *vidarśanādhura*, readily speak of the monks who follow this path with plain contempt. By contrast, middle-class Buddhists typically dismiss all priests contemptuously, declaring that only monks are worthy members of the Sangha.

I use the terms 'clergy' and 'clerics' for priests and monks indifferently; hence I use the term 'clergy' for the members of the *sangha*, which word originally designated the community of *bhikkhu* (mendicants) who had abandoned lay life and donned the saffron robe to follow the Buddha's teaching. I use the term 'novice' (Sinhala *poḍi sādhu* or *sāmanēra*) to designate young men who have joined the Sangha and donned the robe but are still in training for their higher ordination (*upasampadā*) by which they will be confirmed as priests or monks.

4 This is the more left-wing of the two major Sir Lankan political parties; it is about as socialist as the British Labour Party.

5 It is not normal for village priests to devote themselves to social service, but it far from uncommon.

6 The other two are the Buddha and the Dhamma (doctrine). It is a significant characteristic of the Buddhist clergy that they do not so much mediate as manifest the sacred to man.

7 Gombrich (1971:217–18) makes the same comparison. He also remarks that the same words are used at the end of every sermon, a fact I failed to note.

8 From the stage of *savan* one will attain Nirvana after seven more births (Gombrich 1971:285).

9 There are some hints of this in Gombrich's account (cf. Gombrich 1971:64, 223, 321).

10 A Nayaka is a priest who had been elected to seniority in a local chapter of clergy. I shall refer to this sermon again as 'the Nayaka's sermon'.

11 Spiro (1971:79) quotes two Burmese who told him plainly they did not want Nirvana; one simply, and one almost equated it with nothing. Both were middle-class.

12 St. Augustine, *Confessions*, VIII, 7.

13 See Stcherbatsky 1932: vol.I, part II, ch.I. While Stcherbatsky is expounding the theory of one particular school of Mahayanist philosophers, that theory is a special development of a common position in Buddhist philosophy, quite plain, for example, in the Theravada scriptures.

14 In many religions private devotions are important; many Buddhists, for example, say these are more important than public collective rites. But

Durkheim (1912:63–4, 1915:46) is surely right when he argues that 'these individual cults are . . . aspects of the common religion of the whole Church'.

15 When Evans-Pritchard (1976:244) was asked whether, when he lived among the Azande, he believed their notions of witchcraft, he replied that 'in a kind of way I believed them . . . If one must act as though one believed, one ends in believing or half-believing as one acts'.

16 Gombrich (1971:327) is more hesitant in suggesting this conclusion and gives different reasons for it.

REFERENCES

Ames, M.M. 1964a Buddha and the dancing goblins: a theory of magic and religion. *American Anthropologist* 66, 75–82.

—— 1964b Magical animism and Buddhism: a structural analysis of the Sinhalese religious system. In E. B. Harper (ed.) *Religion in South Asia.* Seattle: Univ. of Washington Press.

—— 1966 Ritual prestations and the structure of the Sinhalese pantheon. In M. Nash (ed.) *Anthropological Studies in Theravada Buddhism.* New Haven: Yale Univ. Press.

Beattie, J. 1966 Ritual and social change. *Man* (N. S.) 1, 60–74.

Bechert, H. 1866 *Buddhismus, Staat und Gesellschaft in den Ländern des Theravāda-Buddhismus.* I, Allgemeines und Ceylon. Frankfurt: Institut für Asienkunde in Hamburg.

Burridge, K. O. L. 1960 *Mambu: a Melanesian millenium.* London: Methuen.

Carter, C. 1924 *A Sinhalese-English dictionary* (1965 edition). Colombo: M. D. Gunasena.

Christian, W. A. Jnr. 1972 *Person and God in a Spanish valley.* New York & London: Seminar Press.

Durkheim, E. 1912 *Les formes élémentaires de la vie religieuse.* Paris: Alcan.

—— 1915 *The elementary forms of the religious life* (trans.) J. W. Swain. London: Allen & Unwin.

Evans–Pritchard, E. E. 1976 Some reminiscences and reflections on fieldwork. In E. E. Evans–Pritchard *Witchcraft, oracles and magic among the Azande* (abridged edn.). London: Oxford Univ. Press.

Fairbanks, G. H., Gair, J. W. & De Silva, M. W. S. 1968 *Colloquial Sinhalese.* Ithaca: Cornell Univ. South Asia Program.

Geertz, C. 1966 Religion as a cultural system. In M. Banton (ed.) *Anthropological approaches to the study of religion.* London: Tavistock.

—— 1968 *Islam observed.* Chicago: Univ. Press.

Gombrich, R. 1971 *Precept and practice: traditional Buddhism in the rural highlands of Ceylon.* London: Oxford Univ. Press.

—— 1972 Review of Spiro (1971). *Modern Asian Studies* 6, 483–94.

Gudmunsen, C. 1977 *Wittgenstein and Buddhism.* London: Macmillan.

Jarvie, I. 1964 *The revolution in anthropology.* London: Routledge.

Knox, R. 1958 *An historical relation of Ceylon* (1st edn. 1681). Dehivala: Tisara Prakasayo.

Leach. E. R. 1968 Introduction. In E. R. Leach (ed.) *Dialectic in practical religion*. Cambridge: Univ. Press.

Lienhardt, G. 1961 *Divinity and experience: the religion of the Dinka*. London: Oxford Univ. Press.

Ling, T. O. 1973 *The Buddha: Buddhist civilisation in India and Ceylon*. London Temple Smith.

Lukes, S. 1973 *Émile Durkheim: his life and work*. London: Allen Lane: Penguin Press.

Malalgoda, K. 1972 Sinhalese Buddhism: orthodox and syncretistic, traditional and modern. *Ceylon Journal of Historical and Social Studies* II, 156–69.

Nikam, N. A. & McKeon R. 1959 *The edicts of Asoka*. Chicago: Univ. Press (Midway Reprint).

Obeyesekere, G. 1968 Theodicy, sin and salvation in a sociology of Buddhism. In E. R. Leach (ed.) *Dialectic in practical religion*. Cambridge: Univ. Press.

Ortner, S. B. 1978 *Sherpas through their rituals*. Cambridge: Univ. Press.

Pears, D. 1971 *Wittgenstein*. London: Fontana.

Rahula, W. 1956 *History of Buddhism in Ceylon*. Colombo: M. D. Gunasena.

—— 1967 *What the Buddha taught*. Bedford: Gordon Frazer.

Richardson, A. (ed.) 1950 *A theological word book of the Bible*. London: SCM Press.

Robinson, M. S. 1975 *Political structure in a changing Sinhalese village*. Cambridge: Univ. Press.

Ryan, S. 1958 *Sinhalese village*. Coral Gables: Univ. of Miami Press.

Smart, N. 1964 *Doctrine and argument in Indian philosophy*. London: Allen & Unwin.

Southwold, M. 1978 Buddhism and the definition of religion *Man* (N. S.). 13, 362–79.

Sperber, D. 1975 *Rethinking symbolism* (trans.) Alice R. Morton. Cambridge: Univ. Press.

Spiro, M. E. 1971 *Buddhism and society*. London: Allen & Unwin.

Stcherbatsky, T. 1932 *Buddhist logic*. Leningrad: Academy of Sciences of the USSR.

Turner, V. W. 1969 *The ritual process*. London: Routledge.

Weber, M. 1958 *The religion of India* (trans.) H. H. Gerth and D. Martindale. New York: Free Press.

Winch, P. 1970 Understanding a primitive society. In B. R. Wilson (ed.) *Rationality*. Oxford: Blackwell.

Wittgenstein, L. 1966 *Lectures and conversations on aesthetics, psychology and religious belief* (ed.) C. Barrett. Oxford: Blackwell.

THE AGHORI ASCETICS OF BENARES

Jonathan P. Parry

This paper presents material on the Aghori ascetics of the holy city of Benares.[1] Benares is sacred to Shiva, the Great Ascetic, the Lord of the Cremation Ground, and the Conqueror of Death; and the cornerstone of its religious identity is its association with death and the transcendence of death. All who die here automatically attain 'liberation' or 'salvation' (*mukti*, *mokṣa*)[2]—an inducement which attracts many elderly and terminally sick people to move to the city. Each year thousands of corpses of those who have been unfortunate or undeserving enough to expire elsewhere are brought to Benares for cremation on one of the two principal burning *ghāṭ*; while vast numbers of pious pilgrims come to immerse the ashes of a deceased relative in the Ganges or to make offerings to the ancestors. Death in Benares is big business which —as I have outlined elsewhere (Parry 1980)—involves an elaborate division of labour between a number of different kinds of caste specialists variously associated with the disposal of the corpse, the fate of the soul, and the purification of the mourners.

The Aghori ascetic is intimately associated with death, corpses and the cremation ground. I argue that his somewhat macabre practices are directed at a suspension of time, and represent an attempt to escape from the recurrence of death implied by the endless cycle of rebirths. The singularity of his means to this end lies, as Eliade (1969:296) perceived, in a peculiarly material and literal play on the common Hindu theme of the combination of opposites; but both the end itself and its theological justification are—we shall find—expressed in thoroughly conventional language.

At the outset I should acknowledge that there are many gaps in my data relating to the Aghoris, and I should explicitly state that I have not personally witnessed many of the secret performances with which they are most closely associated. What needs to be kept firmly in mind then is that at various points the account relates, not so much to what these ascetics actually do, as to what they say they do and what other people believe them to do.

The contrast which is implied throughout this account is that between the goal of the ascetic and the message encoded in the mortuary rituals of the householder. Although the last rites of the householder—with their insistence on the complete elimination of the remains of the deceased—recall the ascetic's denigration of the 'gross' physical body and in this respect perhaps reveal the influence of the renouncer's message (Bloch & Parry 1982), it is clear that in many respects these rituals point in an entirely different direction. While the ascetic's endeavour is to arrest time, to escape the endless cycle of rebirths and to attain a permanent state of being unfettered by any material form, the mortuary rites of the householder lead to a renewal of the deceased's existence in a bodily form which is perhaps less 'gross' than the one he has relinquished but which is none the less transient. I have discussed the symbolism of cremation as an act of regeneration in more detail elsewhere (Parry 1981 and 1982), but a few preliminary observations may help to set my discussion of the Aghoris in context.

Given that the death of the householder is a necessary prelude to his recreation it is only to be expected that the beliefs and practices associated with cremation are pervaded by the symbolism of embryology. The body is to be taken to the cremation ground head first because that is the way a baby is born; while the corpse of a man should be laid face down on the pyre and the corpse of a woman face up, for this is the position in which the two sexes enter the world.[3] During the fifth month of pregnancy the vital breath enters the embryo through the suture at the top of the skull and it is from here that it is released during cremation. Throughout pregnancy the baby is sustained by the digestive fire which resides in its mother's belly,[4] and at death it returns to the fire from which it came and is thus reborn (cf. Knipe 1975:1). At both parturitions an untouchable specialist acts the indispensable role of midwife —cutting the umbilical cord at birth and providing the sacred fire and superintending the pyre at death.

In passing I note that at other points the symbolism of the maternity ward is replaced by that of the bridal chamber. The funeral procession of an old person is described as a second marriage party and is accompanied by erotic dancing; while a husband and wife who die within a few hours of each other are placed on a single pyre in what is explicitly represented as a position of copulation. Indeed, the connection between death and sexuality is a theme which is constantly reiterated in both textual and popular traditions. If death regenerates life, it is equally clear that in turn the regeneration of life causes death. The loss of semen, for example, results in disease, old age and death, while its retention confers vitality and even immortality.

At death the soul becomes a disembodied ghost or *preta*, a marginal state dangerous both to itself and to the survivors. The purpose of the rituals of the first ten days is to reconstruct a physical form for this ethereal spirit. Each day a *piṇḍa*—a ball of rice or flour—is offered in the name of the deceased, each of which reconstitutes a specific limb of his body. By the tenth day the body is complete, and on the eleventh life is breathed into it and it is fed. On the next day a ritual is performed which enables the deceased to rejoin his ancestors. The wandering ghost (*preta*) becomes an incorporated ancestor (*pitṛ*). A ball of rice representing the departed is cut into three by the chief mourner and is merged with three other rice balls which represent the deceased's father, father's father and father's father's father. The soul then sets out on its journey to 'the abode of the ancestors' (*pitṛ lok*) where it arrives on the anniversary of its death, having endured many torments on the way—torments which the mourners seek to mitigate by the rituals they perform on its behalf. In order to cross over into 'the kingdom of the dead' (*yamlok*) at the end of its journey, the soul must negotiate the terrifying Vaitarani river which is invariably represented as flowing with blood, excrement and other foul substances.

In a number of ways the symbolism of this whole phase of the mortuary rituals continues the theme of death as a parturition. The word *piṇḍa* is used not only for the rice of flour balls out of which the deceased's body is reconstructed, but also for an actual embryo (cf. O'Flaherty 1980); and the body is completed in a ten-day period which parallels the ten lunar month period of gestation (cf. Knipe 1977). What is more, there is a striking correspondence between the image of crossing the Vaitarani river and the birth passage of the child out of the womb, the latter also being explicitly represented as negotiating a river of blood and pollution. What we seem to have here, then is a case of ritual over-kill; the deceased is reborn out of the fire and then born all over again in the subsequent rituals.[5]

5

In this context it is perhaps also worth noting that, in relation to the twelfth-day rituals, both the textual commentaries and the more knowledgeable ritual specialists in Benares make a rather different kind of link between death and regeneration. If the chief mourner's wife is barren, then in order to conceive a son, she should consume the rice ball used in the ritual to represent her husband's father's father (cf. Kane 1953: IV:345–7, 480). The *piṇḍa* identified with the ancestor thus had the quality of semen and may beget a new *piṇḍa*-embryo (cf. O'Flaherty 1980). Though the notion is clearly inconsistent with the theory of reincarnation postulated by the doctrine of *karma*, the idea is that the great-grandfather comes back as his own great-grandson; and I would add that even those who deny the efficacy of any such procedure often assert an identity of character between the two.

The striking similarity between the regime of mourning and the code of the ascetic can also be related to the theme of regeneration. The chief mourner must not shave, he must wear a single garment, must sleep on the ground, avoid 'hot' food and abstain from sex—all of which recalls the conduct prescribed for the renouncer. Every year tens of thousands of pilgrim-mourners go to the holy city of Gaya in order to make offerings there which will ensure the final salvation of their deceased parents. Many of them wear the ochre-coloured garments of the ascetic and it was several times explained to me that this is a symbol of their temporary assumption of the renouncer's role. Das (1977:126), who has remarked on this parallel, interprets it in terms of the liminality of both statuses. In this context, however, it has an additional significance: my informants explicitly made the point that it is by taking on the role of the ascetic and performing austerities (*tapasaya*) that the chief mourner acquires the power to recreate a body for the deceased.

What all these examples illustrate is that the mortuary rituals are represented as a recreation of the deceased, as a rebirth in a bodily form of one kind or another. For the renouncer, however, the value of such a goal is dubious, since the world is suffering and the corollary of rebirth is the relentless recurrence of death. The real aim of renunciation is rather an escape from this endless cycle, and it is this—I will suggest—that makes sense of the baroque excess associated with the Aghori to whom I now turn.

Before the creation was a void. According to the myth of Vishnu's cosmogony recorded in the best-known eulogy of Benares's sanctity, the *Kāśī Khaṇḍa* (Chapter 26),[6] all that originally existed was Brahma, which cannot be apprehended by the mind or described by the speech, and which is without form, name, colour or any physical attribute. Creation proceeded by differentation from this primal essence, duality emerging from non-duality. Much of the endeavour of the world-renouncer may be seen as an attempt to recapture the original state of non-differentiation and to re-establish the unity of opposites which existed before the world began.

The discipline of yoga is—as Eliade (1969; 1976) has shown—directed at precisely this goal. By his physical postures the yogi subjugates his body and renders it immobile; by concentrating on a single object he frees his mind from the flux of events and arrests mental process; and by slowing down and eventually stopping his breath 'he stops the activities of the senses and severs the connection between the mind and external sensory objects' (Gupta 1979:168). Sexual intercourse may be converted into a discipline in which the semen is immobilized by the practice of *coitus reservatus*, or its normal direction of flow reversed by reabsorbing it into the penis after ejaculation. By thus controlling his body he acquires magical powers (*siddhi*) by which he may defy nature and control the world. But above all, the yogi's immobilization of mind, body, breath and semen represents an attempt to return to what Eliade describes as a 'primordial motionless Unity', and to attain *samādhi*, a timeless state of non-duality in which there is neither birth nor death nor any experience of differentation.

This suspension of time and conquest of death is also the aim of Aghori asceticism. The theological premise on which their practice is founded would appear to be a classical monism. Every soul is identical with the Absolute Being; all category distinctions are a product of illusion (*māyā*), and behind all polarities there is an ultimate unity. But what *is* peculiar to the Aghoris is a very literal working-out of this monistic doctrine through a discipline which insists on a concrete experience of the identity of opposites, and on a material realization of the unity between them. It is a matter of a kind of externalized fulfilment of what is more orthodoxly interpreted as a purely internal quest.

Although there are many similarities of practice, and perhaps also a direct historical connection, between the Aghoris and the skull-carrying Kapalikas of certain late Sanskrit texts, they themselves trace the foundation of their order to an ascetic called Kina ('rancour') Ram, whom they claim as an incarnation (*avatār*) of Shiva, and who is supposed to have died (or rather 'taken *samādhi*') in the second half of the eighteenth century when he was nearly one hundred and fifty years old. The *āśrama* (or 'monastic refuge') Kina Ram founded in Benares (which is also the site of his tomb) is one of the most important centres of the sect—though only one or two ascetics actually live there. Each of the succeeding 'abbots' (*mahant*) of this *āśrama* is supposed to be an *avatār* of (Shiva's *avatār*) Kina Ram; the present incumbent being reckoned as the twelfth in the line.[7]

There are probably no more than fifteen Aghori ascetics permanently or semi-permanently resident in Benares and its immediate environs,[8] but others from elsewhere congregate at Kina Ram's *āśrama* during the festivals of Lolark Chhath and Guru-Purnima.[9] The evidence suggests that at the end of the last century their numbers were several times greater—Barrow (1893:215) gives an estimate of between one and two hundred—though it is very unlikely that they were ever a numerically significant element in the ascetic population of the city.[10] Their hold on the popular imagination is, however, out of all proportion to their numbers, and some Aghoris acquire a substantial following of lay devotees. Recruitment to the sect is theoretically open to both sexes and to all castes. In practice, however, all the ascetics I knew, or knew of, were male and of clean caste origin (though some of their devotees were female).[11]

The Aghoris, wrote Sherring (1872:269), are 'a flagrantly indecent and abominable set of beggars who have rendered themselves notorious for the disgusting vileness of their habits.' Indeed the 'left-hand' discipline (*vām panthi sādhanā*) they embrace was hardly likely to commend itself to the English missionary. The Aghori performs austerities at, and probably lives on, the cremation ground—in some cases in a rough shack, into the mud-walls of which are set human skulls (Morinis 1979:258). He may go naked or clothe himself in a shroud taken from a corpse, wear a necklace of bones around his neck and his hair in matted locks. His eyes are conventionally described as burning red like live coals; his whole demeanour is awesome, and in speech he is brusque, churlish and foul-mouthed.

Rumour persistently associates the Aghoris with human sacrifice, and there is said to have been a notorious case in the recent past just across the river from Benares. What is certain, however, is that during the British raj more than one Aghori was executed for the crime (Barrow 1893:208), and more recently the *Guardian* newspaper (Thursday, 6 March 1980) reported the death in police custody of an old ascetic who was living on a south Indian cremation ground and who was suspected of the sacrifice of five children whose blood he collected in bottles for the performance of rituals by which he sought to attain immortality. The article goes on to cite a recent (unspecified) survey which claimed that there are still probably a hundred human sacrifices offered each year in India in order to avert epidemics, ensure the fertility of crops or women, or confer supernatural powers on the sacrificer.

As part of his discipline the Aghori may perform the rite of *śava-sādhanā*, in which he seats himself on the torso of a corpse to worship. By means of this worship he is able to gain an absolute control over the deceased's spirit, through which he communicates with other ghostly beings.[12] The Aghori sleeps over a model bier (made from the remnants of a real one); smears his body with ash from the pyres, cooks his food on wood pilfered from them[13] and consumes it out of the human skull which is his constant companion and alms-bowl, and which he is supposed to have acquired by some crude surgery on a putrid and bloated corpse fished out of the river. My informant Fakkar ('indigent'/'carefree') Baba, however, shamefacedly admits to having obtained his from a hospital morgue, though he claims to have taken precautions to ensure that it was a skull of the right type (see below). It belonged, he says, to a young Srivastava (Trader) who died of snake-bite. The provenance of Lal Baba's skull is reputedly more immaculate. Several of my friends at Manikarnika *ghāṭ* recall the day when he waded out into the river to retrieve the corpse to which it belonged, and one of them claims to have unwittingly lent him the knife with which he performed the operation. Before eating I have seen Lal Baba offer the food it contains to a dog, thus converting it into the 'polluted leavings' (*jūṭhā*) of the most debased of animals, and one which is also—like the ideal Aghori—a scavenger living off the carrion of the cremation ground.[14] The 'true' Aghori is entirely indifferent to what he consumes, drinks not only liquor but urine, and eats not only meat but excrement, vomit and the putrid flesh of corpses.[15]

While I myself have been present when an Aghori drank what was said to be the urine of a dog, and swallowed what was undoubtedly ash from a cremation pyre, I cannot personally testify to their necrophagy. All I can say with complete assurance is that they readily own to the practice; that as far as my lay informants are concerned the matter is not in question, and that several of them claim to have seen an Aghori eating corpse flesh. One highly revered ascetic has hung a large portrait of himself in the leprosy hospital which he founded, in which he is shown sitting cross-legged on a corpse, a bottle of liquor in one hand while in the other is a morsel of flesh which he is raising to his lips. Apart from its very existence, the interesting thing about the painting is that the corpse which he is devouring appears to be his own (which would conform with the theology of monism I describe below). What is also relevant here is that another of my ascetic informants insisted that the crucial point about the corpse on which the Aghori sits to worship is that it is identical with his own.

Starting with the *Dabistan*, a seventeenth century Persian source (cited by Barrow 1893 and Crooke 1928), the historical records treat necrophagy as an indisputable fact and provide several supposedly eye-witness accounts of the practice—though some of these are far from credible. The narrator of *The Revelations of an Orderly* (a semi-fictional work published in Benares in 1848) claims, for example, that: 'I once saw a wretch of this fraternity eating the head of a putrid corpse, and as I passed he howled and pointed to me; and then scooped out the eyes and ate them before me.'[16] Another nineteenth century British account claims that 'near Benares they are not unusually seen floating down the river on a corpse, and feeding upon its flesh' (Moor quoted in Oman 1903:166); while according to a third, the drunken Aghori 'will seize hold of corpses that drift to the banks of the river and bite off bits of its flesh . . .' (Barrow 1893:206). Or again, Tod (1839:84) reports that 'one of the Deora chiefs told me that . . . when conveying the body of his brother to be burnt, one of these monsters crossed the path of the funeral procession, and begged to have the corpse saying that it "would make excellent '*chatni*', or condiment" '.

While such reports would certainly do little to allay the doubts expressed by Arens (1979) about the nature of our existing evidence for anthropophagy, what is perhaps more authentic witness to its occurrence is provided by the series of prosecutions which followed the special legislation passed by the British to ban—as Crooke (1928) phrased it—'the habit of cannibalism'. One Aghori, for example, who was tried in Ghazipur in 1862 'was found carrying the remains of a putrid corpse along a road. He was throwing the brains from the skull on to the ground and the stench of the corpse greatly distracted the people. Here and there he placed the corpse on shop boards and on the ground. Separating pieces of flesh from the bones he ate them and insisted on begging.' The defendant later admitted that 'he ate corpses whenever he found them' (Barrow 1893:209). Convictions were also obtained in subsequent prosecutions brought before the courts in Rohtak in 1882, and in Dehra Dun and Berhampore in 1884. In one of these cases the accused testified that 'he frequently ate human flesh when hungry' (ibid. p. 210); while the newspaper report of a further incident asserts that it forms 'the staple of their food' (The *Tribune*, Lahore, 29 November 1898, cited in Oman 1903:165).

Despite the impression which such accounts may create, I am convinced that if necrophagy is indeed practised by any of the Aghoris I encountered, it has nothing whatever to do with the requirements of a balanced diet (as Harris [1977] has somewhat implausibly claimed for the Aztecs); but is an irregular—perhaps even a once-off—affair, performed in a ritualized manner at night during certain phases of the moon associated with Shiva.[17] (In view of Arens's caution, it is perhaps as well to retain an open mind on whether necrophagy ever really occurred in any but freak instances. In this context it may be worth pointing out that even the admissions of the ascetics themselves are not beyond suspicion, for—quite apart from the possibility of police duress—the hallmark of an ideal Aghori is that he consumes the flesh of corpses, and any acknowledged failure to do so is a confession of inadequacy. On balance, however, I think that the probability must remain that at least some Aghoris have always taken this aspect of their discipline seriously.) Details of the precise ritual procedure surrounding such an event are supposed to be secret; and there is a considerable discrepancy between the accounts I was given. Some said that the consumption of flesh should ideally be preceded by an act of intercourse on the cremation ground; others that having eaten of the flesh the ascetic should cremate the remains of the corpse and smear his body with the ash. But almost everybody agrees that after eating the real Aghori will use his powers to restore the deceased to life (cf. Barrow 1893:221; Balfour 1897:345–6), and that the flesh he consumes should be that of a person who has died a bad death.

This association recurs in the notion that the skull which the Aghori carries should have belonged to the victim of an 'untimely death',[18] as should the corpse on which he sits to meditate (cf. Morinis 1979:258–9). The preference is not just a question of the practical consideration that, since such corpses are immersed, their remains are the ones most likely to be available. It is also a matter of the power that resides in such skulls, which is said to render even the most virulent of poisons innocuous. That of a Teli (Oil-presser) and of a Mahajan (Trader) who has died a bad death is especially prized. Oil-pressers, it is explained, are a proverbially stupid caste and their skulls are therefore easy to control; while Traders tend to be sharp and cunning and their skulls are particularly powerful.[19] With the proper *mantra* (sacred formula) an Aghori can get his skull to fetch and carry for him, or cause it to fight with another. It is as if life resides in the skull itself, only waiting to be activated by one who knows the proper incantations. It is because the 'vital breath' of a person who has died a bad death has not been released from his cranium on the cremation pyre by the rite of *kapāl kriyā* that his skull remains a repository of potential power (Parry 1982).

Like other sects with a close affinity to Tantrism, the Aghoris perform (or at least claim to perform) the secret rite of *cakra pūjā* involving the ritual use of the so-called 'five Ms' (*pañca-makāra*)—*māṃsa* (meat), *machlī* (fish), *madya* (liquor) *mudrā* (in this context parched grain or kidney beans) and *maithuna* (sexual intercourse). A group of male adepts, accompanied by one or more female partners, sit in a circle. The woman is worshipped as a manifestation of the goddess and is offered the food and drink which is subsequently consumed by the males who feed each other. The first four Ms all posses aphrodisiac qualities and thus lead towards the fifth—in which the adept and his partner incarnate Shiva and his consort united in *coitus reservatus*. As far as my subsequent argument is concerned, the crucial point here is that the female partner should ideally be a prostitute or a woman of one of the lowest castes; and she should also be menstruating at the time and thus doubly polluted. But what is also significant is that the sexual intercourse which is supposed to occur is a calculated repudiation of procreation. (By contrast the duty to sire offspring was frequently represented by my high-caste householder informants as the only legitimate pretext for coitus.) Not only is the semen withheld, but the act takes place at a time when the female partner is infertile. Moreover, she is preferably a prostitute: the one class of women who have a 'professional hostility' to fertility and who provide the perfect 'symbol of *barren* eroticism' (Shulman's [1980:261–2] apt phraseology; my emphasis). Consistent with the discussion of Aghori aims which follows, the act of ritual copulation thus reveals a certain disdain for the regeneration of life, and identifies the male adept with Shiva locked in a union with his opposed aspect which is both without end and without issue. It is a sexual pairing rid of its normal consequences—progeny and death (the latter being commonly used in popular speech as a metaphor for ejaculation, and being caused—as we have seen—by a failure to retain the semen).

This liaison between the Aghori and the prostitute recurs in several other contexts. The prostitutes of the city not only visit the burning *ghāṭ* to worship Shiva there in his form of Lord of the Cremation Ground (Smaśan-Nāth) but each year on the festival of Lolark Chhath they used to come to sing and dance at the tomb of Kina Ram (though the practice was abandoned in the late fifties after a serious disturbance among the university students). Moreover, it is said that the bed of a prostitute is equivalent to a cremation ground in that it is an equally proper place for an Aghori to perform his *sādhanā* (ritual practice).

By his various observances the Aghori acquires *siddhi*, or supernatural powers, which give him mastery over the phenomenal world and the ability to read thoughts. If he is sufficiently accomplished he can cure the sick, raise the dead, and control malevolent ghosts. He can expand or contract his body to any size or weight, fly through the air, appear in two places at once, conjure up the dead and leave his body and enter into another. All this, of course, is exactly what one might predict from the Aghori's dealings with corpses and bodily emissions, for—as Douglas (1966) points out—that which is anomalous and marginal is not only the focus of pollution and danger, but also the source of extraordinary power.

While *siddhi* may, of course, be won by ascetics who follow quite different kinds of regime, it is widely believed that they are acquired more quickly and more fully by those who pursue the path of the Aghori. This path, however, is more difficult and dangerous than that which is followed by other orders; and one whose discipline is inadequate, who is overtaken by fear during his austerities, or who fails to retain his semen during *cakra pūjā*, pays the penalty of madness and death (cf. Carstairs 1957:232). He then becomes an *Aughar-masān*, the most recalcitrant and difficult to exorcise of malevolent ghosts.

The association between madness and the Aghori is not, however, an entirely straightforward one. The genuine Aghori, it is acknowledged, is—almost by definition—likely to seem demented to ordinary mortals, and is apt to talk in a way which they cannot comprehend. But this is merely evidence of his divine nature and of the fact that he has succeeded in homologizing himself with Shiva, who is himself somewhat touched, and with Lord Bhairava —one of whose manifestations in Benares is as *Unmat* ('mad') Bhairava. Moreover, complete lucidity is not the best policy for one who shuns the world and does not wish to be endlessly importuned for spiritual guidance. But while there may be an element of both divine and calculated madness in an authentic ascetic, it is also recognized that some Aghoris are simply insane in the medical sense. Their affliction, however, is generally attributed to a failure of nerve or an insufficiently fastidious attention to ritual detail during the performance of such dangerously powerful rites, rather than to any notion that their attraction to these practices suggests that they were unbalanced already.

By virtue of his magical powers, the Aghori who has—in the local idiom—'arrived' (*pahuṃce hue*), is likely to attract a large lay following who bring their pragmatic problems to him for solution. Baba Bhagavan Ram, for instance, has an extensive circle of committed devotees. Most of them are of high caste,[20] and many are members of the professional middle-class. (Amongst the inner circle of disciples are, for example, a retired Collector and a retired Police Inspector, a post-doctoral research fellow and an administrator from the university, a college lecturer, a student now studying in North America, two lawyers, an engineer, a Customs and Excise officer, a factory manager, a public works contractor, and a well-to-do shopkeeper.) Two other Aghoris I knew also had a significant middle-class following. Even in the presence of an ascetic, other than their acknowledged *guru*, the humility of such devotees—who would in other contexts brook no trifling with their dignity—is really remarkable. When Pagila ('mad') Baba wilfully defecated on the string-cot on which he was reclining, a Rajput police officer and a Brahman businessman undertook the cleaning up.

Although motives are hard to be confident about, for what it is worth I record my strong impression that what attracts many of these people to the Aghori's following are the *siddhi* which he is believed to have obtained and which he may be induced to use on their behalf in an insecure and competitive world.[21] To my knowledge several of them joined Bhagavan Ram's entourage at times of grave personal crisis—the Police Inspector when he was under investigation for corruption, the contractor when his business started to fail, the Customs and Excise Officer when the prospect of providing a suitable dowry for his daughters became an immediate problem. Not of course that this is an aspect of the matter to which they themselves would publicly call attention. As at least some of these middle-class devotees were inclined to present it, the initial appeal was rather the egalitarian social ethic which Baba Bhagavan Ram preaches, and about which I shall say more later.[22] As I would somewhat cynically interpret it, however, his considerable success amongst such people is at least in part attributable to the fact that this message is one which they can identify as 'progressive' and 'modern' and which they can casuistically use to legitimize a more shamefaced and surreptitious concern to tap the source of a fabulous supernatural power.

The paradox of the situation, however, is that in order to gain and maintain a reputation as an ascetic worthy of the name, the laity require miracles as evidence of his attainments; yet the brash display of such powers is regarded with equivocation for it testifies to an incomplete spiritual development. While proof that he has taken the first step, it demonstrates that he has gone no further, for the one who has really 'arrived' is the one who scorns to indulge the laity with such trifles, who is indifferent to reputation, and who pursues his own salvation with a complete disdain for the world. In order to attain his goal of *samādhi*, a double renunciation is necessary: first a renunciation of the world and then of the powers that are thereby acquired (cf. Eliade 1959:89; 1976:106–7).

The man-in-the-world, however, remains thirsty for miracles

and his compromise is the ascetic who is seen to work wonders—as it were, under the counter and in spite of himself, while denying his capacity to do so. It is not uncommon, in my experience, for one ascetic to be disparaged by the followers of another on the grounds that he is a mere performer of supernatural tricks.[23] But at the same time the follower feels obliged to justify the claims he makes for his own *guru* by reference to a personal experience of the marvels he can accomplish. Did he not witness, or even himself benefit from, this or that miraculous cure? Was he not actually with his *guru* in Benares when the latter was unmistakably sighted in Allahabad? The fact that the ascetic himself disclaims such reports merely confirms his spiritual authenticity.

The curse of an Aghori is particularly terrible and virtually irrevocable. The food of the accursed may turn to excrement as he raises it to his lips, or his heir may die. When a filthy Aghori dressed in the rotting skin of a fresh-water porpoise was, some generations ago, refused admission to the Maharaja of Benares's palace during the performance of a magnificent *yagya*, the sacrificial offerings became immediately infested with maggots and the sacrifice had to be abandoned. As a result of this incident, the Maharaja's line has continually failed to produce heirs, and has been forced to perpetuate itself by adoption; while the curse also stipulated that any Aghori who henceforth accepted food from the palace would be afflicted by a fistual in the anus (*bhagaṃdar*). When the late abbot of Kina Ram's *āśrama* was at last induced to revoke the curse and eat from the royal kitchen, the Maharani immediately conceived a son—but the abbot himself succumbed to the foretold disorder.

For the development of my theme the story is particularly instructive in two ways. The first is that it draws our attention to the fact that the curse of an Aghori, and—as we shall see— his blessing too, is as often as not concerned with reproduction and fertility. But what is also significant is that the exclusion of the ascetic from the Maharaja's *yagya* appears to be merely a transposition of the well-known mythological incident in which Siva is excluded from the sacrifice of his father-in-law, Daksa, on the pretext that he is a naked, skull-carrying Kapalika (O'Flaherty 1976:278)—the sectarian precursor of the Aghori. But Shiva is essential to the sacrifice if the evil it unleashes is to be mastered (Biardeau 1976:96). Denied of his share, he spoils the whole event and precipitates a disaster of cosmic proportions. Though the scale of our story is admittedly more modest, it is not difficult to see that the Aghori is merely playing the role which was written for Shiva—as well he might, for we shall find that he aspires to be Shiva.

The blessing of an Aghori is as beneficent as his curse is awesome. By it he may confer inordinate riches, restore the mad, cure the incurable or bestow fertility on the barren. In order to conceive a child, both Hindu and Muslim couples go in large numbers to Kina Ram's *āśrama*, where they visit his tomb, bathe in the tank of Krimi Kund ('the tank of worms')[24] and take ash from the sacred fire which is fuelled by wood brought from the cremation pyres and which is a form of the goddess Hinglaj Devi. The same procedure should ideally be repeated on five consecutive Sundays or five consecutive Tuesdays—days of the week which are special not only to Kina Ram but also to the god Bhairava. An identical procedure will cure children of the wasting disease of *sukhaṃḍi rog* which is caused by a barren woman touching or casting her shadow on the child immediately after she has bathed at the end of her period.[25] She will then conceive, but the child will start to 'dry up' (*sukhnā*) and wither away.

An Aghori's blessing is characteristically given by violently manhandling and abusing its recipient. Bhim Baba, for example, used to live on the verandah of the City Post Office, stark naked, morosely silent, and generally surrounded by a crowd of onlookers and devotees. Every so often, as if infuriated, he would lumber to his feet (for he was massively fat) seize a small earthenware pot and hurl it with a roar into the crowd. The fortunate target of his missile could leave assured that his problem was about to be solved or his aspirations met (cf. Morinis 1979:244; Barrow 1893:226).[26] It is said that on festival occasions Kina Ram would throw his urine on the crowds by way of blessing. Indeed the bodily emissions of an Aghori are charged with a special potency and have miraculous medicinal qualities. The sister of one of Bhagavan Ram's university-educated devotees, for example, was said to have been cured of a grave illness after her brother had obtained for her a phial of his *guru*'s urine. A lay follower may be initiated by the *guru* placing a drop of his semen on the disciple's tongue; while at the initiation of an ascetic the preceptor fills a skull with his urine which is then used to moisten the novitiate's head before it is tonsured (Barrow 1893: 241).

Now my informants continually stress that as a result of his *sādhanā* an Aghori does not die. He realises the state of non-duality I referred to earlier; he 'takes *samādhi*', and enters into a perpetual cataleptic condition of suspended animation or deep meditation. His body is arranged (if necessary by breaking the spine) in a meditational posture (known as *padmāśan*), sitting cross-legged with his upturned palms resting on his knees. He is then placed in a box which—in Benares—is buried in the grounds of Kina Ram's *āśrama* (and which is everywhere oriented towards the north). Unlike the householder or ascetics of most other orders his skull is not smashed during the mortuary rites in order to release the 'vital breath'. A small shrine containing the phallic emblem of Shiva is erected over the site of the grave, the emblem transmitting to the worshipper the power emanating from the ascetic's subterranean meditation.

By entering *samādhi* (the term refers to his tomb as well as to his condition within it)—which he is represented as doing by conscious desire at a time of his choosing—the ascetic unequivocally escapes the normal consequences of death: the severance of the connection between body and soul, the corruption of the body and the transmigration of the soul. Provided that he has 'taken' *samādhi* while still alive (*jīvit-samādhi*), rather than being given it after death, his body is immune to putrescence and decay although it remains entombed for thousands of years. It is still the occasional habitation of his soul, which wanders the three *lokas* (of heaven, earth and the netherworld) assuming any bodily form it chooses and changing from one to another at will. The real ideological stress is here, rather than on the incorruption of the particular body he inhabited before he took *samādhi*. Endless stories nevertheless testify to a conviction that the body of the model ascetic is perfectly and perpetually preserved in its tomb; and it is widely believed that this body is at times animated by his peripatetic soul which may be brought back to its former shell in an instant by the fervent prayers of the devotee.

A *samādhi* (in the sense of tomb) which is re-animated by the presence of the soul is described as a *jāgrit-samādhi* ('awakened *samādhi*'). Baba Bhagavan Ram's disciples credit him with thus 'awakening' the occupants of every one of the fifty *samādhi* within the precincts of Kina Ram's *āśrama* since he took over its effective management;[27] and this makes it possible to induce them to take a more direct hand in the affairs of men. As for himself, Bhagavan Ram denies the appeal of heaven, where—as he wryly informed me—'all the celestial nymphs (*apsaras*) are now old ladies'. His intention is rather to spend eternity 'watching and waiting' here on earth where he is within easy reach of ordinary mortals. It is out of compassion for the sufferings of humanity that such an ascetic denies himself the final bliss of complete dissolution into Brahma, for once he is finally liberated 'who will give the sermons'?

What sense, then, can we make of the ethnography I have provided? One preliminary observation here is that Aghori ideology, if not always their practice, insists that members of the order do not solicit alms. This relates to the familiar South Asian contradiction that, while the ascetic is enjoined to remain completely independent of the material and social order, he must necessarily depend on the gifts of the householder in order to support himself, and can therefore never entirely escape from the lay world. Aghori practice may be seen as one radical solution to this dilemma. His loincloth is a shroud, his fuel the charred wood of the pyres, his food human refuse. By scavenging from the dead (who have no further use for what he takes), the Aghori escapes the clutches of the living, and in theory at least realizes the ascetic ideal of complete autonomy.

We may also note that the Aghori's vigil on the cremation ground may be represented as an unblinking meditation on the classic Hindu themes of the transience of existence and the inevitability of mortal suffering 'Surrounded by death in the place of death, those aspects of reality that end in the fires of the cremation ground become distasteful... attachment to the world and the ego is cut and union with Siva, the conqueror of death, is sought' (Kinsley 1977:100), Like ascetics of other orders, the Aghori aspires to die to the phenomenal world, to undergo the 'Death that conquers death' (ibid.), and to exist on earth as an exemplar of the living dead. But what makes him different from others is that he pushes this symbolism to its logical limits.

The theological line which the Aghoris themselves most forcefully stress, however, is the notion that everything in creation partakes of *paramātmā*, the Supreme Being, and that therefore all category distinctions belong merely to the world of superficial appearances, and there is no essential difference between the divine and the human, or between the pure and the polluted. As Lal Baba represented his own spiritual quest to me, it is to become like that ideal Aghori, the sun, whose rays illuminate everything indiscriminately and yet remain undefiled by the excrement they touch.

The doctrine that the essence of all things is the same may clearly be taken to imply a radical devaluation of the caste hierarchy, since from this point of view there is no fundamental difference between the Untouchable and the Brahman. What is less obvious, however, is whether this teaching is one which relates only—as Dumont's model (1960, 1970) would suggest—to the ascetic (caste is irrelevant for *him* but not for the world at large), or whether the Aghori's devaluation of the social order is to be interpreted as a message for *all* men. My Aghori informants themselves were not altogether unequivocal on the matter—sometimes denying to caste any relevance whatsoever, while at others presenting equality as a matter of the ultimate *religious* truth of the enlightened rather than as the appropriate goal of social policy. This lack of clarity is perhaps only to be expected, since for them the central concern is with dissolving the barrier between god and man (or more precisely between Shiva and the individual ascetic himself), rather than with tearing down that which divides men from each other.

It is, however, clear that the *social* implications of Aghori doctrine are far from absent from the teachings of Baba Bhagavan Ram, their most illustrious representative in Benares, who has derived from its religious truth a this-worldly ethic of equality and community service—though I concede the possibility that this may be a modern re-working of the renouncer's message. The *āśrama* Bhagavan Ram founded just across the river from Benares includes a hospice for lepers, a primary school, dispensary, post office and printing press. Amongst his circle of followers inter-caste marriage is positively encouraged. But what might also be said is that within the egalitarian order which he would have his disciples realize, a position of unquestioned privilege is none the less preserved for the *guru*. He drives about in a jeep, and while he sleeps over a grave, he does so in a well-appointed room under an electric fan. Even his teaching is not without its streak of ambivalence. While caste may be dismissed as a conspiracy of the powerful, the vow by which his male devotees should offer their daughters in marriage leaves considerable doubt about the equality of the sexes within marriage,[28] and the doctrine of *karma* is not in question. Lepers are paying the price of past wickedness. (I regret that I neglected to ask whether the same might not also be held to apply to the Untouchables.) What is at issue, he told me, is rather the right of others to use this fact as justification for their exclusion from society.[29]

If, however obliquely, Aghori doctrine poses questions about the ultimate legitimacy of the social order, there is a rather different way in which their practice reinforces this message of doubt. In orthodox caste society polluting contacts between castes must be eliminated in order to preserve the boundaries of the group, for which—as Douglas (1966) argues—the boundaries of the body often serve as a metaphor. The Aghori's inversion of the same symbols of body margins implies exactly the opposite message. With the destruction of boundaries entailed by the consumption of flesh, excrement and so on, goes an affirmation of the irrelevance of caste boundaries. Coming at the issue in a more general way suggested by Turner (1969), we might also note the relationship which exists between liminal states, the suspension of the hierarchical structure of everyday life, and a stress on a vision of an unhierarchized and undifferentiated humanity. By contrast with that of the initiand in tribal society, the Aghori's liminality is permanent—and it is also of a somewhat extreme character. It is hardly surprising, then, that he should represent something of the equality which is generally associated with those liminal to the routinely ordered structure.

Perhaps the most striking aspect of the data, however, is the remarkable similarity between the character assumed by the Aghori and the person of Shiva. Indeed the description of Shiva given by his disapproving father-in-law perfectly fits the stereotype of the Aghori:

> He roams about in dreadful cemeteries, attended by hosts of goblins and spirits, like a mad man, naked, with dishevelled hair, laughing, weeping, bathed in ashes of funeral piles, wearing a garland of skulls and ornaments of human bones, insane, beloved of the insane, the lord of beings whose nature is essentially darkness (Briggs 1938: 153).

The epithet *aughaṛ*, by which the Aghori is widely known and which implies an uncouth carefreeness, is one of the names of the god. Like Shiva, who ingested the poison that emerged from the Churning of the Oceans and thereby allowed creation to proceed, the Aghori is a swallower of poison who liberates the blocked-up fertility of women. Like his prototype he is addicted to narcotics, is master of evil spirits, is touched with madness and his most salient characteristic is his moodiness. He is *aṛbhangi*—one who follows his whims with truculent intransigence. He adorns his body with the ornaments of Shiva, plays Shiva's part as spoiler of the sacrifice when denied admission to it, is greeted in a way appropriate to the god with cries of Bom, Bom or Har Har Mahādev, and indeed claims and is acknowledged to be Shiva. So, for example, the abbots of the Kina Ram *āśrama* are explicitly said to be his *avatar*. In the rite of *cakra pūjā*, the Aghori becomes the Lord of Forgetfulness wrapped in a deathless embrace with his consort; while his necrophagy on the cremation ground may be seen as an act of communion in which he ingests Shiva (for a corpse is said to *be* Shiva), and thus re-creates his consubstantiality with him. The skull he carries associates him with Shiva's manifestation as the terrifying god Bhairava who—to atone for the sin of chopping off Brahma's fifth head—was condemned to wander the earth 'as an Aghori' with a skull stuck fast to his hand. Dogs, which like the Aghori scavenge off the cremation ground, are his familiars—as they are of Bhairava in whose temples they wander freely. The special days for visiting these temples are the same as those for visiting Kina Ram's *āśrama*; the god too blesses his worshippers in the form of a (token) beating delivered by his priests, and in ritual intercourse the Aghori's female partner is often identified as his consort, Bhairavi. In short, as Lorenzen (1972:80) has noted, the ascetic homologizes himself with the god and acquires some of his divine powers and attributes.[30] Above all, like Shiva—the Great Ascetic and Destroyer of the Universe whose emblem is the erect phallus and whose sexual transports shake the cosmos—he transcends duality by uniting opposites within his own person, and thereby acquires Shiva's role as Mahāmritunja, the 'Conqueror of Death', who amongst the gods is the only one who survives the dissolution of the cosmos and who is truly indestructible (*avināśī*).

This, it seems to me, is the crux of the matter. The theme of inversion and the coincidence of opposites runs throughout the material I have presented. The ascetic becomes the consort of the prostitute, the menstruating prostitute becomes the goddess, beating a blessing, the cremation ground a place of worship, a skull the food-bowl and excrement and putrid flesh food, and pollution becomes indistinguishable from purity. Duality is abolished, polarities are recombined,[31] and the Aghori thus recaptures the primordial state of non-differentiation. He passes out of the world of creation and destruction and into an existence which is beyond time.[32] He attains that state of unity with Brahma which characterized the atemporal and undifferentiated void which existed before the world began. So while in my opening remarks I suggested that the mortuary rites of the householder represent a recreation of the deceased, and a renewal of his transient existence, I am arguing here that by embracing death and pollution, by systematically combining opposites, the Aghori aims to suspend time, to get off the roundabout and to enter an eternal state of *samādhi* in which death has no menace.

NOTES

I gratefully acknowledge helpful comments on an earlier draft from Maurice Bloch, Richard Burghart, Audrey Cantlie, Chris. Fuller, Jean La Fontaine, Edmund Leach and Penny Logan.

1 Fieldwork in Benares was carried out between September 1976 and November 1977 (supported by the Social Science Research Council) and in August 1978 (supported by the London School of Economics and Political Science). I am deeply obligated to Virendra Singh for his language instruction, and to him and Om Prakash Sharma for their research assistance.

2 There is however a wide variation in the meanings which different informants attach to these terms. See Parry 1981.

3 Although the theory is fairly general, the practice of differentiating between the sexes in this way is—in my experience—largely confined to the Bengali community (which is quite substantial in Benares).

4 Cf. Malamoud's (1975) fascinating discussion of both cremation and gestation as a process of cooking.

5 Were it not for the quite explicit parturition symbolism of the pyre and the funeral procession (described above), it would be tempting to interpret cremation as a mere insemination, leading to the ten-day gestation period of the subsequent rites. In this context it is interesting to note that the *Śatapatha Brāhmaṇa* refers to the fire as the womb of the sacrifice, into which the initiand at *dīkṣā* offers his being as semen (Malamoud 1975).

6 The *Kāśī Khaṇḍa* is a portion of the *Skanda Purāṇa*. A short summary of this myth is given in Parry 1981.

7 Siddhartha Gautam Ram was installed in February 1978, at the age of nine. He does not himself yet live in the *āśrama*, but stays with his *guru*, Baba Bhagavan Ram, in the compound of the refuge for lepers which the latter founded. He was given to Baba Bhagavan Ram to raise after Bhagavan Ram had fructified the formerly infertile union of the boy's parents. As *mahant* of the Kina Ram *āśrama* he is clearly the puppet of Bhagavan Ram, who now effectively controls the *āśrama* (having been at loggerheads with the previous *mahant*, who was his own *guru*). It is said that while the young *mahant* is an incarnation of Kina Ram, and hence of Shiva himself, Bhagavan Ram is an incarnation of the god's *śakti* (his active female aspect), and more particularly of the goddess Sarvesvari (the consort of Shiva as the Lord of All). The much-quoted aphorism that 'without *śakti* Shiva is a *śava* (corpse)' seems particularly apposite to the present case.

8 I personally encountered twelve, but with only eight of them did I have any but the most fleeting contact. Although some Aghoris spend a significant amount of time on pilgrimage (in particular to Prayag, Pasupatinath in Nepal and Kamakhya in Assam), most appear to have a home base, and none that I came across was rigorously peripatetic.

9 Guru Purnima falls on the full-moon day of the month of *āsāṛha* (June-July)

and is a traditional time for paying formal respects to one's *guru*. The more spectacular occasion, however, is Lolark Chhath which is celebrated on the sixth day of the bright fortnight of *bhādon/bhādrapada* (August-September). An enormous fair is held at the tank of the sun, known as Lolark Kund, the waters of which provide a cure for both leprosy and human infertility. (This set of associations between the sun, leprosy and fertility recurs in a number of different contexts.) On Lolark Chhath, however, it is the affliction of barrenness which receives the greatest stress, and thousands of childless couples come to bathe in the tank. The festival is also said to fall on the anniversary of a well-known incident when Kina Ram gave an infertile and therefore greatly distressed Brahman woman the blessing of the birth of three sons in the three following years by beating her three times with a stick. (I discuss the violent nature of Aghori blessings later on in the text.) According to the legend, she was a servant of Swami Tulsidas (though in reality it is not certain that the historical Kina Ram had even been born by the time of Tulsidas's death). After consulting with Lord Rama, Tulsidas had told her that it was not in her fate to conceive. As we shall see, fertility may also be procured by bathing in the tank of Krimi Kund, which is situated inside the compound of Kina ram's *āśrama*, and by subsequently visiting his tomb. Hedging their bets, many couples undergo both remedies on the day of Lolark Chhath. It was also then that the prostitutes of the city used to come to sing and dance at the *āśrama* in honour of Kina Ram (see below).

10 For a general account of the ascetic sects represented in Benares, and some idea of their relative strengths, see Sinha and Saraswati (1978). They estimate (p. 50) that there is roughly one ascetic for every 150 lay Hindus in the city's population.

11 A female ascetic who lived in Benares until her death some twelve years ago is said to have been an Aghori, and is certainly described as performing the ritual practices which are the hallmark of the order. Vidyarthi *et al.* (1979:220–4) contains an interview with a householder-ascetic who lives with his wife and who claims to be an Aghori; while Sinha and Saraswati (1978:145–6) provide a brief account of an Aghori couple who live together as Shiva and Parvati. All those I knew had completely renounced family life, though the *guru* of one of my ascetic informants was a householder. (See also Barrow 1893:224).

12 According to the descriptions I was given, the corpse is held fast during *śava-sādhanā* by a silken thread, which binds its wrist or ankle to a stake in the ground. It is then surrounded by a protective circle, within which the evil spirits of the cremation ground cannot penetrate, and outside of which are placed meat and liquor for them to consume. These spirits will try to engage the adept in a dialogue which he must at all costs resist. Provided that he is sufficiently resolute, they will eventually tire and accept the offerings he has left for them. This is a sign that his austerities will be rewarded. The corpse's mouth will relax, allowing the Aghori to feed it a tiny quantity of *khir* (rice pudding). He will subsequently decapitate it in order to acquire the skull, or cut a bone from the spine; and finally immerse the remains in the river. This is followed by a period of severe ascetic restraint which completes his mastery over the deceased's spirit.

The *ojhā*, who is a specialist in the control over the malevolent dead, is also said to perform *śava-sādhanā* for similar ends. But while the Aghori sits on the corpse's chest, the *ojhā* sits on the stomach.

13 In theory Kina Ram's *āśrama* has the right to claim five unburnt logs and five *paisa* for every pyre lit at the nearby cremation ground at Harish Chandra *ghāṭ*. It is alleged that in practice the Dom funeral attendants appropriate this perquisite, though every day somebody goes from the *āśrama* to collect charred wood from the pyres. This is not only used for cooking but also for maintaining the sacred fire which is the embodiment of the goddess Hanglaj Devi (a manifestation of Agni) who came to dwell with Kina Ram in Benares after he had visited her shrine in Baluchistan.

14 Dogs are also the attendants (*gan*) of Shiva in his form as the terrifying Lord Bhairava (see below).

15 In the ritual language of the Aghori, liquor is known as *dāru* or more commonly as *dudhvā*, urine as *amari pān*, and excrement as *bajrī*. *Dāru* means medicine or simply liquor; *dudhvā* would seem to relate to the standard Hindi *dudh*, 'milk'; and *amarī pān* to *amṛt*, 'nectar of immortality'. I do not know what, if anything, *bajrī* means outside this context and the word is not given in the standard dictionaries I have consulted. I speculate that it is derived from the Sanskrit *vajr*, which is the weapon of Vishnu (and Indra), but which also has the connotation of 'hard' or 'strengthening'.

16 Although the account is written in fictional form, it was clearly intended to be—and was—read as an exposé of the reality, confronting an important and corrupt local administration. The selection from, and commentary on, the orderly's revelations which was published in the *Calcutta Review* (1849 vol. 11:318–96) claims that 'the whole is essentially true, the form only is that of a work of fiction'.

17 The night most closely associated with such practices is *caturdaśi*, which is also known as *mahākāl rātri*—the night of Shiva as the destructive Lord of Time. *Caturdaśi* is the penultimate (lunar) day of the dark fortnight of the Hindu month, and is an inauspicious time during which Vedic study is proscribed (cf. Kane 1941 II:395). It immediately precedes the even more inauspicious new-moon day of *āmāvasyā* when ghosts are abroad and easy to contact (cf. Stanley 1977). The *caturdaśī* which falls in the month *phālguna* (February–March) is the day of the festival of Shivaratri, which celebrates Shiva's marriage and is one of the most important days for visiting his temples.

18 My evidence thus contradicts Crooke's (1928) implication that the Aghori is indifferent about the kind of skull he uses.

19 Other informants had a completely contradictory notion of the Oil-pressers, claiming that they are particularly intelligent. But whichever view they favour, everybody is agreed that there is something special about their intellects which creates a special demand for their skulls.

20 The magnetism of the Aghori ascetic for many high-caste householders was reported as early as the first half of the nineteenth century. 'In the holy city [of Benares], many Brahmans, Kshatris, and high Sudras, take instruction from this sage [the *mahant* of Kina Ram's *āśrama*]; but do not venture to imitate his manners' (Martin 1838:II:492). The same source

notes that 'the Rajas and their chief relations have a strong hankering after their doctrine'.

21 If he should fail them, however, they are likely to go elsewhere. Until his son died, the Raja of one of the small states in the region was a devotee of Baba Bhagavan Ram. He subsequently transferred his allegiance to Ram Lochan Baba, another Benares Aghori.

22 One or two devotees frankly acknowledged that membership of his following provided them with a ready-made network of social contacts with other like-minded professional people, not only in Benares, but throughout northern India.

23 More damning still is the accusation that he uses his *siddhis* for material gain. Whether the magical powers in question are those of the Aghori, or those of the old woman who knows a charm for curing piles, in the long term they are completely incompatible with the accumulation of profit, which leads to their inexorable decline.

24 Some informants claim that Krimi Kund is a bastardization of the correct name Krin Kund. *Krīṃ* is the 'seed' *mantra* of the goddess Kali.

25 *Sukhaṃḍi rog* is also cured by visiting Aughar Nath ka Takhiya, which is in another part of the city and which contains the tombs of several Aghoris.

26 A photograph of Bhim Baba (who died before my field-work started) and a light-hearted account of a brief encounter with him and another Aghori are given in Newby 1966:228–34. A special edition of the popular Hindi magazine *Nūtan Kahaniyān* (Allahabad, June 1977) was devoted to stories of miraculous encounters with Aghoris. One of the articles is a profile of Bhim Baba and provides a vivid description of his method of blessing (which was also retailed by several of my own informants). This source also contains an account of Bhim Baba's origins which has extremely wide currency in the city. According to this account he was a Judge who renounced the world and became an Aghori after having to deal with a case in which he was obliged to administer a manifestly unjust law. On a brief visit to Kathmandu I was able to track down Bhim Baba's younger brother (an architect with a poultry business on the side). The family are Maharashtrian Karade Brahmans who settled in Nepal when their father obtained an appointment at the Pasupatinath temple through the good offices of the *rāj-purohit*. Bhim Baba was apparently in continual conflict with his somewhat disciplinarian father, refused to study, and finally left home (completely naked) after a quarrel in which his father reproached him with ingratitude for years of parental support. He was never employed, far less a Judge.

27 On Baba Bhagavan Ram's control of the *āśrama* see n. 23 above.

28 'Oh Shiva this daughter in the form of energy, I am offering to you to be used for the satisfaction of your holy desires and for the benefit of society —that is for breeding to such a progeny [*sic*] as may be useful for humanity, without any restricition of caste, creed or nationality' (cited in a pamphlet entitled *An Introduction to Shri Sarveshwari Samooh*, published by the Awadhoot Bhagwan Ram Kust Sewa Ashram).

29 I encountered a very similar ambivalence in the case of another Aghori whose public pronouncements continually stress the brotherhood of all

men and the meaningless character of the social hierarchy. It was clear that he regarded himself as a member of a small spiritual élite karmically qualified for the attainment of *samādhi.*

What is also striking is that both of these ascetics not only repudiate caste but also the divisions between Hindus and others; and both are prepared to appropriate Christian symbols to make this point. Bhagavan Ram's leprosy hospice is surmounted by a Christian Cross; while Sadhak Basudeb showed me a pictorial autobiography he had made for the instruction of his devotees which contains a drawing in which he is receiving the stigmata from Christ who appeared to him during his wanderings in the Himalayas. This element of religious syncretism is also apparent at the shrine of Aughar Nath ka Takhiya, which contains several Aghori *samādhis* and which is said to belong equally to Hindus and Muslims. The influence of a devotional *bhakti* ideology is also particularly clear in much of the Aghoris' discourse.

30 The Aghoris' identification with Shiva does not, of course, make them unique. The same might, I think, be said of many other Shiva ascetics and even of Shaiva priests. What is again unusual about the present case is the means rather than the end; and perhaps also the aspect of Shiva with which they choose to identify.

31 One obvious symbol of this merging of opposites is the androgyne; and it is perhaps significant that Baba Bhagavan Ram—despite his unambigously masculine physique—has assumed a somewhat androgynous character. He is said to be an incarnation of a female deity (see n. 23); is represented as a swollen-breasted goddess in a picture kept in a shrine within the *āśrama* he founded, and is said to sometimes appear before his followers in a *sāṛī.*

32 In a number of respects all this invites parallels with the annual pilgrimage of the Huichol Indians to the Wirikuta desert, where all the separations of profane life are obliterated and everything is done backwards in order to effect a return to the time of creation (Myerhoff 1978). One crucial difference, of course, is that the Aghori's reversal is a life-long commitment rather than a temporary phase in the annual round. Unlike Rigby's (1968) Gogo rituals of purification, his inversions are not merely aimed at going back to the beginning of things so that time may start again, but rather at arresting time altogether.

REFERENCES

Arens, W. 1979 *The man-eating myth: anthropology and anthropophagy.* New York: Oxford Univ. Press.

Balfour, H. 1897 The life-history of an Aghori Fakir. *Journal of the Royal Anthropological Institute* 26, 340–57.

Barrow, H. W. 1893 On Aghoris and Aghoripanthis. *Journal of the Anthropological Society of Bombay* 3, 197–251.

Biardeau, M. 1976 Le sacrifice dans l'hindouisme. In M. Biardeau and C. Malamoud *Le sacrifice dans l'Inde ancienne*. Paris: Presses Universitaires de France (Bibliothèque de l'école des hautes études, sciences religieuses, vol. LXXIX).

Briggs, G. W. 1938 *Gorakhnath and the Kanphata Yogis*. Calcutta: YMCA Publishing House.

Bloch, M. & Parry, J. 1982. Introduction: Death and the Regeneration of Life. In M. Bloch and J. Parry (eds.) *Death and the regeneration of life*. Cambridge: Univ. Press.

Carstairs, G. M. 1957 *The twice-born: a study of a community of high caste Hindus*. London: Hogarth Press.

Crooke, W. 1928 Aghori. In James Hastings (ed.) *Encyclopedia of Religion and Ethics*, vol. 1, 210–3.

Douglas, M. 1966 *Purity and danger: an analysis of concepts of pollution and taboo*. London: Routledge and Kegan Paul.

Dumont, L. 1960 World Renunciation in Indian Religions. *Contributions to Indian Sociology* 4, 33–62.

—— 1970 *Homo Hierarchicus: the caste system and its implications*. London: Weidenfield and Nicholson.

Eliade, M. 1969 *Yoga: immortality and freedom*. Princeton: Univ. Press (Bollingen series LVI).

—— 1976 *Patanjali and Yoga*. New York: Schocken Books.

Gupta, S. 1979 Modes of worship and meditation. In S. Gupta, D. J. Hoens and T. Goudriaan, *Hindu Tantrism*. Leiden: E. J. Brill (Handbuch der Orientalistik)

Harris, M. 1977 *Cannibals and kings*. New York: Random House.

Kane, P. V. 1941 and 1953 *History of dharmasastra* vols. 2 & 4. Poona: Bhandarkar Oriental Research Institute.

(Sri) *Kaśi Khanda* n.d. Compiled and rendered into Hindi by Baikunthnath Upadhyay. Varanasi: Shri Bhragu Prakashan.

Kinsley, D. R. 1977 'The death that conquers death': dying to the world in medieval Hinduism. In Frank E. Reynolds and E. H. Waugh (eds.) *Religious encounters with death: insights from the history and anthropology of religions*. Univesity Park and London: Pennsylvania State Univ. Press.

Knipe, D. M. 1975 *In the image of fire: Vedic experiences of heat*. Delhi and Varanasi: Motilal Banarasidass

—— 1977 *Sapiṇḍikāraṇa:* the Hindu rite of entry into heaven. In Frank E. Reynolds and E. H. Waugh (eds.) *Religious encounters with death: insights from the history and anthropology of religions*. Pennsylvania State Univ. Press.

Lorenzen, D. N. 1972 *The Kapalikas and Kalamukhas: Two lost Saivite sects*. Berkeley and Los Angeles: Univ. of California Press.

Malamoud, C. 1975 'Cuire le monde', *Puruśartha: recherches de sciences sociales sur l'asie du sud* 1, 91–135.

Martin, Montgomery 1838 *The history, topography, and statistics of Eastern India*. London: W. H. Allen & Co.

Morinis, A. 1979 Hindu pilgrimage with particular reference to West Bengal, India. Unpublished D. Phil. thesis at the University of Oxford.

Meyerhoff, B. G. 1978 Return to Wirikuta: ritual reversal and symbolic continuity on the Peyote hunt of the Huichol Indians. In B. A. Babcock (ed.) *The reversible world: symbolic inversion in art and society*. Ithaca and London: Cornell Univ. Press.

Newby, E. 1966 *Slowly down the Ganges*. London: Hodder and Stoughton.

O'Flaherty, W. D. 1976 *The origins of evil in Hindu mythology*. Berkeley, Los Angeles and London: Univ. of California Press.

—— 1980 Karma and rebirth in the Vedas and Puranas. In W. D. O'Flaherty (ed). *Karma and rebirth in classical Indian traditions*. Berkeley, Los Angeles and London: Univ. of California Press.

Oman, J. C. 1903 *The Mystics, ascetics, and saints of India: a study of sadhuism, with an account of the Yogis, Sanyasis, Bairagis, and other strange Hindu sectarians*, London: T. Fisher Unwin.

Parry, J. P. 1980 Ghosts, greed and sin: the occupational identity of the Benares funeral priests *Man* (n.s.) 15, 88–111.

—— 1981 Death and cosmogony in Kashi. *Contributions to Indian Sociology* N.S. 15, 337–65.

—— 1982 Sacrificial death and the necrophagous ascetic. In M. Bloch and J. Parry (eds.) *Death and the regeneration of life*. Cambridge: Univ. Press.

(*The*) *Revelations of an orderly*, by Paunchkouri Kran (pseudonym) 1848. Benares: Recorder Press. (Selections reprinted in *Calcutta Review* 1849, 11, 348–96).

Rigby, P. 1968 Some Gogo rituals of 'purification': an essay on social and moral categories. In E. R. Leach (ed.) *Dialectic in practical religion*. Cambridge papers in social anthropology no. 5).

Sherring, M. A. 1872 *Hindu tribes and castes as represented in Benares*. London: Trubner and Co.

Shulman, D. D. 1980 *Tamil temple myths: sacrifice and divine marriage in the South Indian Saiva tradition*. Princeton: Univ. Press.

Sinha, S and Saraswati, B. 1978 *Ascetics of Kashi: an anthropological exploration*. Varanasi: N. K. Bose Memorial Foundation.

Stanley, J. M. 1977 Special time, special power: the fluidity of power in a popular Hindu festival. *Journal of Asian Studies* 37, 27–43.

Tod, Lt. Col. J. 1839 *Travels in western India*. London: W. H. Allen.

Turner, V. 1969 *The ritual process: structure and anti-structure*. Chicago: Aldine Publishing Co.

Vidyarthi, L. P., Saraswati B. N. and Makhan Jha 1979 *The sacred complex of Kashi*. Delhi: Concept Publishing Company.

THE INDIAN RENOUNCER: STRUCTURE AND TRANSFORMATION IN THE LINGAYAT COMMUNITY

N. J. Bradford

Most of what has been written about renunciation and renouncers in India has been based on literary sources and has been confined to an appreciation of the philosophical and the esoteric.[1] The social anthropology of those social movements and sects inspired by renouncers is, however, still in its infancy.[2] One of the objectives of this paper is to describe and account for the institution of renunciation in the context of a particular set of beliefs and practices. Furthermore, in pursuing this objective, I shall be presenting the ethnography of the Lingayats of Karnataka in South India, a sectarian community which has fascinated Indianists for a number of decades, but about which no single monograph has yet been written. Indeed, not only has the Lingayat (also called Virashaiva) tradition been largely confined to the footnotes of Indian sociology, but where commentaries have been forthcoming these have followed a naive historical format.[3]

The generally accepted but by no means well-documented historical view of the Lingayat community is of the degeneration into caste of a former radical devotional (*bhakti*) movement which swept Karnataka in the twelfth century A. D. and was led by Basava, chief minister to the Jain King Bijjala, in association with a company of inspired peripatetic ascetics called *jaṅgamaru* (literally 'the moving ones') or *śaraṇaru* (usually translated as 'saints'). The main evidence of the actual existence of these people lies in their sayings, called *vacana*.[4] In the introduction to his translation of some of these sayings A. K. Ramanujan (1973:21) provides the familiar historical vignette to which I have referred, 'The Virashaiva movement was a social upheaval by and for the poor, the low-caste and the outcast against the rich and the privileged; it was a rising of the unlettered against the literate pundit, flesh and blood against stone.' There is little doubt that many of the composers of the *vacana* came from low castes. Where the leadership came from is, however, another matter. Basava was a Brahman aristocrat and Allama Prabhu, another prominent figure in the twelfth century movement, was clearly neither unlettered nor low caste. Dr Lorenzen (1972:167–88) believes that the so-called priests, or *jaṅgama*, were organized before Basava's appearance and that the Lingayat movement was 'a reformist schism from the Kalamukha church' whose priests were organized into large monasteries. Historical speculation is, then, rife, as it should be in the Indian context where legitimacy is closely dependent upon origins. And it need hardly be pointed out that Lingayats themselves speculate as much as any outsider about the history of their tradition (P. B. Desai 1968; Hardekar 1940; Hunashal 1947; Malladevaru 1973; Nandimath 1942; Sakhare 1942; Government of Mysore 1967).

Whatever the situation in ancient times—and there is enough evidence for a case to be made that it was no different—there are today among Lingayats two kinds of *jaṅgama*, two traditions of '*guru*-ship', and two definitions and histories of Virashaivism. Rather than continue to speculate as to their historical relation—an activity which appears to encourage the notion that the renunciatory ideal has been progressively eroded—I shall treat them as interrelated elements in an everpresent structure. The basis for such a treatment lies in the Lingayat organization and conception of *jaṅgama*, whereby a distinction is made between the *jaṅgama* of the inside and the *jaṅgama* of the outside.

The Lingayat Jaṅgama

The Lingayats are generally known as *liṅgavantaru*, literally 'the carriers of the *liṅgam*' (an emblem of Shiva in the form of a phallus), or as *vīraśaivaru* ('staunch Shaivites'). The Lingayats are distinguished from other communities in India by virtue of the fact, amongst others, that they are invested soon after birth by their *guru* with a small personal *liṅgam* (called *iṣṭaliṅgam*) which they wear in a slung casket and worship in the privacy of a household shrine. They live for the most part in the nucleated villages of northern Karnataka where they comprise a 'dominant' community, divided into some eighty endogamous sub-castes (*jāti*) but all bound by allegiances of various sorts to Lingayat priests and preceptors of the *jaṅgama* caste.

A *jaṅgama* is addressed as 'preceptor' (*guru*), 'father' (*appagaḷu*), 'master' (*svāmi*), 'wisdom' (*buddhi*) or quite simply as Shiva. *Jaṅgama* are also referred to as 'the gods' (*dēvaru*). Indeed, the first ritual obeisance (*namaskāra*) a Lingayat child learns is called 'doing *svāmi*', deity and *svāmi* being conceived as synonomous. All *jaṅgama* males have the honorific suffix *-ayya* attached to their names. For example, a *jaṅgama* male might be called Basayya whereas the non-*jaṅgama* would be called Basanna or Basappa. The 'surname' of a *jaṅgama* always ends with the term *maṭha*. By implication, wherever a *jaṅgama* settles a *maṭha* is founded, although in its more ramified form, as we shall see, a *maṭha* comes to be something of an ecclesiastical establishment and, in some cases, a monastery. Every *maṭha* both architecturally and ritually is inevitably focused upon the tomb of the founding *svāmi*. The Kannada term for the tomb of a *jaṅgama* is *gaḍḍige*. *Gaḍḍige* refers not only to the permanent resting place of a *jaṅgama* but also to the place where he sits in his capacity as priest-*guru* during rites held in Lingayat houses. A *gaḍḍige*, in other words, is not so much a tomb as the place where a *jaṅgama* comes to rest. Like the *jaṅgama*, who always sit on their *gaḍḍige* (a raised wooden seat) the 'personal *liṅgam*', which is often taken out of its casket and used in worship, should not touch the ground.

Two further points, both straightforward, need to be made about the *jaṅgama*. First, they are the purest of all Lingayats—but they are more than this. A *jaṅgama* exudes a force which stands impervious to impurity and which, indeed, positively disposes of it. A *jaṅgama* is said by Lingayats to be able to 'burn' those impurities against which ordinary individuals have to take precautionary measures. Thus the *jaṅgama* eats in the houses of those Lingayat devotees (*bhakta*) who are by caste less pure than he. For ordinary Lingayats and Hindus death carries pollution. The death of a *jaṅgama*, however, carries no pollution and occasions not so much a funeral as an enshrinement. Unlike other Lingayats, *jaṅgama* are buried within the bounds of the settlement area and their tombs may become the object of worship.[5] The second point is that as a *guru* the *jaṅgama* has intruded into the relationship between the Lingayat devotee and his personal *liṅgam*. The principal form of worship, and ideally the only form observed by Lingayats, is the 'worship of the personal *liṅga*' (*iṣṭaliṅgapūjā*). In effect the Lingayat movement took up what had formerly been an esoteric rite confined to the realms of Shaivite asceticism and, charging it with new significance, made it available to the common man-in-the-world. The rite is very simple and consists basically of a private act of meditation upon one's *iṣṭaliṅgam.* In its simplicity and directness the rite reflects the onus that the devotional movements put on the individual and his or her relationship with a personal god. There is no priestly mediator here, no go-between administrator of ritual, no gatekeeper to the god-in-the-temple (*sthāvara liṅgam*). The intrusion of the *jaṅgama* into this relationship rests not simply on the idea that the *jaṅgama* is *liṅgam* but on the fact that he appears to transcend *liṅgam.*

Basava in his *vacana* exhorted Lingayats not to save wealth but to give to the *jaṅgama* in support of the cause. Part of this support consisted in the provision of food and shelter by Lingayats for the wandering propagators of their faith. Even today all *jaṅgama* retain the privilege of partaking of ceremonial meals (*binnāya*) in Lingayat households. There are frequent ritual occasions and festivals when it would be considered highly inauspicious for a Lingayat householder not to invite a *jaṅgama* to a ceremonial meal. When a *jaṅgama* is invited to dine, he goes to the household 'god-room', the floor of which will already have been purified with cow-dung paste. Without taking a bath, no member of the family, let alone others, would be allowed in this room. Soon after his arrival the *jaṅgama* is helped, usually by the head of the household, to wash his feet. This is carried out over a large copper vessel so that no drop is wasted of the *dhūlapādōdaka*, that is, *dhūla* meaning dust and *pādōdaka* meaning 'foot-water'. The water, so consecrated, is then sprinkled throughout the house and upon all those present. This act of aspersion is called 'house-peace' (*mane śānti*). Next the two big toes of the *jaṅgama* are adorned with sacred ash (*vibhuti*) and *patri* leaves and are worshipped with incense by the devotee. Water or coconut milk is then poured from a small vessel over the toes of the *jaṅgama* and is collected in a metal cup held underneath. This act is carried out with the devotee clasping the toes of the *jaṅgama* with his left hand. The water or coconut milk which is collected underneath is called the 'consecrated offering of compassion' (*karuṇāprasāda*) and is drunk by both *jaṅgama* and devotee. *Jaṅgama* and devotee then carry out a two-stage worship of their *iṣṭaliṅga.* First the left hand, then the *iṣṭaliṅga* itself, is smeared with sacred ash and *liṅgapūja* is performed. Next a little of the 'consecrated offering of compassion' is run off the fingers of the right hand on to the 'personal *liṅga*' and a little of this is taken back on the fingers and dripped on the tongue. Each member of the household, or any Lingayat on a visit, may if he wishes undergo this ritual act with the *jaṅgama*. When this has been completed, the meal proper may commence, the *jaṅgama* being fed before anybody else. The *jaṅgama* is also given a ceremonial fee (*dakṣiṇa*).

The ritual washing of the dust from the feet of the *jaṅgama* represents a union (*samarasya*) of *guru* and devotee. There is no question of the ritual purity or status of the *jaṅgama* being endangered by contact with the devotee. In the ritual of the 'consecrated offering of compassion', however, an element of inadequacy enters into the devotee's ritual equipment and disturbs the ritual completeness of *liṅgapūjā* in which the devotee held sole responsibility for the worship of *liṅga* and, by symbolic extension, for his personal purification and his ultimate union with Shiva. Just as a plant cannot live without water, so, it would appear, the *liṅga* cannot live without *jaṅgama*. The *jaṅgama* gives life to the Shiva-*liṅga* and as life-giver he transcends Shiva*liṅga*. Priest-the-mediator has been removed, but *guru* the embodiment of god, who indeed transcends god, intrudes.

The *jaṅgama*, then, is a living Shiva; he is a sacred mediator between this world and the other, between the individual Lingayat soul and the cosmic soul (*paramātman*). *Jaṅgama*, however, do a variety of things. They represent a kind of sectarian substitute for the Brahman caste, acting as domestic priests and *guru*; they are astrologers and exponents of Sanskrit lore; they are exorcists and healers associated with miracles. Indeed the notion of *jaṅgamatvā*, as the quality inherent in living *jaṅgama*, may be seen to comprise an array of complementary oppositions, in which the sacredness of kings and priests combines with the sacredness of extra-social holy men in the wilderness.

Paṭṭadevaru and Virakta

Each *jaṅgama* belongs to an exogamous patri-clan (*gotra*, or *bagi*) which descends from one of the five seats (*piṭha*) or thrones (*siṃhāsana*) deemed to represent the original pontifical seats of the five founding Virashaiva *guru*. These five founding preceptors, called *pañcācārya*, are said to have emerged from the five heads of Shiva in the period before Brahma started populating the world. The pontifical seats or head *maṭha* are situated to this day in such far-flung places as Kedar in the Himalayas, Varanasi on the Gangetic plain, Shrishaila in Andhra Pradesh, and Ujjini and Rambhapuri in Karnataka, the home state of almost all Lingayats. In their original setting (the latter two have been relocated in more recent times) they are all found close to one or other of the eleven renowned *jyōti liṅga* of India. The five pontifical seats are at present occupied by the descendents of the original *pañcācārya*, and all of these incumbent *pañcācārya* 'world preceptors' (*jagadguru*) hail from the Kannada-speaking region of India, two of them from the district in which I carried out field-work. In the initiation rite of *jaṅgama* boys and in the marriage rite for all Lingayats, the five *pañcācārya piṭha* are represented by five metal pots which are filled with water and betel leaves and then linked together and tied to the principal subject of the ritual by a thread.

A hierarchy of *maṭha* radiates downwards from the five pontifical *piṭha* seats, through the *upācārya maṭha* (usually situated in large villages or towns), to the small village *maṭha*, or *hiremaṭha*. Each rank of *maṭha* is called a *gurusthala* ('place of the guru') or *pañcācārya maṭha* by Lingayats. An *upācārya maṭha* represents locally a major pontifical seat and is presided over by a *paṭṭadēvaru*, meaning '*royal god*', or '*enthroned god*', who acts as a 'house-*guru*' (*manegurugaḷu*) to non-*jaṅgama* Lingayats. The latter are regarded by the 'royal god' as his disciple-children (*śiṣya-makkaḷu*), and he is regarded by them as a kind of father confessor who should know their family history and advise them in times of crisis. All Lingayats inherit patrilineally this relationship with a *paṭṭadēvaru*. The organization of Lingayats may thus be characterized in the tableau form reproduced in Fig. 1.

In contrast to the kingly *guru* of the *pañcācārya* tradition there is another tradition of Lingayat *maṭha* called *virakta*. The *virakta* are the ascetic *guru*, *vi* meaning 'apart from' or 'aloof', and *rakta* meaning 'blood' or 'passion'. The kingly *pañcācārya guru* can and should officiate as priests on ritual occasions in Lingayat houses; the ascetic *virakta guru* cannot. Whereas the *pañcācārya maṭha* were built in the midst of villages and towns, the *virakta maṭha* were traditionally situated outside the boundaries of settled areas.

Fig. 1. *The Sectarian Organization of Lingayats*

Founder-*Acārya:*		Renukārādhya	Marulārādhya	Ekorāmāradhya	Panditārādhya	Viśvārādhya	
Mythical Origins:		Somēśvaraliṅga	Siddēśvaraliṅga	Rāmanāthaliṅga	Mallikarjunaliṅga	Viśvanāthaliṅga	
Seat:	G	Rambhāpuri	Ujjaini	Himavātkedār	Śrisaila	Kāśi	Pañcācārya
	U	Siṃhāsana	Siṃhāsana	Siṃhāsana	Siṃhāsana	Siṃhasana	Jagadguru
	R						
	U						
Upācārya	V						
maṭha	A						
	R	Paṭṭadēvaru and all Jaṅgama belonging to:					Śiṣya
and	G						Maneguru
	A	Vīra Gotra	Nandi Gotra	Bṛhengi Gotra	Vriṣabha Gotra	Skanda Gotra	
Hiremaṭha		(Padevidi bagi)	(Mali bagi)	(Uddana bagi)	(Muttina pendina	(Pañcāvanni	
	B				bagi)	bagi)	
	H V						
	A A						
	K R	Non-Jaṅgama Lingayat Households					Śiṣya
	T G						Makkaḷu
	A A						

Virakta guru often have no landed property attached to their *maṭha* and if they do, this will have been given by individual devotees rather than by the legal representatives, or 'elders', of the local community. The *virakta*, unlike the *jaṅgama* of the *pañcācārya* tradition, undergo an initiation, called *nirābhāri dīkṣa*, in which they renounce all worldly attachments. They cannot go back on this. Whereas the ascetic svāmi intones the *mantra* of renunciation (*layajapa*) upon succession to the headship of a *maṭha*, the *hiremaṭha svāmi* intones the *mantra* of prosperity and continuance (*sthitijapa*). The overwhelming majority of village *hiremaṭha jaṅgama* are indeed ordinary householder-farmers.

Although the *virakta* are renouncers (*sanyāsi*) who are ideally cut off from the world of the Lingayat sect, they are in fact regarded as being specifically Lingayat renouncers. The heads of the *virakta maṭha* are with few exceptions *jaṅgama* by birth, and most Lingayats are well aware of this. After taking *nirābhāri dīkṣā*, a *virakta* loses his affiliation to his *pañcācārya* patri-clan (*gotra*) but gains affiliation to the 'throne of the void' (*sūnya siṃhāsana*) and, within that affiliation, to a particular order called here *samaya*.

There is another way in which the duality of *jaṅgama* has been institutionalized. Depending upon the mode of succession to the headship, all Lingayat *maṭha* are classified into two types, called *putra varga* and *śiṣya varga*. *Śiṣya*, pupil or disciple, stands here in contrast to *putra*, the Sanskrit for son. These two modes of succession reveal two different notions of '*guru*ship' (*gurutvā*). For the son it is his father or paternal uncle, who is *guru*; for the disciple it is his preceptor or mentor who is *guru*.

A 'royal god', or *paṭṭadēvaru*, is usually only too pleased and proud to recount the unadulterated line of descent (*vaṃsa pārapampāre*) running from the founding *svāmi*-ancestor to himself. As the *paṭṭadēvaru* use the term, *guru* is synonymous with *jaṅgama* which in turn designates status by birth. The *jaṅgama*, as far as this viewpoint goes, are a caste of *guru*, and by corollary no lay devotee can become *guru*. The vast majority of *pañcācārya maṭha* are, as one might expect, of the *putra varga* tradition. The exceptions to this are the five main pontifical seats and the larger of the *upācārya maṭha*. Even in these cases, however, the notion of discipleship is qualified; thus the disciple should be *jaṅgama* by birth and furthermore should belong to the same patri-clan as his *guru*. The transition from *putra varga* to *śiṣya varga* here signifies nothing more than the difference between an affair of the lineage and an affair of the clan. The *jaṅgama*-devotee relation in the *putra varga* tradition is rigidly confined to a universe of kinship by descent. *Jaṅgamatvā* is an inherited quality and has to do with divine rule. Indeed, it is quite clear that in the old days the big *hiremaṭha* functioned as courts in which the *paṭṭadēvaru* judged and arbitrated cases involving the infringement of caste rules. The installation of a *paṭṭadēvaru* has all the trimmings of a coronation and culminates, as would the enthronement of an Indian Maharaja, with *paṭṭabandha* in which the *paṭṭa*, the golden tablet or scroll of royal authority, is tied to the forehead of the king. This emphasis on descent applies not only to the relationship between the *guru* (here called house-*guru*) and his disciples in Lingayat society at large, called 'disciple-children' (*śiṣya makkaḷu*). In keeping with a relationship which is expressed in terms of filial dependency, the house-*guru* is referred to by his children as '*paṭṭa*-father' (*paddadappa*). As with the household deity so with the *guru* a mythical kin link is handed down from father to son.

All *virakta maṭha* are considered to follow the *śiṣya varga* tradition. Even though there are examples of such *maṭha* that have in practice come to be indistinguishable from the ordinary *putra varga hiremaṭha*, this is considered to be a sign of degeneracy. The last thing a *virakta svāmi* will want to admit is that his *guru* was his father's brother. In the *śiṣya varga* tradition one does not inherit the position of *guru*, either through close 'blood' ties or even mythical clan links. One becomes a *guru* by means of religious devotion and austerity (*anuṣṭhāna*). This solitary religious practice gives the *virakta* a certain power (*siddhi*), considered by ordinary Lingayats to be potentially dangerous and harmful but also able to bring about miracles. *Virakta* are said to have *līla*, a word used to refer to the cosmic play of Shiva, and the curses of *virakta* are thought to be deadly. While the kingly *paṭṭadēvaru* sits on a throne and wears gold, the *virakta* ascetic sits on the skin of the wild tiger. Very often a child born under a 'bad star' will be given by its parents to a *virakta maṭha* for training as a novice. The *śiṣya varga*, then, entails that any Lingayat, not just a born *jaṅgama*, may attain the quality of *jaṅgama* (*jaṅgamatvā*) on the strength of devotion. One may become *jaṅgama* by initiation.

One may thus discern in the quality of *jaṅgamatvā* and in the priestly and preceptorial functions of the *jaṅgama* a set of comple-

Fig. 2. *Jaṅgama/Guru*

PAÑCĀCĀRYA/PAṬṬADĒVARU	*VIRAKTA*
born Jaṅgama	initiated Jaṅgama
sthitijapa (prosperity)	*layajapa* (renunciation)
fatherly control	*līla/siddhi*
centre of settlement/village/town	forest/mountain/outside settlement
having *śiṣya-makkaḷu* ('children')	having *bhakta* ('devotees')
guru at life-cycle ritual	*guru* of knowledge/experience (*anubhava*)
icon of *Pañcācārya*'s emergence from *Śiva-liṅga*	icon of Basava
hirsute, crowned, coloured robes.	shaven-headed, saffron-robed.

mentary oppositions (see Fig. 2). The complementarity of sacred ruler and sacred renouncer, temporal and mystical power, is contained within the sectarian head-piece. Indeed, this complementarity finds expression in the way in which one rubs off on the other. Many *paṭṭadēvaru* are celibate, though they would call themselves *brahmācāri*, not *sanyāsi*. Renouncers find themselves as heads of vast ecclesiastical establishments, indeed there are said to be five *virakta samaya* (equivalent to the pontifical sects of the *pañcācārya* tradition) though the historical evidence points to many more. And last, but not least, *jaṅgama* genealogies show that *paṭṭadēvaru* and *virakta* are not infrequently related as agnatic kin.

Lingayats distinguish, then, between the *jaṅgama* at the centre of the settlement and human affairs and the *jaṅgama* outside, the recluse of the hills and the forest. As Ananthakrishna Iyer (1931:88–9) has written: 'Viraktaswamis do not live in towns and villages, but are more of the nature of recluses. They are not allowed to become gurus or spiritual guides, or to exercise any religious authority over the Lingayats.' All *jaṅgama* are divine, but it is the *virakta* and the sites associated with his remarkable power which draw the pilgrim in need of spiritual rejuvenation or the performance of a specific miracle. The sacred places associated with the kingly *guru* lie far afield, it is true, in the ancient Hindu pilgrimage centres, but no one would make a pilgrimage to an *upācārya maṭha* or a *hiremaṭha*, for these are relatively mundane places in which local disputes are sorted out in the presence of the *paṭṭadēvaru* and the caste elders (*kattimane*) who traditionally act as witnesses to adjudications and contracts. On the other hand, the sites associated with the *virakta* tradition are indeed sacred places of pilgrimage where one may enter into contact with the divine through a transforming vision (*darśana*) of the *svāmi*, or simply by being at a shrine-tomb and perhaps becoming possessed. This is the case both with shrines of ancient standing, such as the final retreat of Basava (at the confluence of the Krishna and Malaprabha rivers) and of his sister's son, Channabasava (at Ulivi, near a river source deep in the jungle of the Western Ghats) as well as with shrines of recent standing where a *svāmi* renowned for his powers still lives.

Inside and Outside

The duality of *jaṅgama* is reflected in the ritual topography of the typical nucleated Deccan village and its surrounding territory. Here a division is conceived of between those humans and deities who are on the inside (*oḷaga*) and those who are on the outside (*horaga*). This division is expressed in the fact that it is only on certain occasions, usually involving rites of transition, that it is deemed proper and indeed necessary for those who are outside to come inside. Let me first elaborate, on the basis of my knowledge of a particular village, on the set of oppositions contained in Fig. 3.[6]

The inner area of the village, called the Fort (*kōte*), is associated with the original settlers and is currently inhabited, except for one small pocket of Shepherds (*kurubar*), by Brahmans and Lingayats, those castes which are purest and which provide the village with its dignitaries. The inner village is marked by the ruins of the old ramparts and by the presence, on the northern side, of the village gate (*ūrū-bāgilu*) presided over, as one would expect, by the deity Hanumanta. The Fort is the inner sanctum, the purest and most vulnerable part of the village, and there are restrictions on the movement into it and across it of such sources of pollution as corpses and low-caste people.

Adjacent to the inner village, and beyond the eastern boundary of the Fort lie the residential areas (*keri*) of the meat-eating castes in the middle range of the social hierarchy, who are also considered to reside within the village (*ūru*). Southwards beyond the present

Fig. 3.

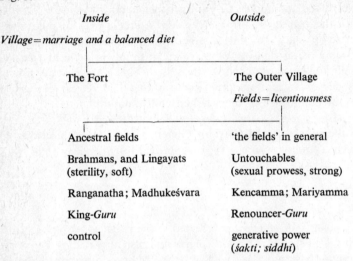

Inside	*Outside*
Village = marriage and a balanced diet	
The Fort	The Outer Village
	Fields = licentiousness
Ancestral fields	'the fields' in general
Brahmans, and Lingayats (sterility, soft)	Untouchables (sexual prowess, strong)
Ranganatha; Madhukeśvara	Kencamma; Mariyamma
King-*Guru*	Renouncer-*Guru*
control	generative power (*śakti; siddhi*)

boundary of the village, marked for the most part by a ring of threshing grounds and a high thorn fence, lie the residential areas of the Adi-Karnataka and Adi-Dravida untouchable castes. Also outside the village boundary are the burial and cremation grounds, the shrine-tomb of a *jaṅgama* ascetic, and a whole complex of deities centred on the temple of the village goddess called Kerekodi Kencamma, the 'Red Lady of the Reservoir'. Outside the village there is also a further distinction between the land close to the village fence comprising the ancestral fields (*manedahola*) of the residents in the Fort and the agricultural land stretching beyond the ancestral fields to the outer perimeter of village territory. The ancestral fields are not sold; in the case of family partition the fields are divided. They are the object of rites associated with the agricultural cycle, and they may become the ultimate resting place of great servants of the family, both human and animal. The lands further afield may change hands and are for the most part the property of middle-caste households and 'newcomers'. Where these fields are owned by the principal families in the village, they will be found to have been bought or leased rather than inherited. These lands are frequented by ghosts and evil spirits. It is in the fields too that people indulge in the sort of licentious behaviour that would not be countenanced inside the village.

The centre of the village is also inhabited by the deities Ranganatha (a blue form of Vishnu) and Madhukesvar (Shiva in the form of a *lingam*). The former is served by a Shri Vaishnava Brahman priest and the latter by a Lingayat priest. Like their priests these deities are vegetarian, and the festivals celebrated in their presence, such as Ram Navami in the case of Ranganatha and Sivaratri in the case of Madhukesvar, have particular significance for Brahmans and Lingayats.

A third of a mile outside the settlement on a track leading to the principal village burial grounds, lives Kerekodi Kencamma, the Red Lady of the Reservoir. The temple icon depicts a fiery-looking goddess with a moustache holding weapons. Immediately in front of the temple, which faces East, a *banyan* tree and a margosa (*nīm*) tree stand intertwined, and beyond them are the shrines of four other goddesses, considered to be Kencamma's sisters or allies. All these goddesses are capable of possessing people and of causing them pain, distress, and disease; each goddess has her local medium (*dēvara hēḷāvaru*) who is called in to help when she is angry and in need of propitiation. The sacrifice of a chicken or goat and a talk with the goddess through one of her mediums usually puts matters right. Some goddesses have very specific powers of retribution. Gullemma (*guḷḷe* means boils) is associated with the plague, and Mukacaudamma is able to strike people dumb. Kencamma and Mariyamma, represented outside the village by a stone under a *nīm* tree, are the major protectresses of the village in general, although Kencamma is associated with cholera in particular. Kencamma's priest belongs to a low, meat-eating caste, that of the Salt-makers (*uppār*). Out of a total of some thirty shrines in and around the village, seventeen are dedicated to similarly fiery goddesses. All except one of these seventeen shrines are situated outside the village fence, some in the colonies of the untouchable castes. The exception is Kukadamma, the 'Lady of the Forest'. She is associated with a particular caste, the Basket-weavers (*myēdār*), who rely on the forest for their basic working material of bamboo and keep a shrine to the goddess in their street. They, along with other villagers, make an annual pilgrimage to the 'parental' shrine of all Kukadammas which lies out in the jungle.

The deities on the outside are death-dealing but they are also life-giving. At a turning point in the year Kencamma, annually, and Mariyamma, triennially, are brought in to regenerate village soil and protect the settlement against the forces of death and decay. The festival of Mariyamma was described to me by the Lingayat 'headman of the temples' (*gudigoudar*):

> The Mariyamma icon, which is kept in the Ambabhavani temple, is taken by the Carpenters and painted in bright colours. Then it is placed outside the house of the Carpenter-priest of the temple facing West, and a sheep is sacrificed to placate the goddess. The icon is brought to a shelter made of *nīm* leaves outside the Ambabhavani temple. Next a he-buffalo is sacrificed by the Adi-Karnataka Untouchables. The head is put in a pit in front of Mariyamma and the blood and parts of the buffalo are mixed with rice and put into a large basket. This is the *caraga* which is carried in procession by untouchables followed by other villagers carrying sickles and weapons. Kencamma, the village goddess, is carried in her palanquin behind. At various shrines around the village sheep sacrifices are made and parts of these are mixed in with the *caraga*. All this is done by the Adi-Karnatakas, guided by me. Later, the *caraga* is taken in procession and sprinkled all along the boundary of the village and on the fields.
>
> On the second day a particular member of the Naik caste—the Potoraj—is called upon. A kid goat is hidden in a house in the village and the Potoraj has to find it by calling to it and making it bleat. The Potoraj must bring the goat to Mariyamma, where he rips its mouth open with his bare hands. The head of the animal is put into the pit in front of the goddess and the rest is given to the Adi-Dravida untouchables. In the evening Mariyamma is taken outside the village to a certain tree beneath which the head of the he-buffalo is buried. The goddess is then brought back to the Ambabhavani temple, her bangles having been broken. All the offerings given to the goddess during the festival go to the village Washerman, one of whom acts as priest for the festival. All this is done to protect the village from diseases and troubles.

The potent ritual material called *caraga* is used to stake out the village boundary and protect the community from the negative, evil forces of the outside. Some villagers take it home and worship it prior to sprinkling it over their lands. The fertility of the soil is something that villagers clearly associate with Mariyamma and Kencamma. It was a vegetarian Lingayat farmer, not one of the low-caste sacrificers, who remarked, 'It's a quality of the soil that it needs blood—if we don't offer it animals, it will take human life.' The armed villagers who carry in procession the *caraga* are perhaps there to ensure that none of the ritual material is stolen by outsiders, thus endangering the fertility of village land. Indeed, the scenario played by the Potaraj, who is of the village Watchman caste, could be seen as the ritual searching out and expulsion of an outsider.

At the time of Kencamma's festival the goddess is married to Viranna (Virabhadra) symbolized in the form of a sword. The part of the divine bride is played by a *dēvadāsi*, and the groom's party by Salt-maker devotees of Mailar Linga called *gōrappa*, who act as priests-cum-shamans for their own caste. The *dēvadāsi* beats the *gōrappa* with a young plantain, and they in turn throw coloured water (*okali*) made from tumeric and lime. Sacrifices are made and Kencamma is taken in procession throughout the village. Although no sacrifice would be made at the shrines inside the Fort, Kencamma visits these on certain ritual occasions. At Dasahra, for instance, she complements Ranganatha in a procession of the two deities inside the village; however, when her ritual penetrations of the village are completed Kencamma always returns to her abode on the outside—the villagers say that she is too fearsome and frightening to be tolerated as a permanent inhabitant of the village and that anyway she cannot abide the sound of grinding hand-mills.

A *virakta svāmi*, like Kencamma and Mariyamma is, I would suggest, a creature of the outside; like them he is a repository of extraordinary powers, although the goddesses perhaps show a greater tendency than the renouncer to expend their inner heat.[7] The *virakta* is structurally appropriate as an agent of transition and regeneration and in this sense complements the normality of the householder-priest.[8]

The Taming of the Virakta

There is, however, another aspect of this structural relation between the inside and the outside, namely that which depends upon fluctuating relations among men. Ritual topography notwithstanding we are talking about living deities and their respective patrons and followers. In short, my use of the ethnographic present to describe *virakta:paṭṭadēvaru* relations is from another perspective inadequate, and I shall now move on to treat the subject of transition in a different dimension. Following Victor Turner's (1972) analysis of pilgrimage we may appreciate that the *virakta* does figure in rites of transition, but what is of interest here is that he is also involved in the processes of social transformation.

The relationship between *jaṅgama* and devotee (*bhakta*) provides the Lingayat sect with its creative vitality as well as its restrictive contours. Recent history has furthermore borne out the strong likelihood that the *jaṅgama* of the outside would figure prominently and positively in the unsettling and divisive social transformations operating within the sect at present. The complementarity of *virakta* and *pañcācāraya* has given way to a schism and a bitter internecine battle. Over the last eighty years, at least in the agriculturally and commercially most prosperous areas of Karnataka, the controlling nucleus of the Lingayat sect has become *virakta.* The pre-eminence of the *virakta* is now so complete that the present generation of Lingayats sees no anomaly in the centrality of *virakta* establishments.

The place where I was able to observe in microcosm the final outcome of what can only be called the 'Virakta Movement' was a relatively new satellite village, which I shall call Somvarpethe, situated on the periphery of a provincial town in North Karnataka.[9] Somvarpethe was, and to a certain extent still is, a notoriously rough locality. For villagers it represents the big city: for those from the classier end of town it is a place of village habits, a place to walk through rather hastily on a pious visit to its now famous *virakta maṭha.* It has always been a place of middlemen, agricultural merchants, and quick-witted, rather unscrupulous people who with iron nerves and an extensive network of resources and contacts seem to make a living, and occasionally a small fortune, out of thin air. It is for these reasons, no doubt, that it is also known locally as 'Thieves' Row' and 'Snake's Nest'. One of the town's notorious crimes of the 1920s, when a rich Brahman was murdered and all his gold taken, involved people from this area. Characteristically it was another Somvarpethe man who informed on them to the British and got 5,000 rupees in the process.

The people of Somvarpethe take a certain pride in being sharp (*biriki*). They recognize that they are exploiters of the rather simple (*sāda*), gullible (*nambigi*) people of the villages, but they also retain a marked respect for village life and peasant values. Those peasants, who made their money in Somvarpetha as merchants, frequently prefer to be called 'sons of the soil' (*ryataru*). The bulk of Somvarpethe people can be characterized as peasants who remain only partially acclimatized to the proverbial madness of the city. Mumbai (Bombay) is a derogatory term in Somvarpethe used to refer to people who behave as if they had gone 'wrong in the head'.

Of Somvarpethe's 333 households 65 per cent have immigrated from villages during the last two generations. There are no ancient temples with elaborate traditions of priesthood and ritual, nor is there that abundance of mythology which usually goes with ancient settlement. Five Lingayat castes—Priest (*jaṅgama*), Agriculturalist (*pañcamasāli*), Merchant (*banajīga*) Oil presser (*gāṇigēr*) and Dyer (*baṇṇagār*) comprise nearly 80 per cent of the population of Somvarpethe. In a village setting one would expect to find each of these different Lingayat castes living in its own locale with a fairly clear sense of its own boundaries. This is not so in Somvarpethe where households belonging to all the various castes live side by side. Intercaste commensality is taken for granted; of approximately eight hundred marriages which I recorded 3½ per cent were cross-caste, all of them amongst the so-called 'Big-Houses' occupied by rich landlord-merchants. Caste caricatures persist, but if the residential separation of each caste has broken down, so too has its monopoly over occupation. Hardly any Oil-pressers or Dyers pursue their traditional occupation; Agriculturalists are merchants, merchants are Agriculturalists, and so on.

Lingayats in Somvarpethe talk of 'Big Houses' and 'Little Houses', 'Big People' and 'Little People'. (The Big Houses are by and large in the main street of the settlement, the Little Houses in the six backstreets branching off it.) This conception of the social structure reflects the socio-economic polarization which emerges from my data on land-holding and on the sources and levels of income for each household in Somvarpethe.

Only 25 per cent of Somvarpethe households depend primarily upon land for their income. This is substantially less than the 35 per cent of households whose principal breadwinners are merchants, traders, shopkeepers and clerks. However, 53 per cent of all households have some connection with agricultural land, either as owners or tenants. This reflects the intermediate nature of Somvarpethe, composed as it is of peasants turning to trade in agricultural produce. When outsiders talk of a Somvarpethe society (*samāja*), they invariably have in mind a community of merchants. Mercantilism goes some way towards providing Somvarpethe with its ethos but does not provide it with a substitute for the land. The relations between one agricultural merchant (*dalāli*) and another, or one merchant and his clerk and his porters, are ultimately no substitute for those that exist in the village between neighbouring farmers, or between a landlord and his tied labourers. The social hierarchy is expressed in terms of 'Big' and 'Little', and although some of the psychology of *jajmāni* relationships remains, very little of the content does. Big Houses are not only the richest but precisely those which have multiple sources of income. Of those persons whose primary sources of income is in professional employment (the younger generation, usually of doctors, lawyers, government officers) 72 per cent also hold land. The biggest landowners are also the biggest agricultural merchants. Of the 109 households falling into the menial labouring category only 27 per cent have any connection with land at all, almost all of these being poor migrants who have leased out their small holdings back in the village. The higher the level of primary income, the higher the level of supplementary landholding. The smaller the supplementary landholding, the more likely it is to be leased out rather than owner-cultivated and therefore less profitable. What emerges from this truncated description of the economy of Somvarpethe is a fairly crude form of socio-economic polarization which stretches the notion of a unitary hierarchy of dependency to breaking point.[10]

The *virakta maṭha* is by far the single most important communal institution in Somvarpethe. The history of this Lingayat settlement and the history of its *maṭha* are inextricably linked, and the regional stature and renown of the people of Somvarpethe has grown alongside that of their *maṭha*. In 1916 the *maṭha* comprised only a neglected tomb and a tiny building surrounded by cacti; at present (1973) the *virakta maṭha* has nearly 150 acres of cultivated land, three clerks, eight permanent agricultural servants, and a complex of buildings covering an area of some five acres. It has a large hall (*mantappa*) for public functions, with rooms attached for visiting dignitaries, and within its pink-walled compound may be found the local post office, the public library, and one of the only four private telephones in Somvarpethe. It has its own printing press, a Sanskrit school (*pāthāśala*), and a high school, and is at present negotiating with the local university for permission to open its own college of commerce. The *maṭha* houses and feeds twice daily nearly four hundred male Lingayat students who come from villages all over Karnataka. The image of Jayaswami, the *jaṅgama* ascetic who came to the *maṭha* in 1916 at the insistence of local Lingayats and was its head until he died in 1964, is worshipped throughout the district and far beyond. Indeed Somvarpethe has recently been renamed Jaya Nagara in his memory. Most of the shops and business premises of the people of the area are adorned with his picture and named after him; the new wholesale agricultural produce market in the town, which is largely controlled by devotees of this monastery, is called Jaya Market. The annual religious fair (*jātri*) instituted by Jayaswami attracts thousands of pilgrims.

Every morning one of the *jaṅgama* inmates of the *maṭha* does the *kadjaya* rounds of the Lingayat houses of Somvarpethe, collecting the millet bread (*roṭṭi*) which will go towards feeding the students living on the monastery premises. Begging for cooked food (*kadjaya*) and begging for grain (*kānti bikṣa*) are two traditional forms of begging carried out by the *jaṅgama*. In the old days, when the *virakta maṭha* had no land, this was a vital part of its income. In fact in the early 1920s, when board and lodging (*prasāda nilaya*) were first provided for students, this, together with annual monetary contributions of around 750 rupees from each of the fifteen or twenty Lingayat agricultural merchant families in the Big Houses of Somvarpethe, and a handful of grain (*pakkikalu*) taken out of each bag sold in the market, were the only income at the *maṭha*'s disposal. Now that the *maṭha* is a big landowner and has a well-organized collection of donations that takes in large areas of Karnataka such begging is of symbolic rather than material value.

With the setting up in the *maṭha* compound of the Prasada Nilaya, which provided cheap board and lodging for rural Lingayats so that they might take advantage of the educational facilities that the town offered, the *virakta maṭha* was given a new lease of life. The Prasada Nilaya is managed by a board of local elders from the Big Houses, and this in itself means that it has in certain respects become a forum for local politics. Indeed, the early involvement of the *maṭha* in the emergent modern educational system and its ability to keep in contact with and make use of those students who have since established professional careers in politics, education, law and medicine has enabled the *maṭha* to become one of the core institutions in the regional network of élite Lingayats. In short, the *virakta maṭha* is a going concern.

This could hardly be said, however, of the Somvarpethe *hire-maṭha* which is in total ruins in an open plot of land with no agricultural land attached to it at all. The recent history of the *hire-maṭha* has been one of ignominy, conflict and decline. One of its *svāmi* was beaten with leather shoes and sent back to where he came from. Another 'fell down a well'. Before the *maṭha* actually caved in, a local landlord used it as a grain warehouse. This *maṭha* which claims allegiance to the Kasi Pancacarya pontifical seat, has not functioned as a *maṭha* for forty years now.

The decline of the one type of *maṭha* and the spectacular rise to power of the other is not a phenomenon confined to Somvarpethe. Throughout Karnataka over the course of the last sixty years *virakta maṭha* have been in the ascendant and the *pañcācārya maṭha* in decline. So great a demand was there for *virakta* ascetics that some of the *virakta* orders (*samaya*) came together and set up a central training establishment, named Shivayoga Mandira, whose novices were then sent out to revive those neglected *virakta maṭha* of the region which lay close to centres of population. The success of the Virakta Movement was not ensured until after a war of pamphlets, conferences, and processions had been waged between what came to be known by Lingayats as the Virakta Party on the one hand, and the Pancacarya Party on the other. Whereas the Pancacarya Party proclaimed that the Lingayat religion was Brahmanical, that Lingayat society was *varṇāśramadharmic*, and that Basava had been an upstart and an aberration, the Virakta Party proclaimed that there were no Lingayat castes, that the *pañcācārya* were frauds, and that with devotion anyone could become a *jaṅgama*. A large part of the proselytizing, whether on the Pancacarya or Virakta side, was carried out by the heads of the *maṭha*. But whereas the Pancacarya cause seems to have been almost wholly in the hands of born *jaṅgama*, the Virakta Party owed a great deal to a leadership of non-*jaṅgama* Lingayats, many of whom were lawyers, teachers, and government officials.

In terms of social organization it was inevitable that the *virakta* ascetics should bear the brunt, as it were, of this period of relative instability for the Lingayat sect. The inflexible, hierarchical organization of the *pañcācārya guru* could not respond to the changing conditions. For the *virakta guru*, however, there were no predetermined channels inhibiting the processes whereby a *guru* might extend his following or a devotee (as opposed to a 'disciple-child') his devotion. According to the household-*guru* system each Lingayat was as a matter of birthright related to his particular 'royal' *guru*. The *virakta guru*, however, is under no such obligation; he is related only to those who are willing and able to relate themselves to him. In contrast to the hierarchical relation existing between a 'royal' *guru*-cum-father confessor and his 'disciple-children', the relation existing between a *virakta guru* and his devotees is characterized by alliance and exchange. All *jaṅgama* subsist on alms-giving: the *paṭṭadēvaru* has a guaranteed source of income, the sources of support for a *virakta* are not so easily defined.

There is another sense in which the mediatory involvement of the *virakta* was appropriate. One of my informants drew a distinction between what he called 'innocent devotion' and 'wide-awake devotion'. It is innocent devotion which motivates the people of the backstreets of Somvarpethe to gather in the late evenings in the temples and sing *bhajana*, devotional songs to Shiva. This kind of devotion means standing equal before God, sharing a common experience in a generous and unselfconscious expression of devotion. 'Innocent devotion' signifies brotherhood, unity, and closeness, albeit within an accepted hierarchical scheme. 'Wide-awake devotion' (which I would call piety, rather than devotion) is much more mannered and cool. Piety is making sure that one's private early morning religious duties—a prolonged and elaborate *liṅga pūjā* or the recitation of a few verses of a Purana at a time when the working farmer is already in the fields—include a visit to the tombs in the *virakta maṭha*, an event which one signals to one's immediate neighbours by carrying a bunch of incense sticks, or in the case of a man by donning a clean *dhōṭi* and leaving bare one's upper torso resplendent with *liṅga*-casket. Piety serves to create distances between people and to provide symbolic confirmation of the new socio-economic division appearing within the sect. Behind the piety of the merchant devotees at the *virakta maṭha* lies a cool detachment born of self-discipline, a form of devotion which comes into its own in any social setting as a linguistic mode appropriate to the re-drawing of social boundaries, which demonstrates a belief in the invulnerability of one's purity, and which supports the act of setting oneself apart and spurning obligations to poor kinsmen.

The anomalous market-place renouncer, has, then, played a mediatory role in the relatively smooth transformation from a consensual Lingayat caste hierarchy in which pure and impure exist in symbiosis to a world of polarization and division signalling the breakdown of traditional social dependencies and the formation of new social boundaries amongst Lingayats. The adventurers, entrepreneurs, and bad boys in that first wave of migration into Somvarpethe stood literally at the margins of traditional Lingayat society. They are now in the Big Houses, at the forefront of Lingayat affairs. They brought the *jaṅgama guru* of the outside with them and made them their *guru*, and, in forcing these *virakta* ascetics into an ideological and organizational mould, tamed them. What was sacred, they made mundane and a part of the *status quo*. The 'Little People' of the backstreets of Somvarpethe, those Lingayats who got left behind in the process of social polarization, refer ironically to the present *svāmi* in the Somvarpethe *virakta maṭha* as 'the dumb Swami' not in recognition of any great power of austerity on his part, but because the 'Big People', committee members, and other devotees who surround him, always speak for him. The Big People whisk him away in their cars to witness their impressive marriage alliances. The Little People, though they would probably like to be able to, cannot afford to have him. The *virakta maṭha* itself is surrounded by high walls and painted in *kyavi*, the colour of the ascetic's robes, but topped with broken glass. In short, the so-called egalitarian ideology of the Virakta Party signals the legitimization of new inequalities, the redefinition of hierarchy.

The processes we have been describing here are all part of a continuing dialectic in which the outside remains as a sacred source, always vulnerable, but accessible nevertheless, to the demands of those living in society. His spiritual power (*siddhi*) sapped by permanent residence among men, the *virakta* ascetic is already being replaced on the outside by other sacred intermediaries, many of them significantly non-*jaṅgama* by birth. The vulnerability of those on the outside to the demands of those on the inside has emerged strongly from this account. As one *paṭṭadēvaru* observed scornfully, 'The *virakta maṭha* have grown big on money, not on the basis of an established tradition (*rokkadindadoḍḍāvaru sthāpanadindalla*)... Who made the *virakta* gurus, anyway? I'll tell you: people!'

The potent deities on the outside are brought in at points of transition in the annual cycle and in such times of communal crisis as an epidemic or the failure of the monsoon rains. Likewise, it would appear, the renouncer is brought in from the outside as a catalyst and agent of transformation in Lingayat society. Not without reason have we chosen to speak of transformation, that permanent, dynamic aspect of structure rather than change, with its attendant implication of progression by elimination and replacement of elements. *Pace* Dumont, (1970:45, 46, 54) we have found in the Lingayat example a complementary opposition of 'man-outside-the-world' (renouncer) to 'man-in-the-world' which has withstood the onslaught of historical decay. The Lingayat renouncer, rather than being 'absorbed' (Dumont 1970:59) has continued to play his part in the Lingayat scheme of things. He may be considered to be outside society, but he is hardly 'man-outside-the-world' (Dumont 1970:54): he is an enduring feature of the collective representation of the world in which Lingayats live.

NOTES

1 See, for example, Oman (1903), Dumont (1970), Heesterman (1964), O'Flaherty (1973), Cantlie (1977), Das (1977).

2 Most accounts focus on literary texts, e.g. Singer (1966), or on leaders, e.g. Fuchs (1966). A notable exception to this is D. F. Pocock (1973).

3 Most of the major sociological works on India contain a brief, and sometimes infuriatingly enigmatic mention of the Lingayats; for example, Hutton (1946), Weber (1958), Dumont (1972). McCormack's output on the subject has been scant (1963, 1973) and shows a premature interest in cross-cultural comparison. The best ethnographic source is still Parvathamma (1971, 1972), though the framework of her analysis is singularly uninspiring.

4 The *vacana*, of which there are many thousands, are the devotional 'poems' of the twelfth-century movement which were retained in folk memory, transposed into devotional songs (*bhajana*), and eventually came to be written down. Local researchers have so far been able to attribute them to some two hundred different composers (*vacanākāra*). Contrary to the impression given by Fuchs (1965:260) the *vacana* are written in an archaic, highly condensed poetic language, so that even though they are in Kannada most of my informants had great difficulty in understanding them. Nonetheless the devotional spirit, which is so wonderfully expressed in the *vacana*, is a continuing tradition.

5 The significant exception to this rule are those *jaṅgama* who live and die outside the settlement area, that is to say, the *jaṅgama* of the outside, who are described later in the paper.

6 I spent October–November, 1969 in this village in the Shimoga District of Karnataka when I was a student at Karnatak University, Dharwar. My knowledge of the village is therefore rather limited and this section of the paper should be taken as a tentative and exploratory statement. Much of what I say is implied in work that has already been done on the Hindu village pantheon. For a fuller account along similar lines, based on fieldwork carried out in a village not far from the one to which I refer, see Gowdra (1971).

7 Here I take for granted the reader's knowledge of a body of literature on the now established subject of the complementary opposition between hot and cold in Hindu belief and practice. See Beck (1969), O'Flaherty (1973), Babb (1975), Hershman (1977), and Cantlie (1977).

8 All this might be seen as part of a basic Hindu vocabulary in which caste, culture, and village complements tribe, nature, and forest. See, for example, Malamoud (1976). Lingayat men have been known to refer to their women as 'forest people' (*kādumandi*) because they do not strictly observe menstrual pollution.

9 What follows is based on SSRC-funded fieldwork which was carried out between October, 1971 and February, 1973.

10 For greater detail on this and, indeed, on the Virakta Movement, see Bradford (1976).

REFERENCES

Babb, L. A. 1975. *The divine hierarchy: popular Hinduism in central India.* New York: Columbia Univ. Press.

Beck, B. E. F. 1969. Colour and Heat in South Indian Ritual. *Man* 4, 553–572.

Bradford, N. J. 1976. Affine and devotee: a study of the Lingayat sect of north Karnataka. Unpublished D. Phil. thesis, Univ. of Sussex.

Cantlie, A. 1977. Aspects of Hindu Asceticism. In I. Lewis (ed), *Symbols and sentiments: cross-cultural studies in symbolism.* London: Academic Press.

Das, V. 1977. *Structure and cognition: aspects of Hindu caste and ritual.* Delhi: Oxford Univ. Press.

Desai, P. B. 1968. *Basaveshvara and his times.* Dharwar: Kannada Research Institute, Karnatak University.

Dumont, L. 1970. World renunciation in Indian religions. *Religion, politics, and history in India.* Paris and the Hague: Mouton.

—— 1972. *Homo hierarchicus.* London: Paladin.

Fuchs, S. 1966. *Rebellious prophets.* London: Asia Publishing House.

Ghurye, G. S. 1953. *Indian sadhus.* Bombay: Popular Book Depot.

Government of Mysore. 1967. *Sri Basaveshvara: eighth centenary commemoration volume.* Bangalore: Government of Mysore.

Gowdra, G. K. 1971. Ritual circles in a Mysore village. *Sociological Bulletin,* 20, 24–38.

Hardekar, M. (ed). 1940. *Social structure of the Veerashaiva saints.* Dharwar: the author.

Heesterman, J. C. 1964. Brahmin, ritual and renouncer. *Wiener Zeitschrift für die Kunde Sud-und Ostasiens,* 8, 1–31.

Hershman, P. 1977. Virgin and mother. In I. Lewis (ed), *Symbols and sentiments: cross-cultural studies in symbolism.* London: Academic Press.

Hutton, J. H. 1946. *Caste in India: its nature, function and origins.* Cambridge: Univ. Press.

Lorenzen, D. N. 1972. *The Kapalikas and Kalamukhas: two lost Saivite sects.* New Delhi: Thomson Press (India).

Malamoud, C. 1976. Village et forêt dans l'idéologie de l'Inde brâhmanique. *Arch. Europ. Sociol.* 17, 3–20.

Malladevaru, H. P. 1973. *Essentials of Virasaivism.* Bombay: Bharatiya Vidya Bhavan.

McCormack, W. 1963. Lingayats as a sect. *Journal of the Royal Anthropological Institute* 93, 59–71.

—— 1973. On Lingayat culture. In A. K. Ramanujan, *Speaking of Siva.* Harmondsworth: Penguin.

Nandimath, S. C. 1942. *A handbook of Virashaivism.* Dharwar: Lingayat Education Association.

Nanjundayya, H. V. and Iyer, L. M. Ananthakrishna. 1931. *The Mysore tribes and castes.* Vol. 4. Mysore: Mysore Univ.

O'Flaherty, W. D. 1973. *Asceticism and eroticism in the mythology of Siva.* London: Oxford Univ. Press.

Oman, J. C. 1903. *The mystics ascetics and saints of India: a study of sadhuism, with an account of yogis, sanyasis, bairagis and other strange Hindu sectarians.* London: T. Fisher Unwin.

Parvathamma, C. S. 1971. *Politics and religion: a study of historical interaction between sociopolitical relationships in a Mysore village.* New Delhi and Jullundor City: Sterling Publishers.

—— 1972. *Sociological essays on Veerasaivism.* Bombay: Popular Prakashan.

Pocock, D. F. 1973. *Mind, body and wealth: a study of belief and practice in an Indian village.* Oxford: Blackwell.

Ramanujan, A. K. 1973. *Speaking of Siva.* Harmondsworth: Penguin.

Sakhare, M. R. 1942. *History and philosophy of Lingayat religion.* (Being an Introduction to Lingadharanachandrika of Nandikeshwara with translation and full rites). Belgaum: the author.

Singer, Milton (ed) 1968. *Krishna: myths, rites and attitudes.* Chicago: Univ. Press.

Tapper, B. E. 1979. Widows and goddesses: female roles in deity symbolism in a south Indian village. *Contributions to Indian Sociology* 13, 1–31.

Turner, V. 1972. The centre out there: pilgrim's goal. *History of Religions* 12, 191–230.

Weber, M. 1958. *The religion of India: the sociology of Hinduism and Buddhism.* Glencoe (Illinois): The Free Press.

INITIATION AND CONSECRATION: PRIESTLY RITUALS IN A SOUTH INDIAN TEMPLE

C. J. Fuller

Introduction

The subject of this paper is the initiation and consecration of temple priests in South India. My data were collected in the Great Temple of Madurai (Tamilnadu), the Shri Minakshi-Sundareshvara Temple dedicated to the goddess Minakshi and her husband Sundareshvara (Shiva).[1] (Hereafter, I refer to the 'Minakshi temple', the shorter name by which it is generally known.) To the best of my knowledge, this paper is the first detailed discussion of the topic to be based on field-work data. Initiation among South Indian Shaivas (the sect of devotees of Shiva) has been briefly discussed, using textual sources, by Rao (1916:10–15) and, in a comparative context, by Gonda (1965a:429–35 & ch. 10 *passim*).[2] However, the authoritative textual work on the subject is by Brunner-Lachaux (1977; see also 1963: xxiii–xxiv; 1968: xv–xvi; 1975) and I shall be frequently referring to it, especially the most recent volume (1977).[3]

The principal purpose of this paper is to make a modest contribution to the ethnography of Hinduism. However, I hope that it will also illustrate the importance of textual scholarship to the analysis of ethnographic data. Without the aid of Brunner-Lachaux's writings, I would have found my material on initiation and (to a lesser extent) consecration virtually incomprehensible. This situation is, in part, a result of the fact that the priests themselves have no grasp of the structure of the initiation rituals and little cognizance of their intended purpose, although this is not equally true of the consecration. (The reason for this difference is one of the topics of this paper.) My indebtedness to the textual scholarship does, of course, only illustrate its practical usefulness for one anthropological analysis, although this in itself is worth stressing. Too much anthropological discussion of 'great tradition' religions has been vitiated by insufficient use of relevant textual material. The theoretical problem of the relation between text and practice is, however, another and infinitely more complex problem, on which I have not attempted to comment directly.

Brunner-Lachaux's books (1963; 1968; 1977) comprise the first three parts of her translation, with extensive interpretative notes, of the *Somaśambhupaddhati*, the ritual manual based on the Agamas and written by Somashambhu. The Shaiva Agamas are the textual authorities for Shaiva rituals, in both temples and homes. Somashambhu's work dates from the eleventh century and much of it was reproduced with little modification in Aghorashiva's manual, written in the twelfth century, which is today regarded as authoritative in most South Indian temples, including the Minakshi temple (Brunner 1975–6:110). Brunner-Lachaux refers extensively to Aghorashiva's manual, as well as to other texts, and thus her work is relevant to the rituals in the Minakshi temple. The basic scheme of Shaiva initiation and consecration is broadly similar in all the manuals known to us and the discrepancies, as we shall see, are not so much between these texts, but between the texts and the rituals as they are actually performed.

'Initiation' translates the Sanskrit *dīkṣā* and 'consecration' the Sanskrit *abhiṣeka*, the ritual in question being the *ācāryābhiṣeka*: the consecration of an *ācārya*, i.e. a *guru* or master (c.f. x–xi).[4] The term *abhiṣeka* specifically refers to a besprinkling or an aspersion (usually with water), the central rite in the consecration. In other contexts, *abhiṣeka* may be translated as 'bathing' and I use this word when referring to the bathing of an image, one of the key rituals of service and offering (*upacāra*) making up ordinary worship (*pūjā*). A clear distinction between these two senses of *abhiṣeka* is required and will be maintained throughout this paper.

The theology of Shaiva initiation is extremely complicated and I shall only sparsely summarize Brunner-Lachaux's discussion (iii–xxx). There are three grades of initiation: *samayadīkṣā* ('regular initiation'), *viśeṣadīkṣā* ('special initiation') and *nirvāṇadīkṣā* ('liberating initiation'). They must be taken by the neophyte in this order. It is important to note that in the theology of Southern Shaivism (*śaivasiddhānta*), the 'liberation' to which the neophyte aspires is neither fusion with the supreme god (as in other monist schools) nor eternal proximity to the god that he may always be adored (as in the dualist schools), but instead an actual transformation into Shiva, which is accomplished through the initiations (xi–xiii). This transformation is required because, in Southern Shaivite teaching, 'only Shiva can worship Shiva' (1963:130; 1977: xxxii). It is believed that initiation is always conferred upon the neophyte by Shiva, but the god usually uses in his stead a human agent, the *guru*, who is himself Shiva during the rituals (ix, xxviii). By most authorities, the liberation of the third initiation is considered to be only conditional and potential. Final liberation is not achieved until the initiate's death and only then if he has scrupulously performed the duties incumbent on him (xiii).

The consecration can only be taken by someone who has undergone all three initiations. Compared with the initiations, it has a relatively minor religious significance and a simple purpose: to convert an initiate into a master able to conduct the public worship (*parārthapūjā*), i.e. worship held on behalf of others. This entitlement is, of course, demanded of a temple priest.[5] Initiates who have not taken the consecration are confined to private worship (*ātmārthapūjā*), that is, worship held on behalf of themselves (xliii; cf. 1963: xxii, n. 10). Compared with the initiations, not normally held in public, the consecration has always been a more spectacular ritual conferring, in front of an audience, the office and status of master. In the modern temples, however, the contrast presented in the texts appears to have developed in such a way that the initiation rituals, wherein the great transformation of the neophyte's soul should occur, have paled before the consecration. Initiations in the temple are carried out simply, speedily and with scant attention to their significance; they are now little more than the requisite preamble to the all-important consecration. The divergence in these respects between text and current practice is one of the central themes of this paper.

The Initiation Rituals performed in the Temple

In this section I shall describe the initiation rituals performed in the Minakshi temple and in the following section I shall comment upon them. The consecration ritual will be described later; although it immediately follows the initiations in the temple, a division in my discussion will simplify the presentation. The data on the rituals come from notes taken by my assistant at the initiation of three new priests (Tam. *paṭṭar*; Skt. *bhaṭṭa*) and their wives in July 1977.[6] (Initiation and consecration rituals are almost always held very soon after marriage.) The description is divided into numbered sections to facilitate cross-reference to the commentary below.

To avoid confusion, I must make it clear that the initiation rituals, which may be undergone by Shaiva devotees other than priests, are not strictly part of the temple's corpus of rituals. They are held inside the temple for reasons of convenience and not, unlike the consecration, because they need to be.

1. The rituals were held on the evening of one day and the morning of the following day; the days and timing must be auspicious according to astrological criteria. Before the rituals on the first evening began, the novitiate priests and their wives (whom I shall refer to collectively as the 'neophytes') bathed their legs in the temple tank to purify themselves and worshipped at the shrines of Minakshi, Sundareshvara, and the subsidiary deities. Such an act of worship is normal before any important ritual; it is intended both to honour the deities and to ask for their blessings on the enactment of the ritual. The neophytes then proceeded to a temporary pavilion (*maṇḍapa*), made out of a canopy supported on decorated pillars, erected in the north-east corner of the corridor around Minakshi's shrine. There the *guru*, an older priest, carried out a series of preliminary rituals, including purification of the pavilion and the pit (*kuṇḍa*) in which the sacrificial fire (*yāga*) would be raised. The *guru* then prepared the cords (*rakṣābandhana*) worn around the wrist, mainly for protection. A second priest tied a cord around the *guru*'s right wrist, before the *guru* did the same for the neophytes (right wrists for males and left for females). The *guru* continued with a further series of preliminary rituals, including the worship of the pavilion itself and all the items contained within it to be used later. These included the design (*maṇḍala*) drawn on the floor in the centre of the pavilion, the small vessels placed around the pavilion's perimeter and the large vessels (*kalaśa*, *kumbha*) eventually employed in the consecration ritual. Apart from the cords, on which I comment below, these preliminaries occur before all important rituals and I shall not consider them further.

2. The regular initiation now began. The *guru*, seated by the large vessels in the pavilion, blessed the neophytes and touched them

with *darbha* grass to purify them. (*Darbha*, also *kuśa*, is a grass extensively used in Shaiva rituals for purification and in many other contexts.) Each of the neophytes then stood up and, blindfolded, dropped flowers on to the design. This design, a square, was divided into five sectors, one in the centre and one at each of the sides, corresponding to the five aspects of Shiva, whose names are taken by the neophytes.[7] As each flower landed, the neophyte's new name was announced.

3. The special initiation followed the regular initiation without a break. The *guru* raised the fire with oblations (*homa*) of ghee, while the neophytes all touched him with stems of *darbha* grass. He then touched each of their heads with the spout of one of the two ladles used for spooning ghee into the fire during the oblations, and took the *darbha* from them before dropping it into the fire.[8] This brief ritual appears to have been the entire special initiation as performed in the temple, and the two initiations together lasted only a short time.

4. Immediately after the special initiation, the preparation (*adhivāsana*) for the liberating initiation began. The *attiyāna* (Skt. *adhiyāna*) *paṭṭar* prepared yellow cotton threads for each of the novitiate priests. (The *attiyāna paṭṭar* is the principal chanter [Tam. *cāstiri*; Skt. *śāstri*] in the temple; the chanters are non-priestly Brahmans responsible for chanting the Vedas, but the *attiyāna paṭṭar* has to be versed in the Agamas as well and often takes a vital role in temple rituals.) He chanted various *mantra* over the threads, each of which had five knots in it, before each priest had one thread placed on his head. The *guru* then dropped flowers on to the five parts of the body (see below) of each of the priests, while pouring oblations of ghee into the fire. The threads were then removed from the priests' heads and deposited in small pots, placed beside the large vessels in the pavilion. The neophytes next received religious instruction from the *guru* (I lack details of this), and then each of them dropped flowers over the large vessels, the design, the fire, and their *guru*. The day's rituals ended with a final oblation into the fire. All the participants then left the temple for their homes.

5. On the morning of the following day, the *guru* began the liberating initiation proper with the normal preliminaries; he worshipped all the items in the pavilion and offered oblations into the fire. The neophytes then came and stood behind the *guru*.

The threads were taken from the pots in which they had been left overnight and tied to the hair of the three new priests. More oblations were poured into the fire before the *guru* touched the first knot in each thread with the ladle (used in the special initiation) and a stem of *darbha*. The grass was then dropped into the fire; the threads were all severed at the first knot and the portions cut off also went into the fire. This ritual was repeated, more hastily, for the other four knots in each thread. Then the neophytes all went to the temple tank to bathe their feet; the two ladles were also washed there. They all returned to the pavilion, where the *guru* again poured oblations into the fire. The new priests then stood beside the *guru*, while the chanter held their right hands; the *guru* touched the joints of the fingers on each priest's hand with the same ladle as used before and poured more ghee into the fire. A further oblation followed before the *guru* performed the ritual of waving the lamps (*dīpārādhana*) in front of the three priests. The initiation was completed by worshipping all the items in the pavilion again, before the chanters recited from the four Vedas, and betel and areca (*tāmbūla*) were offered to representatives of the temple priesthood. The offering of *tāmbūla*, which closes most important religious ceremonies in Tamilnadu, marked the completion of the ritual.

The Initiation Rituals: Commentary

1. As already indicated, I shall not discuss the majority of the preliminary rituals. The protective cords, however, do require some comment. These cords (also known as *rakṣāsūtra*, *kautuka*, Tam. *kāppu*) are used in various rituals, according to Brunner-Lachaux (1968:ix, 106, n.1), although she does not refer to them in the context of initiation or consecration. The principal purpose of these cords, as my priestly informants (in agreement with Brunner-Lachaux) made clear, is protection against harmful influences, especially the evil eye (Tam. *tiṣṭi*, from Skt. *dṛṣṭi*) and the evil spirits (Tam. *pey*), who are believed to harm the participants in any splendid ceremony. The cords are also worn, for the same reason, by the priests in charge of the most important festivals in the Minakshi temple; their use in the initiation and consecration rituals implies that they have an importance in the temple

comparable to that of the major festivals. The cords, however, may also signify intention or determination to complete the ceremony on the part of the wearer; this in turn may be expressed in the form of a vow (*vrata*), which sometimes involves a partial fast or abstinence (Brunner-Lachaux 1968:ix–x; Diehl 1956:252). The second purpose seems to be particularly significant at rites of passage, especially marriages and sacred-thread ceremonies (*upanayana*), in which the cords are respectively worn by the bride and groom, and the boy being initiated. However, the notion of intention does also pertain to the cords worn by priests in charge of festivals and it is, I think, reasonable to presume that both purposes, intention as well as protection, are denoted by the cords worn during the temple initiation and consecration rituals.[9]

2. All the priests with whom I discussed initiation, including those considered to be most knowledgeable, were vague about the structure of the rituals and were mostly unable to explain their significance. According to Somashambhu and Aghorashiva, the neophyte is qualified to worship Shiva after he has undergone the regular initiation (xxxv, 110, n.263), whose basic scheme is as follows. The *guru* leads the neophyte, blindfolded, into the pavilion where he purifies him. He places his hand on the neophyte's head in a gesture of blessing, which also signifies the special protection the initiate will henceforth receive from Shiva (xxxiv). In the textual version, this blessing is the central act of the ritual (96, n.244). The blindfold is then removed, while at the same time the neophyte drops a flower to determine his new name (xxxiv). The *guru* then ends the ritual with oblations into the fire.

In temple practice, the naming ritual has replaced the blessing as the central act and many of the priests, unaware of the original structure of the initiations, synecdochically see it as the core of the first day's proceedings. In some texts, the blindfolding is merely to prevent the neophytes choosing their own names (90, n.235) and this was the only explanation supplied by my informants. Somashambhu and Aghorashiva, however, insist that the blindfolding must be done before the neophyte comes into the pavilion. Symbolically, he enters in darkness and, when the blindfold is removed, gains illumination for the first time by seeing Shiva—represented in the design on the pavilion floor (xxxiv, 90–1, n. 235). The blindfolding ritual occurs in Tantric and Vaishnava initiation as well, and plainly carries a very similar symbolic message. In the Minakshi temple, however, this straightforward but powerful imagery has largely been glossed as a means to stop the neophytes from cheating when dropping their flowers. The climax of the ritual described in the texts—Shiva's blessing followed by a vision of him—almost totally loses its dramatic impact. 3. The special initiation is a continuation of the regular initiation and the two probably formed only one ritual originally (xxxi–xxxiii, 115–6, n.3). The essential feature of the special initiation is the neophyte's rebirth as a son of Shiva, achieved via a series of rituals involving the sacred fire and, as always, the chanting of *mantra*. At the end, the *guru* gives instruction to the neophyte, who then worships Shiva and for the first time performs the fire-worship. A period of asceticism should follow this initiation (xxxv–xxxvi).

In the texts, the regular initiation ends, as the special initiation begins, with the *guru* and the neophyte seated around the fire, the latter touching his master with a *darbha* stem (106, n. 253, 115, n.3). This appears to be the situation in the special initiation in the temple, as described above. The theological exegesis of this communication between *guru* and neophyte—which similarly occurs in the Vaishnavite initiation (Gonda 1965a:405)—is complex and need not be discussed here (cf. 106, n.253 ff.). The rite in which the *guru* touches the neophyte's head with a ladle is possibly equivalent to the tapping (*taḍana*) of his head with a flower (120, n.8) which, in the text, is the first crucial act in the series of rituals to transform the neophyte into Shiva's son. However, even if my assumption is correct, I cannot explain the substitution, although it does seem evident that the brief ritual in the temple is but a highly curtailed, almost nominal, rendition of the special initiation described in the texts. The *guru*, at this stage, gave no instruction to the neophytes and the liberating initiation followed immediately afterwards. Certainly no period of asceticism was observed. Furthermore, the concept of the neophyte's transformation into Shiva's son was never mentioned to me or my assistant, and I doubt that any of the priests could attach any real meaning to the special initiation ritual. I therefore venture to suggest that it is, in the Minakshi temple, a more or less empty ritual nowadays; lacking a clear structure and improperly separated from the initiation before and after it, its meaning to those participating in it is virtually nil.

4. The liberating initiation, *the* initiation, is a long ritual in two parts during which the soul (*ātman*) of the neophyte is purified and freed from the fetters binding it (xxxvii). There are several paths by which this purification and liberation can be accomplished; Brunner-Lachaux describes in most detail the path of the five *kalā*, the mode employed in the Minakshi temple. *Kalā* may be loosely translated as 'element' (cf. xiv–xv for detailed exposition). In the preparatory part of the ritual, the *guru* removes the five *kalā* from the neophyte's body and places them on a thread; his soul is now located on the thread, which is kept overnight. The neophyte sleeps in the pavilion until the next morning, when the initiation proper begins (xxxviii–xxxix). The *guru* then ties the thread to the neophyte's hair and purifies each of the *kalā* in turn, after which he unites the neophyte's soul with Shiva and replaces the transformed soul in his body. The neophyte is now potentially liberated and must carry out his duties, including the daily worship of Shiva, until the end of his life (xxxix–xliii).[10]

The theological interpretation of the ritual of the threads is extremely complex and the reader ought to refer to Brunner-Lachaux's lengthy discussion (168–204 for the preparation and 230–46 for the initiation proper). In the textual version, the *kalā* are transferred to the thread one-by-one, as the *guru* taps the part of the neophyte's body corresponding to each *kalā* with a flower (182–5, n.45–53). The five parts are between the eyebrows, throat, navel, knees and toes. I am not certain whether the *guru* in the temple dropped flowers on to these parts of the novitiate priests' bodies, but his action was clearly equivalent to the tapping prescribed in the texts. However, in the texts, the knots are put into the thread after the *kalā* have been transferred, in order to secure them there (201–2, n.84). When the threads have been deposited in the pots, a rite for their protection should also be performed (204), before a series of rituals (some of which were performed in the temple) ends the first day's ceremonies.

The patent but none the less profound symbolism of the ritual described in the texts has been predominantly lost in the practice of the temple, in much the same way as it was in the case of the blindfolding. By knotting the threads in advance, the symbolic figuration of the transfer and attachment of the *kalā* is lost, the failure to perform the protection ritual leaves the significance of the threads unmarked; the departure of the neophytes to their homes for the night destroys the symbolic representation, so plain in the texts, of a dangerous, liminal stage in which the soul has been removed.

5. Much the same symbolic impoverishment is apparent in the initiation proper. According to the texts, the thread is first tied to the neophyte's hair, as was done in the temple, before each *kalā* is purified in turn (231, n.163–4). The first stage in this purification is tapping the thread (260–2, n.224–6), which is replicated in the temple by touching it with the ladle and *darbha* grass. (As with the special initiation, I do not know why the ladle is used here.) The penultimate stage in the purification—eighteen stages are listed in the text—is severing the thread at each knot in turn. After being cut, each segment of the thread, representing one of the five *kalā*, is burnt in the fire; this is the final stage of the purification, which has to be done for all the *kalā* in order. The scissors to cut the thread are said to represent the power of Shiva, who actually causes the transformation that is completed when the whole thread has been burnt, symbolizing the release of the soul from its old fetters (xli, 282–4, n.257–62). As we have seen, these last two stages were completed in the temple. The neophyte's tuft should then be cut off; this is said to symbolize the elimination of any power restraining the initiate's spiritual progress (338, n.395), although tonsure is, of course, common to many initiation rituals (such as the sacred-thread ceremony) as an expression of the initiate's separation from his previous status (Van Gennep 1960:166–7). The text then states that the neophyte must bathe to remove the pollution induced by tonsure (344–6, n.401), which also apparently attaches to the ladles and scissors.

In the textual version, a large part of the purification is essentially achieved mentally, though accompanied, at various points, by various *mantra* and oblations into the fire. It is clearly an extremely lengthy procedure and equally clearly, it was not seriously attempted in the temple, where only the physical manoeuvres of touching the thread, cutting it, and dropping the severed portions into the fire were carried out. To the anthropologist, particularly because the threads appear as extensions of the head-hair, the last two actions suggest the stereotyped idea of the death of the neophyte—cut and burnt. This inference seems to me reasonable, but it must be noted that it is not consistent with the theological interpretation, for the liberation of the initiate's soul is clearly not a transformation equivalent to his death.[11] However, the representation of this transformation—death or liberation—is weakened in the temple ritual by omitting the tonsure, so that the neophyte's purification in the temple tank is now an almost pointless gesture. The ritual of touching the finger-joints appears to be an abbreviated version of 'placing' the *mantra* on the hands and body (*sakalīkaraṇa*); this ritual is part of the purification procedure for the Shaiva initiate and occurs in the liberating initiation before the unification of the neophyte's soul with Shiva is begun (346, n.403; cf. 1963: xxxviii, 323–5). In the texts, this unification, together with the replacement of the neophyte's soul in his body, is, like the preceding purification, a lengthy procedure. Once again, it was not seriously attempted in the temple, except for another brief series of oblations into the fire.

If the cutting and burning of the threads partly expresses the idea of the initiates' deaths, then the waving of lamps before them would seem to represent their rebirth. This action closes virtually all rituals of worship in the temple and by itself it constitutes an abbreviated form of the complete worship. Thus in this context, as more elaborately in the consecration to follow, it indicates that the novitiate priests are like gods; more specifically, it suggests that they have now been transformed into Shiva. (The reader may have noted that the liberating initiation, unlike the first two initiations, is not performed for the novitiate priests' wives—a curious problem to which I return below.)

In my comments on the initiation rituals, I have tried to draw attention to the fact that the immense significance accorded to the initiations in the Agamic texts is not reflected in the rituals performed in the temple. However, that is not perhaps particularly remarkable. The rituals described in the texts are mostly arcane and are meant to bring about a complicated spiritual metamorphosis, which is largely achieved (especially during the liberating initiation) by mental means. It is unsurprising that the rituals performed in the temple by ordinary priests deviate considerably from those described in the texts and lack the structure and symbolic impact of the latter, without which there can be little coherent meaning for anyone. In the final analysis, what is clearly left is a ritual of naming and an emasculated representation of death and rebirth as Shiva, with whom the new priests are identified at the end. This pattern is, I think, significant. The new names (which are actually hardly ever used) seem to be regarded by the priests mainly as honorific titles connected to their office, which distinguish them from ordinary devotees more than they indicate any special relationship with one aspect of Shiva. The identification with Shiva is, as we shall see, a central theme of the consecration, where it is much more elaborately displayed; the initiations thus appear as a kind of rehearsal for the spectacular consecration ritual in which, in contradistinction to the texts, the major transformation of the neophytes is made to occur. Symbolic significance is, for the participants and their witnesses, primarily located in the consecration, whose symbolic meaning appears to have been dimly projected back on to the initiations.[12]

The Consecration Ritual performed in the Temple

My data on the consecration ritual partly come from notes taken by my assistant at the ceremony in July 1977 and partly from my own observations of a ritual held for two new priests and their wives in September 1976. There were slight differences between the two consecrations, but little is lost by presenting a single account.

The priests in the Minakshi temple belong to two groups: the Vikkira (from Vikkirama) Pantiyas and the Kulacekaras (Fuller 1984: 25). Both the consecrations described were for Vikkira Pantiyas and were held at the entrance to the ante-chamber of Minakshi's shrine. Those of Kulacekaras are held in the equivalent site before Sundareshvara's shrine. The allocation of separate sites was decided upon in the nineteenth century, as a result of disputes between the two groups over their consecrations. I shall return to the issue of priestly disputes in more detail below.[13]

The consecration began immediately after the end of the liberating initiation. Another temporary pavilion had been erected on the stone platform in front of the ante-chamber of Minakshi's shrine. Low wooden benches, representing thrones (*siṃhāsana*), were placed inside this pavilion. The neophytes sat on the thrones facing east (the same direction as Minakshi's image) with their palms pressed together in the gesture of obeisance known as *namaskāra*. Each new priest had his wife seated on his left. Meanwhile, the large vessels kept in the initiation pavilion were carried in procession to the consecration pavilion. Each vessel was carried by a priest on his head. These priests were accompanied by musicians and led by men carrying silver staffs, royal insignia which precede any important temple procession. At one of the consecrations, the procession only went around Minakshi's shrine; at the other, it took the longer route round Sundareshvara's as well.

When the procession reached the consecration pavilion, the vessels were put down inside it. Water was sprinkled from mango leaves all over the neophytes to purify them and twists of *darbha* grass (known as *kūrca*) were positioned on the heads of each of the new priests, as is usually done before any besprinkling ritual.[14] The *guru* in charge of the initiations was now assisted by other senior temple priests, so that each new priest and his wife had their own *guru* for the consecration. The besprinkling ritual then began. Various liquids—sesame oil, milk, *pañcamṛta* (a preparation including milk, curd, ghee, sugar and honey), honey and sandalpaste—were poured over the heads of each of the neophytes by their *guru*. These liquids make up a standard, ordered series, used frequently in the bathing ritual for images in the temple, and the *guru* poured them over the neophytes exactly as they pour them over images of the gods. All of the *guru* then raised the large vessels and emptied them over the neophytes' heads to the sound of loud drumming, which marked, as it normally does, the climax of the ceremony. Finally, the small vessels of water, which had been kept around the large vessels in the initiation pavilion, were poured over the neophytes.[15] After the besprinkling, sandalpaste spots (*tilaka*) were applied to the neophytes' foreheads and a camphor lamp was waved before each of them. Then they all departed to change into new silk clothes; they returned heavily ornamented and garlanded, the young priests wearing elaborate silk turbans. (Some, but not all, of the *guru* wore white turbans and ornaments during the consecration.)

The neophytes went next to the shrine of Dakshinamurti (Shiva as the *guru*) in Sundareshvara's temple. They sat before it and the novitiate priests, guided by a chanter, performed the standard rituals of purification for themselves. The chanter then gave each of them a new sacred thread (*yajñopavīta*) to replace their old ones, which they discarded. These threads had twelve strands. A priest acquires the first three strands at his sacred-thread ceremony (*upanayana*), the next three at his marriage, a further three at his consecration and a final three when his wife is pregnant with her first child, although the last three are not always taken. However, in the ritual before Dakshinamurti, it is said that twelve strands must be given, however many are normally worn. After taking the new thread, a cloth was placed over the heads of each new priest and his wife, and the *guru* whispered a series of *mantra* into his and then her ears. These included the Shiva *gāyatrī mantra* and a number of others which I have unfortunately been unable to identify.[16]

After Dakshinamurti had been worshipped, the participants all returned to the consecration pavilion, where the neophytes were reseated on their thrones. Flowers were placed on their heads and sandalpaste on their foreheads, then the *guru* offered plates of food and waved a series of lamps (oil and camphor) in front of them. The chanters then recited from the Vedas and the temple's singers (Tam. *otuvār*) sang Tamil devotional hymns, after which another camphor lamp was waved by the *guru.* The food-offering (*naivedya*) and waving of lamps (*dīpārādhana*), followed by the chanting, singing and waving of a final camphor lamp, were all performed exactly as they are during worship before an image. In other words, the neophytes were treated as if they were images of the gods, an important point to which I shall return below.

The new priests then stood and, as a gesture of homage, touched the feet of their *guru.* Each priest was given a bell and a water-pot by his *guru.* These two articles are both required by a priest performing worship in the temple; he rings the bell while offering food and waving the lamps, and sprinkles water from his pot around the food as part of the act of offering. The *guru* (and in some cases their wives) then sat on the thrones and the new priests, in their turn, now offered food and waved the lamps before them.

New silk clothes were next presented to the neophytes by other priests, and to all the *guru* by the neophytes. These presentations appear to have been made slightly differently at the two consecrations, but on both occasions the neophytes exchanged garlands with the senior priests and temple officials who were in attendance.

The consecration closed with a procession in which the neophytes were borne in a palanquin around the streets outside the temples led by elephants, camels, musicians and the other regal paraphernalia included in all major temple processions. The procession ended at the two streets, near the north gate of the temple, in which most of the priests reside. In front of each priest's home, a woman from the household poured a red liquid (Tam. *āratti*) on the ground beside the palanquin, which was intended, much like the wearing of protective cords, to ward off the evil eye and other malevolent influence. The ceremony concluded with a feast for the new priests and their wives.

The Consecration Ritual: Commentary

The consecration, as already indicated, is in the texts a relatively simple ritual compared with the initiations, and it has none of the complex theological underpinning of the latter. In the texts, before the besprinkling ritual is carried out, the *guru* should rub the neophyte's body with a variety of substances having purificatory and apotropaic qualities: rice gruel, earth, ashes, *darbha*, cowdung, mustard, curds and water (474–6, n.27). In the temple, these have been replaced by the various liquids, also used for the bathing of images, that are poured over the neophytes' heads. The besprinkling with water from the main vessels is the climax of the ritual in both text and temple practice. This water has been powerfully charged by reciting over it the *mantra* of Shiva and its cascade over the neophyte's head symbolizes the devolution of Shiva's power to him (xliv), as was consciously understood by my informants in the temple. After the neophyte has been decked in new clothes, which is done by the *guru* in the texts and, perhaps, represents his adoption of new functions (478–82, n.33–5), the *guru* performs homage to him by offering flowers, perfume, etc. (482, n.37). The *guru* then gives the new *ācārya* his emblems of office, some of which are regal and denote his prestige and authority, and some of which are specifically required by a ritual officiant (482–5, n.38–43). In the temple, the latter would comprise the bell and water-pot, whereas the regal symbols, although they include the silk cloths and turbans (worn by some of the *guru* as well), are more strikingly visible in the final procession. The *guru* next gives instruction to the neophyte (486), before the consecration is concluded by a ritual involving the burning of the neophyte's fingers (494–5, n.55); both these were omitted in the temple.

The reader will note that after the besprinkling, the temple ritual deviated considerably from the textual description summarized above. My priestly informants explained that the ritual held before the shrine of Dakshinamurti was partly a recognition of the role of Shiva as the *guru*, whose deputy is the *guru*-priest in the consecration.[17] In its central features, the acquisition of a new thread and whispering of the 'secret' *mantra*, this ritual almost exactly replicates the sacred thread ceremony. It implies that for Shaiva temple priests there are two analogous rites of passage: a young man becomes a Brahman at the sacred-thread ceremony, when he learns the Vedic *gāyatrī mantra*, and later a Shaiva priest, or even Shiva (Dakshinamurti) himself, at the consecration, when he learns the Shiva *gāyatrī mantra*. The interpolation into the consecration of this rite of passage appears to divest the earlier initiations of yet more of their significance, by implying that the crucial change of status, which is visibly marked by new threads, occurs during the consecration and not the initiations.

The homage paid to the neophyte by the *guru* in the textual version has been replaced, in the temple, by offering food and waving the lamps, an action then repeated for the *guru* by the neophyte. The reciprocity present here deserves particular attention. In the texts, there is no equivalent of the *guru*'s worship by the neophyte. Almost certainly, this is because the ritual described in the texts presumes a transfer of powers from *guru* to neophyte, followed by his retirement. This does not occur in modern temples and, as Brunner-Lachaux remarks, it is quite normal for a *guru* to consecrate a number of neophytes who afterwards take their places by his side (xliv-xlv, 486–91, n.47). If the ritual described in the texts indicates a transfer of powers, the ritual of the temple plainly implies that the *guru* and the newly-consecrated priest possess equal powers.

The most striking feature of the entire consecration in the temple is the ritual identification of the neophytes with the gods, in that they are worshipped by their *guru* almost exactly as worship is performed before an image. The besprinkling is carried out in precisely the same way as the bathing ritual for an image, and this is also true of the food-offering and waving of lamps, as well as other details, such as the application of sandalpaste to the forehead. Only the decoration (*alaṃkāra*) differs, because the neophytes dress themselves in new clothes and ornaments, instead of having it done for them by the *guru*; modesty, particularly in respect of the new priests' wives, is probably the explanation for this. In the temple, these four rituals, which are always performed in the same order—bathing, decoration, food-offering and waving of lamps—are considered to form the core of the ritual of worship before an image (Fuller 1979: 460–1). The precise parallel between the latter and the consecration ritual could scarcely be missed by anyone attending it. Frequently, however, an abbreviated form of worship, comprising only the food-offering and the waving of lamps, is carried out before an image. These two actions, as we have seen, were performed for the neophytes by their *guru*, and then *vice versa*, after the ritual before Dakshinamurti. Thus the *guru*, although they do not undergo the besprinkling, are also plainly identified with the gods during the consecration ritual. On no other occasion in the temple's rituals is this identification between priest and god so clearly made, although priests do worship each other and themselves (Fuller 1979: 467–8) during other temple rituals. However, in the latter cases, the worship is done quickly and simply. Only in the consecration is the worship of a priest performed fully in exactly the same way as it is for a god in the temple. The implications of this will be discussed in more detail below.

The Role of the Priests' Wives

At this point, however, I must consider the role of the novitiate priests' wives. Although the reasons are less than clear and Brunner-Lachaux's text gives us no real clues, it is agreed in the Minakshi temple that the wives' participation is vital. All men must be married before they become priests and all priests should have a living wife, if they are to perform any of the more important rituals, including the daily worship. If widowed, a priest must remarry in order to continue to work, although his second wife will not undergo the initiation and consecration rituals. In part, this rule may simply reflect the precept, current since Vedic times, that demands the co-operation of husband and wife in all religious acts (Kane 1941:556). Brunner (personal communication) suggests that wives may indeed have been introduced into these rituals in a late imitation of Vedic practice; they find no mention in any Agamic text from Somashambhu's or Aghorashiva's period. This historical hypothesis is not, though, inconsistent with the assertion made by those few of my informants who claimed to know the reason for the rule that a priest is 'incomplete' without a wife and that he must, in order to worship Minakshi properly, have access to *śakti*, the divine power personified as a female and incarnate in the goddess. A priest can only legitimately gain access to this power, which is inherent in all women, through sexual relations with his wife. This notion is reminiscent of the Tantric doctrine that in ritual intercourse the female incarnates the goddess's power (Gonda 1965b:62), although it also has Tamil antecedents. More pertinently, it has significant parallels with the conceptualization of the relationship between Minakshi and Sundareshvara that finds expression in the temple rituals (Fuller 1980). The relationship between male and female, on both human and divine planes, is certainly a crucial aspect of the temple rituals and the priests' role in their performance. Furthermore, the priests also stress their status as married householders (*gṛhastha*) in contrast to the ascetics (*saṃnyāsin*), who are not permitted to perform rituals in the temples; this opposition between priests and ascetics is important to the definition of their role and status. Further discussion of these questions, however, cannot be attempted here (see Fuller 1984: ch. 3).

If the priest depends upon his wife for the proper performance of his role, it is not illogical that she should undergo the ritual passage with her husband. However, it is also claimed that the consecration confers upon the priests' wives the right to perform public worship and that they do actually possess residual rights in the temple, so that if all the priests were somehow incapacitated, their wives could do their work. This is evidently hypothetical, but informants did tell me that the priests' wives used to conduct worship in the temple for the Nayaka queens, who observed purdah (sixteenth-eighteenth centuries). I have found no documentary confirmation of this information. However, the important point is that, in addition to the notion that a priest requires a living wife, the idea also exists that the wives themselves acquire the priestly powers at the consecration.

Finally, I must consider the differences between the roles taken by husband and wife in the various rituals. Whereas the regular and special initiations are conducted for both of them, the liberating initiation is apparently undergone only by the men. The reason for this discrepancy is obscure. If the wives do not receive the liberating initiation, then they ought to be ineligible for the consecration. There are some differences between the two spouses' roles in the latter ritual. In particular, although the *guru* worships the new priest and his wife together, he only gives the bell and water-pot to the husband, who alone worships his *guru* in return. But this, I think, merely reflects the fact that only the husband will actually work as a priest and his wife will never need a bell and water-pot to perform worship in the temple. The differences do not pertain to the central features of the consecration, particularly the be-sprinkling, which are performed for both husband and wife. It thus seems clear that the couple really are consecrated together. We must therefore conclude either that the wife is supposed to receive the liberating initiation by proxy through her husband, or that the practice in the temple simply contravenes what is prescrib-ed by the textual authorities.

The Impoverishment of Meaning in the Initiation Rituals

In my commentary on the initiation rituals, I have already suggest-ed some reasons for the virtual absence of any symbolic signifi-cance in them. Brunner-Lachaux, however, has explained the diver-gence between text and practice differently and because the issue is relevant for an understanding of the significance of the consecra-tion ritual, I shall briefly review her arguments. She suggests that the liberating initiation (and by implication the first two as well) only persists—nowadays as a caricature—because it is a precondi-tion for the consecration (420–2, n.457). No one, she contends, still believes in the efficacy of this initiation. It is, among contempo-rary temple priests, 'no longer considered as the Door which leads to Shiva, but as a ritual which has to be undergone if one wants to become an *ācārya*—a status giving immediate and tangible benefits. Nowadays, it is practically never performed for its own sake. . .' (xxxvii). With this argument I am in basic agreement. However, she attributes this debasement mainly to the quality of latter-day priests, who are loath to waste time, money and effort on complicated rituals (cf. 1975–6:113). The *guru*'s failure to retire after the consecration is explained in much the same way; Brunner-Lachaux specifically links the latter deviation from the texts to a rise in the number of temples, which led to a vast expansion in the priesthood and a concomitant deterioration in its quality and prestige (xliv–xlv, 491, n.47).

Let me consider this argument a little further. The very composition of Somashambhu's and Aghorashiva's manuals does indicate that in their epoch (eleventh-twelfth centuries), there prevailed a climate of religious devotion and knowledge sufficient to nurture them. No more than any other scholars are they likely to have emerged from nowhere. But this climate might have embraced only a religious minority and it seems more than likely that there was, then as now, a sizeable contingent of religious officiants whose worldly concerns matched their spiritual ones. In the case of the Minakshi temple the disputes between priests, almost certainly mainly about the perquisites attached to their rights in the temple rituals, apparently date back to the sixteenth century. They may indeed go back to the fourteenth century or earlier, only two or three hundred years after Somashambhu and Aghorashiva. The historical material on the Minakshi temple (Breckenridge 1976:180–7; Fuller 1984:ch.4.) reveals that the two groups of priests, the Vikkira Pantiyas and the Kulacekaras, have argued with each other over their different rights and duties for at least four centuries. In the sixteenth century, their antagonism actually took the form of an attempt by the Vikkira Pantiyas to prevent the Kulacekaras from holding consecrations, and *vice versa.* Both groups sporadically persisted with these attempts to thwart each other until the nineteenth century, when the British Collector of Madurai intervened. His attempt to solve the conflict included an order to separate the consecrations of the two groups: the Vikkira Pantiyas were to conduct theirs before Minakshi's shrine and the Kulacekaras before Sundareshvara's. It is, I think, beyond doubt, in the light of the historical record, that the mutual obstructiveness of the two priestly groups was motivated by the desire to deny prospective priests belonging to the opposite group access to the pecuniary rewards of the temple. Prestige and status were probably involved as well, but it seems unlikely that anyone was much inclined to hamper the spiritual progress of others. The evidence also suggests that the *guru* have never retired in favour of their disciples in the Minakshi temple during the last four hundred years at least, and this has probably been the situation in many other temples as well (Brunner 1975:441).

It is conceivable that things were otherwise in Somashambhu's time, as Brunner-Lachaux insists (xliv). However, it does seem to me that it is equally likely that the Agamic texts have always been theological disquisitions primarily prescribing what ought to be done, rather than descriptions of what was done. Of course, their authors were probably inspired by contemporary practice. But the connection between text and practice need never have been very close and it is, I suggest, much safer to admit that we are mostly ignorant about what really occurred during initiation and consecration rituals in the temples of the past.

In spite of what I have just said, I would not dispute Brunner-Lachaux's assertion that modern temple priests lack belief in the efficacy of initiation rituals and are disinclined to expend resources on them. I am not convinced that this state of affairs was ever wholly otherwise nor, more specifically, that the putative decline is attributable to an expansion in the priesthood. However, the absence of belief does seem to be a fact and this must, of course, be linked to the virtual absence of any significant, meaningful content in the rituals as they are now performed. Credence can only be undermined by meaninglessness and meaninglessness promoted by unbelief.

The Consecration as a Ritual of Office

Our problem, however, is not only the apparent impoverishment, when compared with the texts, of the temple's initiation rituals; it is also that the consecration ritual performed in the temple is, by contrast, at least as elaborate as that described in the texts, and also considerably longer and more complicated. This latter fact is also important.

Although, in the texts, the primary function of the consecration is the provision of spiritual leaders, capable of conducting initiations, for the Shaiva community, its main *raison d'être* today is to admit a man into the temple priesthood. The consecration can be done for the heads of monasteries, but it is otherwise restricted to members of the Shaiva priestly subcaste and, in the case of any particular temple, to members of those groups which possess traditional, hereditary rights in that temple.[18]

The consecration ritual in the temple can be seen to have a number of analytically distinct functions. It confers the office of temple priest on a man by devolving to him the power of Shiva, with whom he becomes identified, as he must if he is to perform the god's worship. It also expresses and legitimates the fact that married males belonging to the Shaiva priestly subcaste are alone entitled to this office and, within the Minakshi temple, it more specifically legitimates the monopolistic priestly rights of the Vikkira Pantiyas and the Kulacekaras. These rights, as I have mentioned, have important economic aspects and thus the consecration is effectively legitimating the traditional 'closed shop' of the two priestly groups. I must now explain how the ritual fulfils these various functions.

But we must first ask why the initiations could not fulfil these functions. There are, I think, two main reasons. Firstly, the initiation rituals, although they are in practice undergone by few people other than novitiate priests and their wives, are not in principle debarred to others and, further, it is not the initiations, but the consecration, which confers on a man the ability to conduct the public worship. Without drastic modification, the initiation rituals could not, therefore, serve as rituals of priestly office. Secondly, the consecration has always been a public ceremony and it is therefore very much more suitable as a vehicle for the legitimate accession to priestly office. Precisely because it is a question of public recognition of accession to a public office, and not of an essentially personal spiritual transformation, a private ritual, like the initiation, would be an inappropriate mode of conferment.

The central act of the consecration, in both text and temple practice, is undoubtedly the besprinkling which, as I have said, is consciously understood to be the devolution of Shiva's power to the neophyte, who is thereby made into a person able to assume the priestly office. In the temple's ritual, this action most plainly appears to convert the neophyte, now charged with divine power, into the god, although in the texts this fundamental transformation has already occurred during the initiations. In the temple, this central rite is also, however, the first stage in a ritual of worship; identical in form to the bathing of an image, it is followed by the rituals of decoration, food-offering and waving of lamps, the last two of which are also performed by the neophyte for the *guru*. Thus the neophyte's acquisition of Shiva's power is immediately confirmed by worshipping him as a god, and the *guru*'s continued divinity is simultaneously reaffirmed. As I have said, no one familiar with the temple's ritual could fail to appreciate the equivalence of priest and god that is displayed here. I do not mean to suggest by this that anyone actually believes that an ordinary priest is identical to the Lord of the Universe. No one does and discussion of this problem would take us far from the central issues of this paper; all that is important here is to see that the equivalence between priest and god appears to ensure Shiva's sanction for the consecration, through his participation in it. Further endorsement is supplied by the ritual before Dakshinamurti, which reiterates that Shiva in his *guru*-form is the true master of the rituals.

To the priests and the minority of onlookers with some knowledge of Shaiva theology, the logic of automatic divine legitimation has another stage. *Guru* and neophyte are divine because the ritual has made them so and it has done this because it was enacted according to Shiva's instruction, which were, it is believed, written down in the Agamas. But this belief poses a problem because, as we have seen, the ritual deviates widely from Agamic prescription. How then can the Agamas perform any legitimating function? Because, most simply, they are asserted to have this function. Although few priests have ever read any of the Agamic texts, there are a handful (in the Minakshi temple and elsewhere) who are acknowledged by their peers as experts in their study. In most cases, their expertise is open to dispute, but precisely because the texts are so intractable—as the volume of Brunner-Lachaux's footnotes itself shows—next to no one is competent to deny the pretensions of the acknowledged experts. As priests themselves will readily admit, who in the end, other than Shiva himself, really knows what the Agamas mean? Like the arcane sacred texts of many other religions, it is the very obscurity of Shiva's dictated instructions that makes them into powerful founts of legitimate religious authority. If all else fails, there is a further line that can be taken: the devotionalist concern with intention, rather than formal correctness, may be stressed. Thus the priests will, if necessary, maintain that the efficacy of rituals is primarily a product of their devotion to Shiva and this, of course, makes the literal meaning of the Agamas inconsequential (cf. Fuller 1989: 135–46).

An important feature of the consecration ritual is that the priests conduct it for themselves. They alone can act as Shiva and create new incarnations of the god from among their own ranks. In this respect, the consecration of a priest obviously differs from the very similar consecration ritual for a king, in which the priest legitimates the monarch's accession to the throne. Thus the granting of priestly office to one of their number also serves to show that the temple priests, a self-perpetuating body, are endlessly able to legitimate themselves and are answerable only to the god of whom they are themselves earthly forms.

However, the office of priest, as already stated, is not purely religious. Rights in the public worship used to be valuable economic assets and even today the priestly office, though less lucrative, continues to provide its incumbents with most of their income. Only if they can maintain their monopoly over worship in the temples can Shaiva Brahman priests remain financially secure. In the Minakshi temple itself, the hereditary monopoly belongs to the Vikkira Pantiya and Kulacekara groups, and it is in their own vital interests that this remains so, although in the past (but less often today) each group has sometimes seen the other as its most dangerous rival (Fuller 1984: 73–4). The economic component of hereditary priestly rights has certainly been important for centuries and thus it has long been a function of the consecration to reaffirm the legitimacy of the priests' valuable monopolies.

Significant in the legitimating function of the consecration ritual is the attendance of delegates of both priestly groups, as well as representatives of the priesthood from other nearby Shaiva temples. The holders of most of the other major offices in the temple are also present. These include the powerful officials of the Devasthanam, the bureaucratic governmental authority which now controls the Minakshi temple. The most important of these men is the temple's Executive Officer, who had to give permission for the consecration in the first place. In this and other matters, the authority of the Executive Officer, an appointee of the Tamilnadu Government's Hindu Religious and Charitable Endowments Department, does now effectively circumscribe the priests' power in the temple, so that their ability solely to legitimate themselves is no longer complete.[19] The gathering of representatives from all the main interest groups in the temple, together with large numbers of ordinary devotees, plainly gives public sanction to the proceedings, the model for which is not modern. The priestly consecration, in which the novitiate priests sit on thrones before their court and afterwards go in regal procession, is explicitly similar in form to that of the traditional consecration, also a devolution of divine power, performed for a Hindu king (484, n.38; Brunner 1975:422). Overall, therefore, the consecration, held before a court that includes the powers-that-be in the temple, serves, in addition to its other functions, to legitimate the perpetuation of the traditional monopoly over the temple priesthood held by Shaiva Brahmans belonging to the Vikkira Pantiya and Kulacekara groups.

In the absence of adequate historical data, it is impossible to explain fully the development of the initiation and consecration rituals over time.[20] However, I hope I have shown that in the Minakshi temple today—not, I believe, an exceptional case in this respect—the consecration is predominantly a ritual of accession to priestly office which simultaneously legitimates, because it is sanctioned by both divine and human power, the ritual prerogatives of the priests as well as their economically valuable hereditary monopoly. Today, as has probably been the case for centuries, the consecration ritual is mainly about legitimate succession to office; lacking any real relevance to the latter, the initiations are little more than an almost meaningless preamble, a superficial rehearsal for the great public spectacle that follows.

NOTES

Research in the Minakshi temple was conducted for twelve months (August 1976–July 1977), financed by the Social Science Research Council, and a further two months (July–September 1980), financed by the Small Grants Research Fund in the Humanities of the British Academy; I thank both organizations for their support. I also thank my informants and assistants in Madurai, Mme Hélène Brunner for her invaluable, detailed criticisms of an earlier version of this paper, and Dr. Richard Burghart, Dr. Audrey Cantlie, Dr. Penny Logan and Dr. Martin Southwold for their useful comments.

1 All technical ritual terms are transliterated from their Sanskrit forms, except for a handful of words transliterated from their Tamil forms and indicated as such.

2 Cf. also Diehl (1956:51, 56); on Tantric initiation see Hoens (1965) and Renou & Filliozat (1947:597–8); on Vaishnava initiation see Rangachari (1931:101–14); for comparisons, Gonda (1970:64–5).

3 All page references given without author and date are to Brunner-Lachaux (1977) throughout.

4 See Gonda (1965a: ch. 10 *passim*) for the relation between initiation in later Hinduism (our concern here), on the one hand, and the Vedic *dīkṣā* and other rites of passage (*saṃskāra*), particularly the boy's sacred-thread ceremony (*upanayana*), on the other. For the *saṃskāra*, see particularly Kane (1941: ch. 6—especially pp. 192–3 for their purposes) and Brunner-Lachaux (1977: ii).

5 It is probable that Somashambhu and Aghorashiva were mainly concerned with the consecration of the head of a monastery (*maṭha*), a position they both held. It is possible that the consecration ritual for a temple priest was originally rather different, but Brunner (personal communication) states that no firm evidence on this point has yet been found.

6 Initiation and consecration rituals occur rather infrequently, even in a large temple like Minakshi's. I was therefore fortunate that any occurred while I was in India. However, the first (in September 1976) took place only five weeks after I had begun my research. At that time my first assistant and I were still very ignorant about the temple and we had few close relationships with any of the priests. We saw only the consecration ritual and did not find out about the initiation rituals until later; the priests, significantly, did not think they would interest us. The second set of rituals were, to my dismay, held just two days after I had to leave Madurai at the end of my fieldwork (in July 1977). My second (and by then very experienced) assistant attended the whole ceremony and has given me reasonably full notes on it, but there are some lacunae. My data are obviously not as good as I would wish, but owing to the importance of these previously undescribed rituals, I have thought it worthwhile to do what I can.

7 *Iśāna* (centre); *tatpuruṣa* (east); *aghora* (south); *sadyojāta* (west); *vāmadeva* (north).

8 Two ladles are used for oblations into the fire; one (*sruc*) in which Shakti is invoked and another (*sruva*) in which Shiva is invoked (Brunner-Lachaux 1963:246, n.1). My assistant states that the feminine ladle was employed here and later, but he wrongly describes this as the *sruva*. I do not know whether he, or his priestly informants, were in error here.

9 A full discussion of these cords would also have to deal with the problem of why they are so frequently tied on to images of the gods in the temple—a problem because it seems to imply that the gods need protection against relatively feeble malevolent forces. I cannot attempt to resolve this issue here.

10 The Minakshi temple priests are aware of their duty to worship Shiva daily, but many of them do not fulfil it. Some seemed seriously troubled that Shiva might punish them for this lapse. However, the priests also believe that it is far worse to discontinue the daily worship once begun, than never to begin it in the first place. They thus feel that it is less sinful to admit one's weakness at the outset, than to pretend to a resolute self-discipline that one does not possess.

11 In the Vaishnava initiation, threads are wound around the neophyte's body and then cut (Gonda 1965*a*:406; Rangachari 1931:112–3); a symbolic death is suggested here too, but with the same qualifications.

12 According to the texts, the initiation ritual is repeated for the soul of an initiate at his funeral ritual (*antyeṣṭi*) before the body is burnt. The *kalā* are again purified before the soul is finally united with Shiva (xlix-li, 594–600). Priestly informants in the temple, however, understood the *antyeṣṭi* to be a ritual in which *kalā* were taken out of the body and they did not appear to see it as the final initiation. Some perceived it as the removal of the divine powers acquired at the consecration, thus reflecting again their idea that the crucial transformation occurs in the consecration, not the initiations. This ritual, I was told, should be done for all who had been consecrated, both priests and their wives. However, as I have never seen a priestly funeral, I do not know what is in practice done, nor have I been able to question informants at the time of a death when better data could almost certainly be obtained.

13 Both groups of priests belong to the Shaiva Brahman priestly subcaste and their members intermarry. However, the Vikkira Pantiyas have rights in the temple superior to the Kulacekaras; in particular, only the former can perform the daily worship (Fuller 1984: 32–4, 72–5). I have been told that in the past the Kulacekara consecration was slightly less elaborate, reflecting their inferior rights in the temple, but I could obtain no definite data on this supposed difference. The initiations preceding a Kulacekara priest's consecration are conducted in the corridor of Sundareshvara's shrine. Many Minakshi temple priests also have rights in other smaller temples in the region and in recent years (1977–80), several new priests have been consecrated in these other temples before coming to work in Madurai. This practice has been started to save money, for the rituals held in smaller temples need not be so elaborate and therefore cost the neophytes' families less.

14 In September 1976, the *darbha* twists were placed on only the husbands' heads, but this may have been an error. In July 1977, I think they were

placed on all the neophytes' heads, but my assistant's notes are rather vague about this.

15 In September 1976, according to my notes, the small vessels were emptied before the large ones. In July 1977, the large ones were poured first and this is the order normal in other similar rituals of besprinkling and bathing. In the earlier consecration, it is probable that either the priests made an error or my notes are incorrect.

16 The Shiva *gāyatrī mantra* is modelled on the famous *gāyatrī mantra* from the Rig Veda (see Brunner-Lachaux 1963:58, n.4). There are also *gāyatrī mantra* for all the other important deities in the temple.

17 It is possible that Dakshinamurti's prominence in the consecration partly stems from a misinterpretation of the texts (cf. 481–2, n.351).

18 All the priests in the Minakshi temple have rights in the public worship, which are allocated between them by a number of different rotas, so that the public worship in its entirety is divided into various sets of distinct rights. (The general pattern is, I believe, typical of all major South Indian temples.) To give an example: one such set comprises the daily worship before Minakshi's shrine; this is divided, according to the days in the Tamil month, so that one particular priest might, for instance, have these rights on the tenth and twentieth days of each month. Similar divisions operate for all the other sets, and different priests vary greatly in the total 'quantity' of rights that they possess. Only priests with rights in the public worship can perform worship for private individuals in the temple, today their main source of income. Rights in the public worship are regarded by the priests (and the law) as heritable property, but it is important to note that because of the working of the inheritance rules, these rights are sometimes held by women and uninitiated or unmarried males, who are unable to exercise them and must appoint deputies from among the working priests. I have discussed the complicated subject of priestly rights in the Minakshi temple in more detail in Fuller (1984: ch. 4).

19 The Minakshi temple has been administered by Executive Officers appointed by the H. R. & C. E. Department since 1937; over the years since then, the priests' power in the temple has been steadily undermined (Fuller 1984: ch. 5). The statement in the main text, true for 1977, now requires modification. In 1980, a committee of trustees had been appointed for the temple by the Tamilnadu Government, and the chairman of the trustees has now replaced the Executive Officer as the most powerful figure in the temple. He would now, I presume, attend any consecration held in the temple. This change does not however, affect my argument substantively.

20 In the past, priests did sometimes work in the temple before being consecrated, although they never performed the more important rituals. Some of my older informants, who started working in the temple in the 1930s, only underwent the consecration ritual some time afterwards. This may not have been exceptional. Consecration appears to have become compulsory for all new priests since Executive Officers began to administer the temple.

REFERENCES

Breckenridge, C. A. 1976. *The Śrī Mīnākṣi Sundareśvara temple: worship and endowments in South India, 1833 to 1925*. Thesis, Univ. of Wisconsin-Madison.

Brunner (-Lachaux), H. 1963. *Somaśambhupaddhati, pt. 1: le rituel quotidien*. Pondicherry: Institut Français d'Indologie.

—— 1968. *Somaśambhupaddhati, pt. 2: rituels occasionnels, I*. Pondicherry: Institut Français d'Indologie.

—— 1975. Le *Sādhaka*, personnage oublié du Śivaisme du sud. *Journal Asiatique* 263, 411–43.

—— 1975–6. Importance de la littérature Āgamique pour l'étude des religions vivantes de l'Inde. *Indologica Taurinensia* 3–4, 107–24.

—— 1977. *Somaśambhupaddhati, pt. 3: rituels occasionnels, II*. Pondicherry: Institut Français d'Indologie.

Diehl, C. G. 1956. *Instrument and purpose: studies on rites and rituals in South India*. Lund: Gleerupska.

Fuller, C. J. 1979. Gods, priests and purity: on the relation between Hinduism and the caste system. *Man* (N. S.) 14, 459–76.

—— 1980. The divine couple's relationship in a South Indian temple: Mīnāksī and Sundareśvara at Madurai. *History of Religions* 19, 321–48.

—— 1984. *Servants of the goddess: the priests of a South Indian temple*, Cambridge: University Press.

Gonda, J. 1965a. *Change and continuity in Indian religion*. The Hague: Mouton.

—— 1965b. *Les religions de l'Inde*, vol. 2. Paris: Payot.

—— 1970. *Viṣṇuism and Śivaism: a comparison*. London: Athlone Press.

Hoens, D. J. 1965. Initiation in later Hinduism according to Tantric texts. In C. J. Bleeker (ed.), *Initiation*. Leiden: Brill.

Kane, P. V. 1941. *History of Dharmaśāstra*, vol. 2. Poona: Bhandarkar Oriental Research Institute.

Rangachari, K. 1931. *The Sri Vaishnava Brahmans*. Bulletin of the Madras Government Museum (N. S.), vol. 2, no. 2.

Rao, T. A. Gopinatha 1916. *Elements of Hindu iconography*, vol. 2. Madras: Govt. Press.

Renou, L. & Filliozat J. 1947. *L'Inde classique*, vol. 1. Paris: Payot.

Van Gennep, A. 1960. *The Rites of passage*. London: Routledge.

VAISHNAVA REFORM SECTS IN ASSAM

Audrey Cantlie

This paper is concerned with the reform movement that arose in the 1930s among Vaishnavas in the State of Assam. The movement can be termed 'reform' from two standpoints. From the viewpoint of its adherents it represents a purge of the accretions and distortions—as they see them—which have attached themselves to the tradition over time; it is a reform in the sense of a return to a pristine state. From the viewpoint of the external observer, on the other hand, the term 'reform' is understood in quite a different way: it implies that a change has taken place in the tradition through the incorporation of alien ideas (albeit often in disguised form) such that the tradition has become something other than completely Hindu. In other words, the nature of the change is judged to be in some respects a break with the past. Here the view of the external observer is directly opposed to that of the adherents of the movement, although it may coincide with that of its Hindu critics.

In order to understand the nature of the 'reform' movement, it is necessary to give a brief description of the traditional system which it seeks to reform. Assamese Vaishnavism follows the path of devotion (*bhakti*) based on the teachings of the *Bhāgavata Purāṇa* and is associated in its origins with the name of Shankaradeva (1449–1548) who is regarded by his followers as an incarnation of Vishnu. Soon after his death his disciples established centres of worship, called Satras, which provide the permanent organization of the sect. A Satra consists of a *guru* and the disciples initiated by him. Physically it comprises the house of the *guru*, a large prayer hall for daily worship called a Name House (*nām ghar*) and, in some cases, rows of huts for celibate devotees who have renounced the world. The Satra is supported by the dues of its disciples and by grants of revenue-free land made in the name of the Satra image. Traditionally every Assamese Vaishnava, prior to marriage, journeys to a Satra to take initiation (*śaraṇ*) when he is instructed by the *guru* in the mysteries of the sect. In theory he is free to choose any *guru* he pleases, but in practice he receives initiation from the *guru* of his father so that Satra affiliation is now hereditary. The legitimacy of the *guru* rests on a line of succession recorded in the family book of his Satra which links him, either by birth or—in the case of celibate *guru*—by initiation, to the original founder of his sub-sect and, through him, to Shankaradeva as an *avatār* of Vishnu. At initiation the novice receives knowledge (*mantra*) from the *guru* as a form (*murti*) of Vishnu and becomes identified with him. Thereafter he is required to lead the life of one who has surrendered himself to God and to pay annual dues for the upkeep of the Satra. The Satras are the traditional repositories of Shankaradeva's religion as it has been transmitted from Gosain to Gosain down the generations. The Gosains or Satradhikars, as they are called, are either Brahman, in which case they take the title Gosvami, or Kayastha, in which case they take the title Mahanta. They were, until recently, the recognized authorities on all religious questions and are worshipped by their disciples as living gods. There are estimated to be over six hundred Satras distributed throughout the State. Worship is chiefly congregational, different castes combining to sing together hymns in the vernacular before the *Bhāgavat*, into which the God is invoked for the duration of the performance. The hymns consist largely of the many names of God and performances of Name, as it is called, are held on all seasonal festivals, *rites de passage*, and other contingencies of life.

The Vaishnava reform sects originated in the 1930s, in the Nowgong District of Assam, from a controversy concerning the period of death pollution (*aśōc*) to be observed by non-Brahman castes. Traditionally in Assam the Brahmans observed impurity for ten days on a death in the family, performing the first *śrāddha* on the eleventh day, and the non-Brahmans observed impurity for thirty days, performing the first *śrāddha* on the thirty-first day. The basis of this distinction was the belief that the soul of a Brahman, being superior to the soul of a Shudra, reached heaven more quickly. A number of prominent Shudras now began to conclude their funerary rites on the eleventh day on the grounds that they were not inferior to the Brahmans and that after death the soul was not distinguishable by caste. The movement spread rapidly, especially after Independence, and the non-Brahman population is now divided into the following sects: (1) the Monthly people (*māhakīyā*) who continue in the traditional observance of one month's impurity; (2) the Eleven-day people (*eghāradinīyā*) who observe ten days' impurity on the model of the Brahmans; (3) the Thirteen-day people (*teradinīyā*) who observe twelve days' impurity as an assertion of Kshatriya status; and (4) an extreme group of Haridhaniyas, also called Harijaniya or Nam Kirtaniya, who do not observe ritual pollution on death and who no longer employ Brahman priests to perform Vedic rites. One or other of the new sects is now to be found in almost every Hindu village.

The movement is associated with two main social changes. The first is the spread of education and the second is the Congress movement. The spread of education and literacy to the masses, which accelerated after Independence, enabled many non-Brahmans for the first time to read both Sanskrit and Assamese religious texts and to question traditional interpretations. More importantly, the non-Brahmans became qualified by education to compete for posts in government service, teaching and law which, in the old days, had largely been Brahman preserves. The introduction of universal franchise and of special privileges for scheduled castes and tribes and backward classes (categories which cover two-thirds of the population) further altered the balance of power in favour of the non-Brahman castes. The Congress movement also had a considerable impact on the structure of society. After the social upheaval of the 1921 Civil Disobedience movement, which was widely supported in Assam, Kaibarttas and Brittial-Banias (exterior castes) and Naths (marginal), formerly excluded from upper-caste prayer halls or Name Houses, as they are called, gained access to the exterior portion of the hall at the west end (*ṭup*).[1] After the 1930 movement they were admitted in many parts of lower Assam into the body of the hall where they worshipped together with other castes. The first leaders of the new sects were in the main active members of the Congress party who after Gandhi's Harijan movement became interested in religious reform as a means of reforming society. Haladhar Bhuyan, President of the Nowgong branch of Congress, combined with the celibate devotee, Rama Kanta Atoi, to found in 1933 an organization called the Shri Shankaradeva Sangha. In his Presidential Address he described the aims of the Society as the restoration of the true *dharma* which had been overlaid by superstitions, the publicizing of a monotheistic religion, the abolition of untouchability and the extension of equal rights to people of all castes. The universalistic ethic of the *Bhāgavata Purāṇa* which opens salvation to all irrespective of caste or tribe was seen as an anticipation of the modern emphasis on equality and the abolition of caste distinctions. Sonaram Chutiya, another President of the Shankaradeva Sangha, observed: 'The climate of opinion today, the policy of the present government, the fundamental rights of the constitution, all tend to a casteless and classless society. But our custom was from before. Accidentally they match.' These reformers made no distinction between restoring what they regarded as the fundamental principles of their religion which had become corrupted over time and moving forward to the creation of a modern egalitarian democratic society.

> In our Vaishnava *dharma* man is Vishnu. There is a saying: 'The service of man is the service of God'. Nehru and Gandhi also believed that man is God.

> Mahatma Gandhi is the *guru* of this sect. There is no difference between the ideas of Shankaradeva and Mahatma Gandhi.

> Shankaradeva founded a casteless society. Vishnu was incarnated as Shankaradeva only to uplift backward people. Like Gandhi he worked for Untouchables. The Shankaradeva Sangha came into existence by the will of God for the purpose of restoring the actual principles of Shankaradeva. It has all castes eating and worshipping together. It is a new era in Assam.

The aspirations of the lower castes largely took the form of resentment of the dominant position of the Brahmans who, although they numbered only some 100,000 in the Brahmaputra Valley at the time of the 1931 Census, were over-represented in government service and the professions. Although anti-Brahmanism is publicly disavowed by the leaders of the Sangha—'We do not hate Brahmans, but the priest'—it is widespread among their followers and has been a dominant feature of the movement since its inception.

> I am a living witness to the start of the Shri Shankaradeva Sangha. I was a member of the District Congress Committee in Nowgong at that time; Haladhar Bhuyan was the President. We ran our candidate for the Assam Assembly. He was opposed by one of the

most powerful persons in Nowgong, Rai Bahadur Bindalan Chandra Gosvami [Brahman] . . . Wherever we went, we were frustrated. No one came to vote for us. We not only had no supporters, even the candidate suggested we should not spend another farthing and not go into any more villages canvassing votes, for he received so many insults.

We sat dejected. At that moment a man came to Haladhar Bhuyan's house, Rama Kanta Atoi, on cycle. Seeing us brooding, he asked us the matter. We expressed our frustration. He said, 'Give me Rs. 20 and a good bicycle. I will defeat Bindalan Chandra Gosvami.' Although at that time Rs. 20 was something, we gave and the office bicycle.

He went first to the village where our candidate was born and started speaking ill of the Brahmans from generation to generation. That worked like anything. Our candidate was returned . . .

When we won, there was another meeting among ourselves. In order to preserve the basis of our support Haladhar Bhuyan said we should go on preaching against Brahmans and Brahmanism. And so the Sangha came into being.

In 1933 Jogendranath Barua, a District Judge in Golaghat, performed the *śrāddha* of his father on the eleventh day on the grounds that he was not inferior to the Brahmans. This was the first Eleven-day ceremony by a prominent non-Brahman and caused a sensation in society.[2] At that time the right of a Shudra to end death pollution on the eleventh day was not socially accepted and many Brahman priests refused to assist at the rites.[3] Meetings were convened of pandits from all over Assam to discuss whether the performance of *śrāddha* by non-Brahmans on the eleventh day was supported by *śāstra*. Gopikabhallub Gosvami of Golaghat, one of the pioneers of the Eleven-day movement, argued that he could find no bar in *śāstra* to Eleven-day observances for all castes, quoting in support of his position *Garuda Purāna*, *Preta Kalpa*, verse 19, ch.13:

> It is authoritatively stated in the *śāstras* that in the Kali Age there are ten days' purification for all castes after births and deaths.[4]

The majority of Brahman pandits, however, took a different view. At one of these meetings Haladhar Bhuyan said:

We respect the Brahmans always. Whatever is quoted in this meeting, it is all written by Brahmans. But times are changing. If you press the people under your feet, the people will revolt. So you should conclude that both Monthly and Eleven-day forms have religious authority. Otherwise people will leave the Brahmans and become Nam Kirtaniya (translated from Haladhar Bhuyan's Presidential Address of 1962 in which he gives a history of the Shankaradeva Sangha).

The scholars, however, subsequently printed a leaflet to the effect that Shudras could not perform *śrāddha* at all: it had no sastric authority. On receipt of this leaflet Bhuyan consulted with Mahantas and pandits of Nowgong. They called a meeting and founded the Shri Shankaradeva Sangha with Rai Sahib Dambarudhar Barua as President and Haladhar Bhuyan as Secretary. Six months later the All-Assam State Sangha was established under the Presidentship of the Satradhikar of Garamur.

At first the Sangha took the position that non-Brahmans were entitled, like Brahmans, to end death pollution on the tenth day. Later their proposals became more radical. In his pamphlet on death observances written for the guidance of Shudras in 1945 the Garamuriya Satradhikar discussed the problem of finding a priest fit to be fed at the *śrāddha*. He cited Manu as saying that the soul of the deceased has to swallow as many mouthfuls of boiling lead as morsels of food eaten in his name by a Brahman who is not versed in the Veda. For those who were unable to find a suitable Brahman he advised that the safest course was to perform Nam Kirtan instead for the benefit of the soul. The Shri Shankaradeva Sangha now forbids its members to employ Brahman priests on pain of expulsion and ridicules much of the funerary ritual, notably the offering of *piṇḍa* to crows and dogs. The following stories (probably apocryphal), which were still circulating in Nowgong District in 1971, illustrate the bitterness of anti-Brahman feeling in that area:

A Sut died near Nowgong town, leaving a wife and baby. The Brahman priest asked for her cow which was her only possession. She said she needed the cow or her baby would die. The Brahman insisted. She refused. He said he would not perform the funerary rites unless she gave him the cow. She burnt her husband without Vedic rites.

A Brahman came to perform the funerary rites of a prominent Sut. The son of the dead man was an undergraduate with no belief in ritual observances. Sixteen gifts are offered in the name of the deceased in order to extinguish the attachment of the soul to this world. If he gets these articles over there, he will not hanker for them here and his soul will rise upwards. The Brahman accepts certain of these gifts in the name of the dead. He generally wants something to which the deceased was particularly attached. In this case the Brahman knew the family well. He said, 'Your father was very fond of his bicycle. If possible, offer that bicycle to me.' The son became annoyed and said, 'Do you insist on something very dear to my father?' He replied, 'Yes.' The son went inside the house and returned with his mother. He said to the priest, 'My father loved my mother very much. I offer my mother to you. Take her away.' The priest replied, 'Because you have said this, you will get no benefit from the *śrāddha*', and left without taking anything. After that the village gave up employing Brahman priests.

The rejection of Brahmanical ritual is justified by reference to the monotheism of Shankaradeva. The Vaishnavas describe their religion as 'taking shelter in One' (*ekaśaraṇa dharma*) and traditionally strict Vaishnavas refused to participate in Durga Puja and similar festivals. Now, however, for the first time the principle of monotheism was applied to domestic ritual in the course of which, it was pointed out, the priest makes offerings to a great number of gods and goddesses. All such rites were therefore condemned as explicitly forbidden by Shankaradeva (*Bhāgavata* II, v.545):

> Do not bow down before other gods and goddesses;
> Partake not of their offerings;
> Look not upon their images, enter not their temples,
> Lest thy faith be vitiated.

Those who continue to perform Brahmanical rites do not deny the authenticity of this verse, which they explain in a number of ways, but they point out that Shankaradeva was married by *hom* and offered *piṇḍa* to his father and to his father's mother.

The first biography of Shankaradeva was written by Ram Saran Thakur, Madhavadeva's nephew. Here it is said that Shankaradeva observed thirty days' impurity for his father's death and for his father's mother's death. Madhavadeva observed thirty days for Shankaradeva. This nephew was with Madhavadeva all the time as his cook. He records marriage with *hom*, he records *piṇḍa*, he records *laguṇ diyā*. In the ten or twelve biographies which I have read, the same story is told. All cannot be wrong.

Members of the Sangha reject these passages as spurious additions interpolated by the Brahmans, preferring to rely on the writings of Shankaradeva himself rather than on his biographers. Much of the argument is conducted in homely analogies:

Is it not said in the *Bhāgavatu Puraṇa* that if water is poured on the base of a tree, then all the branches and leaves suck up nourishment? All gods and goddesses are mere manifestations of Vishnu so their worhip as independent deities is unnecessary.

If one wants some corrugated-iron sheets, one does not go directly to the Deputy Commissioner but to the Supply Officer. So we poor devotees, if we want wealth, we must go to Lakshmi.

It is true: God is one. But this does not mean we should disrespect other gods. To dinner we invite a guest of honour. But there are other guests. We must feed them too. What is the harm if we feed them too?

As the prohibition on the worship of deities other than Vishnu provides the only rationale for the rejection of Brahmanical rites and the opposition to Brahman priests, it is insisted upon in the Shri Shankaradeva Sangha with a rigidity uncommon among Hindus, and members have been suspended for attending Durga Puja. At the same time the concept of Untouchability has been redefined to apply to worshippers of many gods, described as 'the unholiest thing in the world', more polluting than beef cooked in wine by an outcaste woman (cf. Shankaradeva's *Daham*). 'Shankaradeva wrote,' observed a Vice-President of the Sangha from the Untouchable fisherman caste, 'that he who believes in more than one God is an Untouchable. That was the opinion of Shankaradeva. That was the opinion of Lord Krishna.' Members of the Sangha eat with Untouchables who have joined the organization but they refuse to eat with Brahmans observing Brahmanical rites.

The Sangha was formed with the assistance of a number of Satradhikars. Some, like Garamur, were attracted by their programme of social reform. Others saw in the substitution of Nam Kirtan for Brahmanical ritual more work for the poorer Gosains. But as the Sangha became more extreme in its views, the majority, including the Garamuriya Gosain, withdrew. Today the Satradhikars are criticized for corrupting the religion of Shankaradeva by the leaders of the Sangha, who appeal over their heads to the authority of the written text:

> After Shankaradeva's death the Satradhikars neglected his ideals and vitiated his principles. They did not consult his books and did not do what the books said. They became self-indulgent. *Dharma* became a money-making business (Vice-President of the Shankar Sangha).
>
> There are many Satradhikars who regard Shri Shankaradeva as *guru* but never follow his instructions (President of Shankar Sangha).
>
> The Satras were established to carry out Shankaradeva's teaching but the Satradhikars are groping in the darkness. They have forgotten the real motto of Mahapurusha and are ruining the society. Some Satradhikars have become zamindars. They have no time to preach *dharma* and occupy themselves with land accounts (former President of Shankar Sangha).
>
> If this state of affairs continues in the Satras, in twenty years they will go to hell.

The Satradhikars are in a difficult position. For a number of reasons they have become unpopular today. Visitors to the Satra are expected to wash their utensils. They sit on the bare ground while the Gosain sits on a mat. These customs are resented by the educated youth. When the Gosain is invited to lower-caste Name Houses, he takes his own distributor to prepare the offering. Today the lower castes resent these distinctions and mock the Gosain, 'Why are you bringing that distributor wearing a dirty *dhuti*?' The Satradhikars depend for their livelihood and for the maintenance of the Satra on the support of their disciples. This limits their freedom of action.

> I don't know what I am. I would like to be Eleven-day but I associate with the Monthly people. My father supported the Shri Shankaradeva Sangha. He addressed meetings and wrote books, but he could not practise because of the obstruction of Monthly disciples (Purna Chandradeva Gosvami, Noruva Satra, Bardoa).

The Sangha claims the support of five or six Satras with Kayastha Gosains, but of these only two are actively involved in the organization. At first many Gosains refused to initiate Eleven-day disciples but, as their numbers grew, this became impractical. The majority of Satras still refuse to initiate Haridhaniyas.

> I allow people to be Monthly or Eleven-day. What I object to is this revolutionary Haridhaniya doctrine which has nothing to do with Shankaradeva's religion or with Hindu *śāstra*. Some of my disciples have become Haridhaniya. I have almost severed connection with them (Mohan Chandra Mahanta, Diciyal Satra, Nowgong).

Dissociation from the Gosains has created problems with initiation. Traditionally the rite of initiation was the only portal to the sect. 'Without a *guru*,' Shankaradeva said, 'you cannot enter into my religion (*dharma*).' Few men ouside the Satras are versed in the stages of higher initiation with their attendant *mantra*. The Sangha in consequence minimizes the significance of the rite —'If a man reads the *Bhāgavat*, initiation is unnecessary'—but the public continue to expect it. In an attempt to undermine the authority of the *guru* the Shri Shankaradeva Sangha published in 1969 a manual for initiation containing the esoteric *mantra* which they describe as 'fake things introduced by the Satradhikars for their own power'. The first leaders of the Sangha initiated converts who became attached to them personally as their disciples. This system led to schismatic tendencies in the organization and allegations of corruption. They have now introduced in each district an Initiation Committee, three to seven of whose members are required to be present at initiation. Initiates thus belong to the organization and not to an individual *guru*. In the form of initiation adopted by the Sangha, Shankaradeva and his successor Madhavadeva are presented to the initiate as the *guru* of the sect and not those who give initiation. A Gosain made the following practical comment on the revised system:

> The religion of Shankaradeva is based on initiation. The particular instructions are not important. They are kept secret and handed down from Mahanta to Mahanta and from Gosain to Gosain. But it creates belief in the system. By publishing the *mantra* they have destroyed this framework and modified the religion of Shankaradeva . . . Initiation taken from a committee of seven members is meaningless.

The impact of the reform sects has hastened the decline of the Satras which are seen as increasingly irrelevant to the needs of modern life.

> The whole system is disintegrating. Shri Shankaradeva Sangha is the main cause. Unless the disciples support the Satra, it cannot thrive. I sit in the town. Practically I do nothing. The Satra system is a rotten and decaying business (Mohan Chandra Mahanta, Diciyal Satra).

> Formerly we used to have two hundred families nearby. Now we have only twenty Monthly families giving full co-operation. All the rest have become Eleven-day and Harijaniya. We can no longer hold big functions. I have to contribute to the Satra and so has the Gosain (Lakshmi Kanta Deva Gosvami, Bholaguri Satra).

> Ten years ago we gave up disciples. It is troublesome to go and visit disciples fifty miles away. In the old days the disciples used to help us ploughing. Now we have no disciples so we have taken to the professions (Rebat Chandra Mahanta, Daukasapari Satra).

It is claimed that indirectly the new sects have benefited both the Satradhikars and the priests. The Gosains of many small Satras, driven by economic necessity, have profited by turning to western education and taking gainful employment; their Satras exist today only as a postal address. Similarly the Brahman priests, with a diminishing clientele, are abandoning their traditional occupation and only the fool of the family is said to enter the priesthood. Some are to be seen cultivating with hoe or buffalo, others have entered the professions.

The commonest reason given for the change to eleven days is that one month's impurity is incompatible with the conditions of modern life.

> Nowadays one cannot stay in the house doing nothing for one month after the death of parents—that is certain. That is not a crime.

The Shankar Sangha is opposed to the renunciation of the world:

> We oppose *bhakat* who have long hair and go from house to house begging. The *śāstra* say we should marry and do our duty in the world —that is *dharma*. In Kali Yuga the Sannyasis are eaters of night soil (former President of Shankar Sangha).

They have devised a shortened version of the various *mantra* and other daily rituals which is compatible with active participation in business and office life. For the traditional *hom* sacrifice at marriage they have substituted a new ceremony in the vernacular. The simplification of ritual extends to many folk customs either suggestive of spirit worship or rejected as superstitious. Traditionally, for example, it is the custom for the mother of the bride and the mother of the groom, when they go in procession to draw water for the ceremonial bath, to place an areca nut, a pan leaf and pice in the tank saying, 'I draw water for the marriage of so-and-so'. This is objected to on the grounds that, 'We worship Vishnu, we do not worship water'. The marriage customs that have been discontinued in some areas include the throwing of sugar balls (*lāru*) over the head of the groom on arrival as a protection against evil spirits, the rubbing of the bride and groom with turmeric and pulse, the erection of a ceremonial quadrangle of banana trees (*bei*) for the bath, the burial of a duck's egg under the quadrangle, the pounding of wild turmeric by seven married women (*gāthiyan khundā*), the exchange of ceremonial water pots between the bride's house and the groom's house, the drawing with rice flour of a circular pattern (*maral*) as a seat for the sacred water pot, the hanging of auspicious mango leaves across the gateway to the house, the ribald dance of an old woman with a winnowing mat on her head, the contest between drummers, the ritual fast of the bride and groom, and the offering of spiced food to the spirits of envy (Khoba Khubi) on the third day of the wedding. On folk custom there is a division of opinion within the Sangha. Some reject all such customs as superstitious, others wish to preserve their distinctively Assamese character provided they do not contravene the monothestic principle.

> We want to preserve the old customs unless they clash with Shankaradeva. I build a *bei* but I do not bury a duck's egg under it. I have no objection to mango leaves and other things. They will be used in my daughter's marriage. It is play. Some say: 'Why should we use mango leaves?' But I say, 'Why should we not?' My children will throw vegetables on the cattle on Cow Bihu. Play (President of Shankar Sangha).

Members of the Sangha do not observe fast days, the forbidden months for marriage or the forbidden days for ploughing. They do not recognize ritual pollution—'Pollution does not exist'—for which they have substituted the western notion of hygiene:

> We think as you do. When a fly falls on food, that food is impure.
>
> Others put on ritually pure (*dhuti*) clothes to eat. We put on clean (*cāphā*) clothes to eat.

The attenuation of ritual is criticized on the grounds that it has made religion too easy: the leaders may be devout but the followers will simply observe the forms and the forms have been so reduced so to mean little.

> If you take the line of the Shankar Sangha, just burn a man and finish him. They are too drastic. The danger is that when the rites become a habit, the religion will disappear. They are making religion too easy. Of course it is all right if done with feeling—that will not remain. In their ardent enthusiasm they will destroy everything.

The Shri Shankaradeva Sangha now claims to be the largest religious organization in Assam with over 100,000 registered members. Unlike the Satra, it is not based on the traditional link between *guru* and disciple and its organization is modern. The primary unit of association is a local branch with a minimum membership of twenty-five. Members are listed in a register kept by the Branch Secretary and pay a subscription of four annas a year. In each District there is a District Commitee which elects representatives to the Central Executive Committee. The President of the Sangha, who holds office for two years, is elected by secret ballot from three men nominated by the Central Executive Committee. In 1971, according to the President, there were some six hundred primary units in the State, of which half were in Nowgong District. From Nowgong the movement spread to other parts of the State and today the Sangha represents only a small proportion of those who have become Eleven-day or Haridhaniya under the influence of the ideas which led to its inception. Members of high castes—Kalita, Keot, Kooch—tend to become Eleven-day, i.e. they seek to abolish in this respect the distinction between themselves and the Brahmans, whereas the Haridhaniyas who wish to abolish caste distinctions altogether find their adherents chiefly among the lower castes—Chutiya, Ahom, Nath—and the tribals of the plains. The Untouchables—Kaibartta, Brittial-Bania, Hira, Namasudra—who are highly Sanskritized in Assam with their own 'Brahman' priests, are reluctant to forfeit the status which they have achieved by more traditional methods and the majority continue to observe one month's impurity as before. Taken as a whole the reform sects can be said to draw their support from the lower castes rather than the higher and from the younger generation rather than the older, a fact which causes much family conflict.

The effect of the movement has been to create new social divisions in the village. In every Hindu village there is at least one, and usually several Name Houses, consisting of a restricted association of households which combine for the specifically religious purpose of maintaining a centre of devotional worship. This group acts as the local community within which its members ordinarily live their lives and exercises not only religious but also social and jural functions which, in other parts of India, are commonly vested in village or caste councils. There is no village organization except in the rare cases when the whole village belongs to a single Name House and there is no local caste or sub-caste organization except where the Name House is composed of members of a single caste. The houses of a Name House describe themselves as one people (*rāij*) who eat together, share the same beliefs and customs, and interact in the day-to-day vicissitudes of life. When a group of households decides to become Eleven-day or Haridhaniya—usually on the death of a prominent man—it divides itself from the rest of the village to form a separate religious association with its own Name House. The different sects do not associate or interdine and, as one or other of the new sects is now to be found in almost every village of Upper Assam, the reform movement has become the major vehicle for the expression of caste and other local animosities.

The following data, collected in 1969 in the village of Panbari in the Jorhat subdivision of Sibsagar District, provide material on two reform sects found in the village, the Haridhaniyas and the Thirteen-day people. The village consists of 161 households divided into five religious congregations owning four Name Houses. Three of the Name Houses are of long standing; their congregations are Monthly. The Haridhaniya movement started in the village twenty-five years previously and now numbers eleven households who have raised funds to build a Name House of their own, completed in 1970. The fifth congregation consists of the Thirteen-day people who seceded two years previously from one of the existing Name Houses which they continue to use for their meetings but at different times from the other members, a common temporary arrangement in such cases. The three established Name Houses inter-dine but none of their members will eat in the houses of the Haridhaniyas or the Thirteen-day people.

The Haridhaniyas are usually to be found among the lower castes of the village. In Panbari six of the Haridhaniya households are Chutiya, three are Duliya Kalita, one is Kooch (who joined the Haridhaniyas after being expelled from his Name House for disorderly conduct), and one is Miri (tribal). With the exception of the Miri these households were formerly disciples of two major Satras (Auniati and Bengenati) but the Gosain now refuses to accept their dues. They in turn reject the Satradhikars on the grounds that they have corrupted the teachings of Shankaradeva by the adoption of Brahmanical rites.

> Five hundred and twenty-one years ago Shankaradeva was born in Nowgong. He translated the *Bhāgavat* into Assamese and spread the Haridhaniya *dharma*. He died in Cooch Behar at the age of one hundred and twenty-five years. His chief disciple, Madhavadeva, continued his work. He died at the age of one hundred and seven years. After his death this *dharma* was lost. There are many Satras today, 530 Satras. They take the name of God in their mouth, but they perform the worship of gods (*devatā pūjā*), not the worship of God (*īśvar pūjā*).

The leaders of the Haridhaniyas give initiation but they make no distinction among themselves between *guru* and disciple, substituting for the authority of the *guru* the text of the *Bhāgavat* which, with the spread of literacy, can be consulted directly as the word of God.

> The *Bhāgavat* is my *guru*. I learnt the Haridhaniya *dharma* from *Bhāgavat*.
>
> The Brahman Satras observed Vedic rites and massacred the followers of Shankaradeva. At that time the people could not read. The British came to Calcutta and started a school there. Then they came to Assam and started schools here. Gradually the people came to read the scriptures and to understand.

In the absence of the *guru* there has been a shift in favour of the lay devotees as the living representative of God and the traditional form of worship has been adapted to emphasize this:

> When we invite devotees, the devotees are God. We have no need of *thāpanā* (the establishment of a sacred book into which God is invoked for worship). We worship the devotees, not the *thāpanā*. We do not invoke God into the *Bhāgavat*. We do not invoke god into the offering (*prasād*). We prepare the offering but we set it down before the devotees. God does not come to eat, so we eat. We ourselves are God.

The devotees here substitute for the visible symbol of God which is dispensed with altogether.

The Haridhaniyas do not make caste distinctions and say they are prepared to accept even Christians or Muslims as one of themselves provided they accept the Haridhaniya *dharma*, but they will not eat or associate with caste Hindus outside their faith. They do not recognize ritual pollution and are not therefore required to preserve the ritual purity of the kitchen although, like other Hindus, they do not usually eat in their working clothes, nor do they consider it obligatory to bathe and observe a period of fast after cremating the body of a kinsman. They do not employ Brahmans and have subtituted for the *hom* sacrifice at marriage a brief ceremony in the vernacular. They no longer observe the three seasonal festivals (*bihu*) and the son-in-law is not required to visit his wife's parents on these days. They do not recognize the forbidden days for ploughing when they can be seen in the fields driving their oxen. All this runs counter to village ideas of propriety.

> We do not like the Haridhaniyas, we do not understand them. We have seen customs we do not like. The Haridhaniyas plough on forbidden days. They do not fast after death. They eat food on the cremation ground, shouting 'Jai Ram'. We no longer visit these houses.

The prohibition on inter-dining between different sects creates particular problems for kin and affines. In this conflict of loyalties some men sever all connection with their relatives. Others, more liberal, continue private informal visits, but to attend a public gathering such as a marriage or funerary feast is seen as a statement of political alignment and leads to expulsion from the Name House. The pattern of kinship obligations thus becomes difficult to sustain.

> Last year our mother's brother invited us to the marriage of his daughter. He performed by Vedic rites so we did not attend the ceremony. In other ways we helped. We went to the groom's house, we helped in selection. But on the day of the marriage we did not go. Tonight we invited him to the marriage of a daughter in our house but he refused. As he is not coming today, we will not visit his house again.

Marriage arrangements also cause difficulties and many matches are broken off because the parties fail to agree on the form of ceremony. Religious scruples, however, often yield to the advantages of obtaining a good son-in-law whose scarcity value is reflected in the shift within one generation from bride-price to dowry. If the groom's house insists on marriage by the traditional fire sacrifice, a Haridhaniya is usually prepared to compromise his principles to the extent of asking a relative to substitute for him as the 'giver of the bride' (*kanīyā dātā*) and absenting himself from the house on the wedding night.

The exclusiveness of the reform sects places the individual in a situation of conflicting obligations in which his decision to adhere to a particular set of ritual observances is often determined less by religious considerations than the practical advantages of continued support from kin and neighbours.

Padma was attracted by the Haridhaniya *dharma* and attended several of their meetings. His elder brother rebuked him and his wife's father took the lead in rebuking him. Although he still supports the ideas of the Haridhaniyas, he paid a fine and returned to his Name House.

Santi is a poor widow with a young daughter. After her husband's death, his brother became a Haridhaniya and her Name House warned her that she must sever connection with him. She replied that she was often hungry and had to accept food sometimes in the houses of her relatives. She is no longer a member of the Name House and is considered a Haridhaniya because she eats with Haridhaniyas.

Deben Dutta, one of the Haridhaniya leaders, persuaded his elder sister's husband and his two brothers to join the Haridhaniyas. They did so willingly to avoid the cost of employing Brahmans. The brothers' wives continued to visit the Monthly houses nearby whereupon Deben reproved them, 'Why are you going to Mountly houses?' They replied, 'They are our neighbours. We must visit them.' Shortly afterwards the three brothers left the Haridhaniyas and upon payment of a fine of Rs. 5 and a piece of cloth were readmitted to their old Name House.

Deoram became a Haridhaniya fifteen years ago when his eldest son died and he cremated him with Brahmanical rites. His wife's parents and her brothers ceased to visit him. Two years later he became Monthly again.

There is little difference in the religious observances of the Haridhaniyas and those of the Shri Shankaradeva Sangha, who are themselves often referred to as Haridhaniya (a term which they resent). The majority of Haridhaniyas, however, prefer to remain as autonomous local groups rather than become members of a State organization. There are a number of reasons for this. The Sangha has a reputation for intolerance and exclusiveness and is criticized as a destructive movement, based on communal hatred, which has divided society. Its members are forbidden to associate with houses who employ Brahmans, that is, with most of the population. The Haridhaniyas in Panbari also take this position, but other groups of Haridhaniyas are not always prepared to cut off connection with their affines and relax these rules in practice. Again, there are many local variations of custom amongst them. In some villages the Haridhaniyas observe the forbidden days for ploughing with oxen, in others they take initiation from the Gosain: in these matters they have no wish to follow the Sangha line. More importantly, however, each group of Haridhaniyas has its own history of local struggle and has little wish to be merged as a primary unit in a large scale organization when it can retain its pride of achievement and its sense of separate indentity.

The Thirteen-day movement started in Panbari in 1967 when Ganesh Parasad's wife died. He consulted the other eight houses of his descent group and they agreed to complete their death pollution on the twelfth day and to perform the first *śrāddha* on the thirteenth day. Ganesh engaged a new Brahman priest who was prepared to officiate at the rites. These were the wealthiest houses in the village, engaged in business or clerical occupations in the nearby town, and they gave as their reason for shortening the period of ritual impurity on death the economic disadvantages of staying at home and losing a whole month's work. All nine houses claimed to be Kayastha by caste. Six months later they were joined by a Keot called Lakhi Barua. Lakhi had settled in Panbari, his wife's natal village, after his retirement in 1960. He was a man versed in the scriptures. One night when the usual Name Leader at the Name House was ill, he attempted to take his place and lead the service. The congregation refused to co-operate and, angered by this insult, he left the Name House and became Thirteen-day together with his wife's brother. Another rich Kayastha house became Thirteen-day about the same time. The local Name House sat to discuss the Thirteen-day people and ruled that if any house attended Thirteen-day rites, it would be expelled. When Lakhi Barua arranged his daughter's marriage, he invited the Thirteen-day people and three or four houses from his old Name House. Of these a Kayastha attended and a Keot widow who was not on good terms with her relations. They were in consequence expelled from the Name House and joined the Thirteen-day group. In the beginning of 1969 another Kayastha woman died in the village. The dead woman's sons performed her *śrāddha* on the thirteenth day and, together with three Kayastha houses who attended the funeral feast, they were expelled from the Name House. The Thirteen-day people now number twenty households, of which seventeen are Kayastha and three are Keot. The Kayasthas in Assam are an open caste, largely recruited by infiltration from below, and it is the general opinion of the village that it is open to any Kalita to become a Kayastha by giving up cultivation. The transition is validated by affinal connections and in particular by the marriage of daughters. These houses are, however, for a number of reasons at odds with the villagers and their claim to Kayastha rank is not recognized. One house has four unmarried girls who attained the menarche twenty-one, thirteen, twelve and ten years ago respectively. Their father, unable to find suitable bridegrooms, prefers to keep them unmarried rather than compromise his caste aspirations. Another house has three unmarried girls, the eldest over forty, in a similar situation.

The Thirteen-day movement is confined almost entirely to Kayasthas living in towns or sub-urban villages who wish to differentiate themselves from the Shudra population as Kshatriya. They do not seek to equate themselves with the Brahmans and have no quarrel with Brahmanical rites. In general they show little interest in doctrinal matters—most of the Kayasthas in Panbari have not yet taken initiation, saying they are too busy—and the change to Thirteen-day is to be interpreted as a move to upgrade their caste status within the traditional system rather than as a challenge to institutionalized religious observances or a desire for widespread social reform.

It was open to the reform sects to take the position that ritual requires adaptation and simplification in response to the changed conditions of modern life. Their critics, indeed, see what they are doing as essentially something new.

> Let them found a new religion. Why claim to derive from Shankaradeva? Shankaradeva's teaching has been handed down to us unchanged in an unbroken line from Gosain to Gosain. They say what we have been doing for five hundred years is a mistake. No, what they do now is a mistake.

The Shri Shankaradeva Sangha, on the contrary, has adopted the opposite strategy of claiming that their revisions of current practice represent a return to the original purity of Shankaradeva's religion as set out in his writing and that they in consequence are the only true Vaishnavas.

> Our basis is the writing of Shankaradeva and Madhavadeva only. It is no new thing. What we believe is that it is Shri Shankaradeva's own teaching. The Satras were established to continue his teachings, but the Satradhikars are groping in the darkness. There are many Satradhikars who regard Shri Shankaradeva as their *guru* but never follow his instructions. The people have been misled. The Shri Shankaradeva Sangha was started forty years ago in order to teach people exactly what their religion is.

The uncompromising ridigity of the Shri Shankaradeva Sangha is often criticized: 'If a man's religion cannot tolerate other religions, it is not worth the name of religion.' It serves, however, two important functions for its adherents. In the first place, it provides them with a platform for the abolition of caste and the rejection of the Brahmans so that the social reforms which provide the impetus of the movement can be implemented in the name of religion. Secondly, it acts as a form of legitimation for a new middle class élite composed of men from the lower castes who have benefited from the changed conditions of education and employment to gain a new secular standing. These men are not willing to acquiesce in the inferior rank held by their caste in the traditional system. At the same time, by virtue of being brought up in this system, they also share its values. A highly-educated Chutiya, attracted by the ideas of the Sangha and engaged with his co-villagers in a protest to the Gosain at the low place given to Chutiyas at feasts in the Satra Name House, commented on his caste rank as follows: 'It is not only the high castes who think we are inferior. We also feel we are inferior.' The effect of the reform movement is to provide such men with an alternative system in which caste distinctions are not only disregarded as irrelevant to spiritual salvation but condemned as heretical social practices on the authority of the scriptures.

The reform sects draw a parallel between the teachings of the *Bhāgavata Purāṅa* and the egalitarian values of democratic India. The path of devotion was traditionally associated with an emphasis on one chosen god as the object of worship, a condemnation of blood sacrifice, a disregard of the complex paraphernalia of Vedic rites as inferior, if not unecessary, forms of worship, and a denial of the relevance of Untouchability and caste to the practice of devotion itself. The tendency towards monotheism was not, however, carried to the point of denying the existence of other Hindu gods whose worshippers were considered to be within the religion although outside the devotional path. For the devotee his chosen God was elevated above other gods and identified with the supreme principle (*ātman-brahman*) so that his worship came to include their worship. Similarly, although it was recognized that the path of devotion existed within the wider spectrum of Hinduism, to the devotee his path represented not *a* path to salvation but *the* path, and was held both to supersede and to include all previous paths (in the same way as the *Bhāgavat* was described as the essence of the Vedas). The rituals associated with the path of works, although considered unnecessary for the true devotee, were recommended as useful aids for those who had not yet attained this final stage, and the renunciation of the world associated with the path of knowledge was transformed and adapted to the life of the lay devotee who was able to fulfill all the duties of a householder provided only that he performed his actions without desire for their fruits. The existence of different classes (*jāti*) of men was accepted as given, but the relevance of these classes was denied in respect of devotion which opened a way to salvation for all men irrespective of their social origins. In these ways the path of devotion maintained continuity with the tradition out of which it developed.

The reform sects have taken up the distinctive features of the devotional path and placed them within a different conceptual system, influenced by Western ideas, where they assume a different meaning. The worship of one God is taken as the rationale for abolishing caste distinctions—'God is one; therefore man is also one'—and is interpreted as the basis of a universalistic ethic which will convert Vaishnavism into a world religion:[5]

> This religion will unify not only Assam, including tribals and Muslims, but the whole world. The worship of one God is the only religion of mankind. Islam and Christianity are simple forms of Vaishnavism.

The idea of Brahmanhood as the possession of knowledge, traditionally vested in the Brahman caste and extended to the *guru*, has given place to the diffusion of divinity among the laity regarded as the living representatives of God. The privileged intermediary roles of the priest (in respect of Vedic ritual) and the *guru* (in respect of *bhakti*) have been rejected in favour of the text of the *Bhāgavat* which is accessible to all who can read. The rite of initiation, traditionally regarded as the only portal through which the devotee can approach God, has been diminished to the point that it is no longer considered essential for membership of the sect. The rite itself has lost both its esoteric character and its personalized link between *guru* and disciple conceived in terms of an exchange of substance such that the initiate is identified with the *guru* as the embodiment of God. In its revised form the various *mantra* have been greatly simplified and the system of higher stages of initiation has lapsed. The Shri Shankaradeva Sangha is hostile to the idea of renunciation as withdrawal from the world and advocate a short and straightforward set of rituals appropriate to the daily life of a Vaishnava actively involved in wordly affairs. The complex observances of ritual purity have also been abandoned in favour of the modern notion of hygiene. The sect has rejected the concept of caste—'Caste does not exist'—and the gradations of the caste hierarchy, formerly expressed in terms of ritual purity, are replaced by a dichotomy between those within the faith and those without, Untouchability being re-defined in terms of those outside the faith who worship many gods. The belief that devotees are 'one and the same' by virtue of a shared spiritual condition is translated into the modern idiom of equality and democracy. The worship of the devotee as the embodiment of God—'The service of man is the service of God'—is secularized as the idea of public and national service. The leaders of the Sangha see themselves as social reformers, faithful to the teachings of Shankaradeva, who are striving to regenerate their religion and their society in accordance with his principles. But in the eyes of their critics the conversion of Vaishnavism into Everyman's religion has necessitated a radical transformation in the structure of the religion which they no longer recognize as their own.

The nature of this transformation can be summarized in terms of the categories of religious thought. The path of devotion, as traditionally understood in Assam, involved a re-ordering of the conceptual categories of Hinduism. The Gosain appropriated from the Brahman the role of the *guru* as the possessor of knowledge—a role which became greatly enlarged—leaving with the Brahman the role of the priest. The Gosain, no less than the Brahman, was considered a living god. As the Gosain might or might not be a Brahman, the category of *guru* overlapped the division between Brahman and non-Brahman. The householder appropriated the idea of renunciation and adapted it to life in the world so that the category of devotee, who might be either an ascetic or a householder, overlapped the division between renouncer and householder. At the same time, although caste was taken as given, its relevance for devotion was denied so that the devotee, in respect of devotion, could be said to be without caste. In sum, the basic categories of traditional thought persist in the devotional path but are differently emphasized and combined.

The position of the reform sects is as follows:

They do not recognize the category of Brahman.
They do not recognize the category of renouncer.
They do not recognize the category of caste.
They do not recognize the category of *guru* (except in so far as it is vested in someone no longer living or in a sacred text).

They divide the social world into two categories only, devotees and non-devotees, and the religious world into God, sacred text and devotee, the text providing in respect of the devotee an avenue of direct access to God. The social reforms advocated by the reform sects are thus accompanied by an equally radical transformation in the world of religious forms.

NOTES

I am grateful to Richard Burghart, Chris. Fuller, Friedhelm Hardy and Adrian Mayer for their helpful comments on an earlier draft of this paper.

1 The main features of the distribution of castes in Assam are set out in the Census of India 1901, vol. III, Assam: 153. 84.4% of the Hindu population are Shudras—Kayastha, Kalita, Patia, Keot, Saloi, Kooch, Rajbansi, Shaha, Ahom, Nath, Mukti, Chutiya, Jogi, Boria—55.2% being respectable Shudra castes from whom Brahmans take water and 29.1% Shudras from whom Brahmans do not take water. There is a small proportion (9.8%) of exterior castes—Hira, Kaibartta, Brittial-Bania, Namasudra—and a still smaller proportion (5.8%) of twice-born castes—Brahman, Ganak. There are no indigenous Kshatriyas or Vaishyas, although the Kayasthas sometimes claim to be Kshatriya today. The majority of castes are racial, rather than occupational, in origin. These include the Kalita, Keot and Kaibartta, Kooch, Rajbansi, Ahom, Chutiya, Boria, Nadiyal and Chandal which account for 83% of the indigenous Hindu population (ibid.: 116). The picture has not greatly altered today.

2 My father was District Commisioner of Nowgong at this time. He remembers that he had in his office a non-Brahman clerk called Dambarudhar Barua who prayed a great deal. He arranged his daughter's marriage without employing a Brahman to perform the customary rites. The feeling in the office became so acrimonious that the clerk had to be transferred.

3 Brahman priests today are divided into those who serve Monthly houses and those who serve Eleven-day houses. If a Brahman serving Monthly houses were to assist at an Eleven-day rite, he would lose his Monthly clients.

4 The story is told of how Gopikabhallub Gosvami journeyed to Benares in order to obtain an 'authentic' copy of the *Garuda Purāṇa*. The edition current in Assam was published in Bengal and omitted this passage—or so it was said—at the instigation of the Brahman priests.

5 The movement also serves as a vehicle for ideas of Assamese nationalism. The Shri Shankaradeva Sangha takes the view that all who live in Assam are Assamese and not only proselytizes actively among tribals and tea-garden labour but claims three Muslim converts. This view is partly a response to the dismemberment of Assam and the carving of five hill states out of what was once a single province.

LORDSHIP AND CASTE IN HINDU DISCOURSE

Ronald Inden

This essay is an attempt to bring to light the Indian concepts of mastery and lordship as fundamental to an understanding of India's political and religious history.[1]

Lords at Large

The makers of Vaishnava and Shaiva ritual discourse in India during the eighth to twelfth centuries constructed worlds that were populated with lords seemingly endless in their variety. There were, according to them, lords of the entire earth and of single villages, lords of provinces, lords of armies, lords of plants and of animals, lords of the cardinal and intermediate directions, the zenith and the nadir, lords of the gods in heaven and of the demons in the underworld. Every conceivable category of thing, place, animal, and person had its lord.

How did one of these lords present himself? He appeared seated on an ornate throne at the centre of a place marked off as his, his smooth-skinned, healthy, oiled body dressed in a *dhoti* of fine cloth. His head was adorned with a crown and he wore a necklace, upper and lower-arm bracelets and anklets, all of gold or silver set with gems. At his side sat his consort, full-bosomed and beautiful, also finely clad and bejewelled. One leg of the lord was folded beneath him, the other hung down, resting perhaps on a footstool. To the rear and at both sides of this enthroned couple stood attendants gazing reverently at their master and waving palm-leaf fans or yak-tail whisks, while yet another servant held an umbrella over his head. The lord himself, his hand, palm up, extended out and downward, conferred a boon on a petitioner; or, elbow bent, hand open and bent back at the wrist, he granted him protection. This lord also presented himself in a complementary manifestation, standing, ready to act, or mounted on his favourite vehicle, holding his distinctive weapon and riding, almost effortlessly it would seem, into battle to despatch a potential rival.

Whether he appeared as a protector bestowing favours or as a warrior prepared to fight, this image of an Indic lord would seem to contrast sharply with the typical depiction of men of the highest of the four castes of India, the Brahman. These were supposed to be men of special knowledge, ritualists and renouncers, not soldiers. Nor would the men of the third and fourth castes, those of merchants, agriculturalists, and herders and those of servants and artisans seem to provide us with this lordly figure. Masters of their households they might have been, but not lords. If any of the castes was the source of this image it was, thus, the second caste, the Kshatriya, the caste of warriors and princes, the heroes of Hinduism's basic text, the Mahabharata. And it is no surprise that kings, supposed to be born as Kshatriyas, appeared as lords *par excellence* in the Hindu discourse of our period. Yet it was not only *kings* who were depicted as lords. In fact, the greatest of kings, the king of kings, overlord of the entire earth, was not himself considered the greatest of lords. Greater than he were the invisible gods and the greatest of these gods, the royal god, Vishnu and the ascetic god, Shiva, were belived to be the most powerful lords of all. They were not overlords of the earth alone, but of the entire cosmos.

So prolific is lordship in the Hindu world of this period that I would not hesitate to call it the root metaphor for the orders of gods, people, and things constituted by Hindu discourse and instituted by Hindu rulers in their kingdoms. However, I do not wish even to suggest that concepts of overlordship, lordship, and mastery were not constitutive of Indian society before the eighth century or outside of Hinduism. As early as the time of Asoka one finds such notions in their specificity and I am fairly certain that the industrious indologist could find them inchoately in the Rig Veda itself. One also finds ritually enlivened, visible images of the Cosmic overlords, Vishnu and Shiva, otherwise invisible to the naked eye, established in temples before this period. Yet in the eighth century the lordship of the gods gained new ontological ground when Vishnu and Shiva triumphed over their rivals, the Buddha and Jina. Although images of the latter two, depicting them as lords, had been established in large shrines of their own, their ontological status as Cosmic Overlords continued to be a matter of dispute among their followers. For at least some of them, the overlordship of the Buddha or Jina was perhaps only metaphoric. But there was no doubt about the ontological status of Shiva or Vishnu among their adherents. There was nothing metaphoric about their lordship. They were omnipotent lords who commanded the cosmos and manifested themselves in their images. With their triumph, the figure of lordship suddenly acquired a predominance it had not had before.

That the concept of lordship took on a new power and richness in this period is certain. The most cursory study of Hindu iconography in this period shows a proliferation of the signs of lordship, evident in the consorts, thrones, vehicles, weapons, banners, crowns, gestures, and temple shapes displayed by the visible images of the gods. The texts portray this world of lordship as a culturally-constituted order with a commanding centre and a commanded periphery and carefully demarcated zones in between. It contained lords of the past, future, and present, and lords of creation, preservation, and destruction. Most of all, it was a hierarchic order of lords. A higher lord was carefully distinguished from a lord lower in relation to him. At the same time, however, the higher also included the lower, much as Dumont (1970:65–72) puts the matter in his classic formulation. The higher lord contained and commanded the lower lord's power, his competence to act, the things and people of which he was lord, not in the sense that he added these powers to his own, but in the sense that he was capable of producing, arranging, or dissolving them as he wished under certain circumstances.

Lordship Constituted

Sanskrit is rich in terms related to a concept that can be translated as master or lord in English. Some of these are *svāmin* (owner), *īśvara* (ruler), *nātha* (protector), *pati* (controller), *bhartṛ* (supporter), *bhoktṛ* (enjoyer), *prabhu* (wealthy, powerful), *vibhu* (omnipresent, pervasive), and *bhagavān* (possessor of shares, fortune). Any of these terms could be used to designate a man as a lord or master. Some of them tended to be used also to signify master in the sense of the master of a house. Such were *svāmin*, *pati*, and *bhartṛ*, all of which also had the meaning of master of a wife, husband. Some, however, were used to designate a man as a lord, a man whose mastery was more comprehensive than that of a simple householder. These were *prabhu*, *vibhu*, *bhagavān*, and, and, above all, *īśvara*. Derived from the verbal root *īś*, to command, order, own, have possession of, this term was used to refer to and to address Kshatriyas, Brahmans, kings, ascetics, sages, and gods. Above all, it designated the gods who were construed as lords of the cosmos, Vishnu and Shiva, the term *parameśvara* being more commonly applied to the former, the term *maheśvara* to the latter. In certain contexts the term *īśvara* and its variants, *íśa* and *īśāna*, referred to Shiva rather than Vishnu, the synonyms *bhagavān* and *svāmin* being more or less reserved for the latter. A strengthened form of *īśvara*, *aiśvarya*, can be translated in English as lordship. But it also had a very specific referent. A group of eight *aiśvarya*, or lordly powers, was said to be possessed by certain kings and ascetics, by the gods and, of course, by the god designated as the Cosmic Overlord himself. Of these, perhaps the most important power, *īśitva*, from the same verbal root, *īs*, as *aiśvarya*, was the illusionist's power to create, order, and destroy tangible, visible beings or things at will.

A lord was, by definition, a male, *puruṣa*, the same word which denotes the personal Absolute, a Cosmic Man. He had his domain (*viṣaya*) or field of action over which he exercised his lordship. This domain could consist of things, animals and people, and the places where they were properly to be found. But a lord's domain did not consist only of what was outside of himself. The senses were described as the gates (*dvāra*) of the body, itself described as a fortified city (*pura*), the residence of a lord. And the mind or heart (*manas*), the intellect (*buddhi*), and the inner self (*ātman*) were variously spoken of as commanding or governing the lower constituents of a person. Indeed, the innermost constituent of a person according to the *Viṣṇudharmottara Purāṇa* (*V.Dh.P.*), the one that ruled all the rest, the *puruṣa*, a portion of Vishnu, the Cosmic Purusha, was itself described etymologically as the one lying (in a meditative sleep), *śī*, in the fortified city, *pur*. And one spoke constantly of the need for the king as well as the ascetic to master (*ji*) his senses.

The domain of a lord was often described as female. She was referred to in cosmology as material nature (*prakṛti*). In Hindu theology, the female consort of a god was frequently the hypostatized domain of which the god she accompanied was said to be the lord. Sarasvati, the wife of Brahma, was true knowledge (*vidyā*) and speech (*vac*) its manifestation, two of the elements making up the domain of which Brahma was the lord. Furthermore, the female divinity, while being the domain of her lord, was often considered a lady or mistress (*bhagavatī*, *īśvarī*) who could herself grant boons (*vara*) and give assurances (*abhaya*) to her worshippers with respect to the domain she constituted. For example, Durga, referred to as Bhadrakali in the *V.Dh.P.*, was the weaponry of the triad (*trimūrti*) of Brahma, Vishnu, and Shiva. Standing as a warrior in a chariot drawn by four lions, she had eighteen arms—in addition to the standard weapons of a warrior, the sword and shield, bow and arrow—the hands of which held the distinctive 'weapons' of those three lords: the large and small sacrificial ladles of Brahma, the conch and lotus of Vishnu, and the trident and rosary of Shiva (*V.Dh.P.* 3.71. 8–12). On the same occasion of the year that he honoured an image of Bhadrakali, the king also honoured his regalia (*rāja-cihna*) and weapons (*śastra*) (*V.Dh.P.* 2.15). At a more parochial level, the wife of a householder was considered synonymous with the good fortune and wealth, *śrī* or *lakṣmī*, of his household, the domain of which he was the master, to be honoured to the best of her husband's ability (*V.Dh.P.* 2. 33 20).

But even though a female could herself be a mistress of her own domain, male and female were not considered to have the same ontological status. As in cosmology, the male, the *puruṣa*, was the higher reality, so in the household the lord was the higher in relation to his domain. The former was the commanding and independent element, the latter, the commanded and dependent. And as in cosmology the *puruṣa* was the element that encompassed and confined *prakṛti*, so in the household the lord encompassed and confined his domain. She was one part of the whole, he was both the other part, and at the same time, the whole itself.[2]

A particular human lord or master was distinguished from the others with whom he had relations by his *adhikāra*, his competence to act in a certain way with respect to his domain.[3] This competence was also referred to as his *dharma*, his 'orders', that set of acts, *karma*, by the performance of which he not only sustained or held up (*dhṛ*) himself and his domain, but the product of these acts, *dharma* as the cosmo-moral order itself. The competence of a lord or master was his nature, his inherency (*svabhāva*), acquired at birth as the result of his acts in previous lives. But certain competencies could also be acquired from a higher lord after one's birth. A king, for example, could appoint (*ni-yuj*) people who were not born in royal families to certain tasks (*karma*) which were part of his orders as king (*rāja-dharma*). Indeed, one of the marks of a higher lord was his competence to cause things to be done by his servants rather than by himself directly. The term *adhikāra* and certain of its variants were used to designate such appointees, e.g. *dharmādhikārin*, Officer of Cosmo-moral Order (here, in the sense of justice), and their offices, namely, *dharmādhikaraṇa*, Office of Justice.

The very people, places, things, or animals that constitited a lord's or master's domain also constituted his *śakti*, his capacity or power to act. But no opposition should be drawn between the power he possessed internal to himself and the power constituted by his domain outside of himself. That is, the power of a lord consisted not only of the lands and servants, livestock and grain he might possess, but also of the strength of his body, the quality of his speech, and the state of his emotions and intellect. Indeed, the outer powers were typically considered to rest upon these inner ones and, most of all, on the special knowledge a lord or master might possess.

The domain of a lord not only constituted his external capacity to act in accordance with his competency; it was also his to enjoy (*bhuj*). The people, places, things, and animals that made it up were his 'field of enjoyment' (*bhukti*), they were his enjoyments or pleasures (*bhoga*), his to consume, even to enjoy erotically where appropriate.

Enjoyment of one's domain, however, was always and at every turn conditional in Vedist and Hindu discourse. It was only if a master used his domain in accord with *dharma* that he continued to enjoy its pleasures. Good results were synonymous with pleasurable enjoyment. Bad results were synonymous with the 'enjoyment' of misery (*duḥkha*). Even more, good results entailed the increase of one's domain and the people, places, animals, and things of which it consisted. Such increase was not a mindless, quantitative proliferation, but an ordered, proportionate, qualitative increase. Healthy and virtuous sons would be born, bounteous crops ripen in season, and the older would precede the younger in death.

The outcome of this increase was, by the end of one's life, a realization or completion of the mastery or lordship to which one was born. Because he had not only increased the visible entities which comprised his domain but had also augmented his store of moral merit (*puṇya*), he would attain a heavenly paradise where he would do nothing but enjoy pleasures. Then, he would be reborn in a higher place in the Hindu chain of being and become a higher lord or master is his next life. On the other hand, bad results were accompanied by a decrease of one's domain. People grew hungry and thin, livestock died, wives became barren, children died before parents, disease became rampant, one lost one's wealth and land, and had no sons. And as a consequence of the demerits or moral offences (*pāpa*) that a master had accumulated in the course of his misconduct, he was sure to go to a hellish underworld to 'enjoy' various punishments. Once he had used up his store of offences, he would then return to earth, but he would be reborn not at a higher level in Hinduism's hierarchically ordered universe, but at a lower level. The ultimate goal was to rise to the top of this hierarchy of lordships and masteries where one would attain release (*mokśa*) from birth and death and gain union (*yoga*) with the Cosmic Overlord himself, a permanent state beyond the fluctuating worlds of enjoyment (*bhoga*).

The indigenous concept of lordship unites in one field a number of seemingly discrepant institutions—the householder, caste, kingship, that best of Brahmans, the Shrotriya, and the Vaishnava or Shaiva temple and its devotees—without reducing one to the other. Within the compass of this essay, however, it is possible to show how the idea of lordship organized only one aspect of a Hindu kingdom. The aspect I have chosen to discuss here is that classic topic of South Asian anthropology, caste. I shall discuss not how the indigenous concepts of lordship and mastery were constitutive of any particular caste system in any one kingdom, but how these concepts organized the concept of caste as presented in the texts on *dharmaśāstra*, the 'instructions on cosmo-moral order'. Though I have drawn directly and indirectly upon the statements made in other, earlier *dharmaśāstra*, such as the *smṛti* of Manu, Yajnavalkya and Vishnu, the main text on which I rely is the *Viṣṇudharmottara Purāṇa*.[4] This text places the rules of the earlier *smṛti* on caste and householdership in a Pancaratra Vaishnava environment and in so doing alters them in ways that are significant but can only be touched upon here. For example, the *Viṣṇudharmottara* gives prominence to the householder as the subject of a Vaishnava king and devotee (*bhakta*) of Vishnu and relegates to the background his place in the hierarchy of castes. Consistent with Vaishanva doctrine, the text also devalues the life-stage of the homeless ascetic (*saṃnyāsin*), giving precedence at the apex of the social order to the Vaishnava householder devotee over the ascetic.

Caste

The people of a kingdom were supposed to be organized into a definite set of four *varṇa*, or 'colours', and a number of 'mixed' (*saṃkara*) colours derived by intermarriage from these four. These are the social groups described under the rubric of 'caste' (from the word *casta*, first used by the Portuguese to describe them). The four are the Brhaman or ritualist and preceptor, Kshatriya or warrior prince, Vaishya or cultivator, cowherd, and merchant, and Shudra or servant and artisan. Their respective colours—white, red, yellow, and black—were not associated with racial origin, as Hocart (1950: 27–33) long ago showed, but were, as we shall see, visible signs of qualities that predominated in their constitution (*V.Dh.P.* 1. 7. 9–12).

Twice-born

A major distinction in the hierarchy of *varṇa* was that between the three Twice-born (*dvija*) castes on the one hand and the Shudra on the other. A Twice-born was, as this term itself indicates, a man who had undergone an initiation that was considered a second birth. This rite not only brought the initiate into direct relationship with the privileged knowledge of the Veda; it also entered him into the first of the four life-stages (*āśrama*) of Vedism. Here, as a celibate student (*brahmacārin*), he became a practitioner of *brahman*, the Vedic knowledge and rites leading ultimately to union with *brahman* as the Absolute of the Vedists.

Once he had completed his stay with his preceptor—which could be very short indeed—he was to be married and enter the life stage of the householder (*gṛhastha*). Properly initiated and married men of the Brahman, Kshatriya, and Vaishya *varṇa* thus became householders, masters of houses with Vedic fires and masters of the Veda, competent to perform, or have performed, Vedic household (*gṛhya*) sacrifices and to recite Vedic *mantra*. These were two of the three parts of his code of conduct, his *dharma*, his nature. A third, given primacy over the performance of the household sacrifices in the *V.Dh.P.* was to make gifts—altruistic donations to the poor and masterless, to learned Brahmans, and, best of all, to gods who had been invoked into images and enshrined in temples (*V.Dh.P.* 2. 80. 6; 2. 31; 3. 299–317, 341). By doing this a Twice-born man realized his mastery, increased the prosperity of his household and accumulated an invisible store of merit toward a higher life. A Twice-born man realized his competency as a householder, of course, only after his father died and he inherited his house, or, if he had brothers, a share of it and the other items—land, people, animals, and movable wealth that constituted his householdership. To be a man of the Brahman, Kshatriya, or Vaishya castes presupposed initiation. Men of Twice-born fathers who were not initiated became like Shudras. Note the use of the language of mastery in this injunction of the *V.Dh.P.* (2. 80. 10). 'The Twice-born live like Shudras if they do not attain mastery in relation to the Veda (*na prabhavanti vede*).'

Shudra: Servant and Artisan

The Shudra did not, like the Twice-born, have mastery with respect to the Veda and the Vedic fire. He was merely once-born and not initiated into the Veda; he did not receive the sacrificial thread. He did not, accordingly, have competence to perform Vedic sacrifices or recite the accompanying Vedic *mantra*. A debased notion of the Shudra in the *dharmaśāstra*, states that the Shudra's *dharma*, his duty and nature, lies in domestic service (*sevā*) of the Twice-born and considers that the Shudra are similar to servants (*dāsa*)—we might call them slaves—who had lost mastery with respect to the enjoyment of movable wealth (*dhana*), wife, and son. That is, they were not masters of their own households, they were parts of the households of the men of the Twice-born castes who were their masters (*Manu* 8. 412–417). Such a Shudra can barely be said to have mastery even over his own body, over the work of his own hands. His body was commanded not by his own mind, but by the words and mind of his Twice-born master.

A less debased idea of the Shudra accorded a certain mastery to him in regard to the crafts or arts (*śilpa*), of which there were said to be sixty-four in the special instructions on this topic, the *śilpa-śāstra*. Here the Shudra had a greater mastery over his own body, over his hands, his *par excellence* 'organs of work' (*karmendriya*). And he himself directed his own efforts to a large extent. Since the craft of this sort of Shudra constituted a means of livelihood (*vṛtti*), he could be master of a household.

The crafts seem to have been associated with the numerous 'mixed castes' that were supposed to have originated from the intermarriages of the four *varṇa* and were classed as Shudra in most instances (there being no fifth *varṇa*). Some of these castes classified as Shudra, for example, the Vellala of Tamilnadu or the Kayastha of Bengal, resembled the Vaishya or Kshatriya in some respects, to wit, competence at fighting and the collection of wealth in the form of the king's revenue. Apart from these few, however, the Shudra artisan, even though a householder, was not, like the Vaishya, supposed to accumulate wealth (*na kāryo dhanasamcayah*) beyond his and his dependents' immediate needs (*Manu* 10. 129 with Bharuci's commentary). His mastery over his own productivity was so tenous that if a Twice-born needed two or three articles to complete a Vedic sacrifice, he could simply take them from the house of the Shudra, 'for a Shudra has no right to possess goods (*parigraha*) in connection with sacrifices' (*Manu* 11. 12 with Bharuci).

Consistent with his lowness, his deficient mastery, the Shudra was to have a name meaning wretched, miserable in the sense of weakened (*jugupsita*), poor, and ending with the word *dāsa* (servant). His colour, black, was the mark of his inner nature (*svabhāva*) in which dull darkness (*tamas*) predominated over the other two qualities, stirring activity (*rajas*) and quiescent goodness (*sattva*) of which every person, animal, and thing was constituted. Since Shudras had mastery over only their own bodies, seniority among them was to be gauged not by the extent of their mastery over a domain outside of themselves, but merely by the extension of their bodies in time, birth or age (*V.Dh.P.* 2. 85. 11–12; 3. 233. 84; *Manu* 2. 31 with Medatithi's commentary). Poor Shudras in particular were depicted bearing loads (*bhāra*), the strength of their bodies from the tops of their heads to the soles of their feet as their only power.

Vaishya: Cultivator, Cowherd, Merchant

Of the three Twice-born *varṇa*, the Vaishya was the lowest. In relation to the Kshatriya and Brahman he was the ordinary 'householder' and 'commoner'. The term from which Vaishya is derived, *viś*, signifies household or people. Within a kingdom, the category of Vaishya was synonymous with that of ordinary people or subject (*prajā*, *jana*). The domain over which the Vaishya householder exercised mastery was wealth (*dhana*, *dravya*, *vṛtta*, *artha*, *sva*, *riktha*), primarily in the form of what we would call movable wealth. His very name was to connote wealth and end with the word, *dhana*, meaning wealth; and among themselves, seniority was to be determined by wealth. Wealth also constituted his external source of power. Like his tutelary deity, Kubera, the prosperous Vaishya had as his bodily sign a pot-bellied (*lambodara*) physique. His colour, yellow, was the visible badge of his invisible 'inherency' in which restless activity, predominating over dull darkness, preponderated over quiescent goodness. The Vaishya's *dharma* called for him to engage in agriculture (*kṛṣi*, ploughing), the tending of cattle (*go-rakṣā*), and commerce or trade (*vāṇijya*) These three, comprising the topic called *vārttā*, or livelihood, formed his field of competence in the moral code and by nature. 'He should know,' says Manu (9. 329–330):

> the values and good and bad qualities of gems, pearls, and coral, of metals, of woven cloth, of perfumes, and of flavourings. He should have knowledge about the sowing of seeds, and of the qualities of fields and seeds, and should know about weights and measures from every angle.

If he was to be a master with regard to things, even more was he to be the master of domestic animals, and especially of the all-important cow (*Manu* 9. 327–328):

> Prajapati (impersonal *brahman* as Progenitor of the cosmos) emitted cattle and entrusted them to the Vaishya, while he entrusted living creatures in their entirety to the Brahman and king. The Vaishya should never wish that he not keep cattle, and so long as the Vaishya desires to, they are not to be kept by another.

Thus, the Vaishya was the master of valuable *things* and certain valuable *animals* yet not of 'all creatures.' Not only that, he was to make this wealth accumulate, though not for himself alone (*Manu* 9. 333):

> He should exercise the greatest diligence in the increase (*vṛddhi*) of goods (*dravya*) in accord with *dharma* and he should exert himself in giving food to every creature.

The hierarchic relationship of the Vaishya with the Shudra is clear. The Shudra was master of his body, his own labour, his own household, if he had one, but he was not the master of wealth beyond what he required for subsistence. The Vaishya was not only master in all of these domains, he was master of wealth, of things produced and traded, and of animals domesticated, expert at causing them to increase.

Kshatriya: Warrior and Prince

The duty-cum-nature of the Kshatriya was to protect his people (*prajā-pālana*) and to do this by fighting in war Indeed, his highest goat was not to accumulate wealth, but to gain fame (*yaśas*) which he did by never turning back in a battle. He was higher than the Vaishya and his mastery embraced that of the Vaishya in much the same way that the mastery of the Vaishya included that of the Shudra. Yet there is a difference, for with the Kshatriya we may begin to speak of 'lordship', of mastery in a more potent form.

The term *kṣatra* itself means *dominium* or lordship and the Kshatriya is, literally, the one who possesses *dominium*, though many of our texts prefer to emphasize the protective function of the term stating that he is the one who protects (*trā*) from being 'harmed' (*kṣata*).[5] Furthermore, many of the other words that can be glossed as 'king' were also used synonymously with Kshatriya. And a king, the lord of a kingdom, was supposed to be a Kshatriya, according to the *dharmaśāstra*. Like a king, the Kshatriyas of a kingdom were also lords of the land (*bhūmīśvara*, *bhūpa*, etc.) and lords of people (*janeśvara*, *nṛpa*, etc.) and like him, they were masters of the weapons of war.

The Kshatriya was to have skill in the use of the sword and shield and, in particular, of the bow and arrow. The special knowledge of which he was to be master was called the Dhanurveda or Knowledge of the Bow, though it included rules on the use of lesser weapons as well. He was also the master of animals: his vehicle of war, every bit as important as his weaponry, was the horse or, if he were a king, a horse-drawn chariot or an elephant. The Kshatriya was, as our texts would say, born to bear weapons, to exert his mind and body in warfare. His physique was specially suited to this. His arms (*bāhu*) were the locus of his power; he was supposed to overcome difficulties 'by the strength of his arms' (*bāhu-vīrya*), he had 'long arms' (*mahābāhu*), 'his strength was in his arms' (*bāhubala*), 'he had arms that reached to his knees' (*ājānubāhu*). His first name was to denote bodily strength (*bala*), his last name, armour (*varma*). Among Kshatriyas, seniority was to be determined by the relative degree of 'heroic valour' (*vīrya*). His colour, red, was the identifying mark of his inner nature in which restless activity predominated over quiescent goodness, both of which predominated over dull darkness.

Yet, even though the categories of Kshatriya and *rājā* were closely related, they should not be conflated. The king of a kingdom might be a Kshatriya, but not all of the Kshatriyas were kings. Nor were they necessarily nobles. Instead they were lesser kings or part kings, as the term *rājanya*, one of the synonyms for Kshatriya, indicates. This is a diminutive of the term *rājā*, king, best translated as lesser king or prince. Other terms such as *rājanyaka*, (princeling) and *rājaputra* (son of a king) also convey the idea of lesser or partial kingship. These lesser kings or princes were lords of parts or shares of the land in a kingdom and of the people on these lands; the king was lord of the land and people of his kingdom as a whole.

Since these people were none other than the Vaishya (and Shudras), his lordship over them also made him lord over the things and animals (and labour) of which they were masters. Another way to put it is that the mastery of the Kshatriya was more complete than that of the Vaishya (and Shudra). The Kshatriya had mastery over not only movable wealth—cash, grain, and the like, but also over immovable wealth, namely the land, which was thought to be the ultimate source of movable wealth. Similarly, he had mastery over not only domestic animals, but also over people as well. He was not simply master of a productive household, he was lord of a fraction or share of a kingdom. The relationship between the kingly Kshatriya and the Vaishya was, thus, clearly hierarchic.

Brahman: Ritualist and Preceptor

At the top of the hierarchy of four *varṇa* was the Brahman, whose *dharma* was to impart the Veda (*adhyāpana*), perform Vedic sacrifices for others (*yajana*), and accept the gifts respectfully offered by others (*parigraha*). He was supposed to be the master of the *brahman*, the Absolute in the form of the Veda, and of the special knowledge (*jñāna*, *vidyā*) it contained. The word *veda* itself means knowledge and the knower of the Veda was to be accorded seniority among his fellow Brahmans by virtue not of his age, wealth, or strength, but by virtue of the special knowledge he possessed. His name was to signify not riches or armed strength, but the more diffuse yet more embracing notion of auspiciousness (*maṅgalya*) and end with *śarma*, that is, 'delight.' The distinctive part of the Brahman was not his arms, but his mouth, whence flowed those potent sounds (*śabda*), the formulae of the Veda. White, his emblematic colour, was the symptom of his 'nature' in which quiescent goodness predominated over the two lower *guṇa* or qualities, stirring activity and dull darkness.

The Veda (comprising in its broader sense not only the four Vedas themselves but the Brahmanas, Aranyakas, and Upanishads as well) was the body of knowledge that not only contained injunctions (*vidhi*) on the performance of sacrifices (*yajña*), those acts of *dharma par excellence* by which *dharma* as cosmo-moral order was to be sustained, but also included esoteric knowledge relating to the highest goal, *mokṣa*, of leaving the differentiated world and attaining union with or absorption in the Absolute itself. The words of the Brahman and the sacrificial acts and meditations enjoined in them were his domain, his proper field, of action, and, at the same time, his power, the means by which he obtained his ends. In the form of his curse (*śāpa*), they could be even more menacing than the weapons of the Kshatriya. The Brahman was, of course, not the only *varṇa* to have a relation with Vedic sacrifice and the Veda itself. As we have seen, all three of the Twice-born *varṇa* had or could have some knowledge of the Veda; but the

Brahman was the only one whose knowledge embraced the whole of it, whence the special efficacy of his words.

The lordship of the Brahman, his mastery of the Veda, the sacrifice, and the special knowledge which both maintained the cosmos and led to release from it, did not perhaps appear to the untutored eye to comprehend the lordship of the Kshatriya, for the Brahman, unlike the Kshatriya, did not live in a large mansion in the centre of his landed domain and did not have command of the people and wealth of the land, did not ride to battle on a horse or elephant armed with sword and shield or bow and arrow. On the contrary, he was supposed to lead a life of relative austerity, devoting himself during most of his waking hours to the performance of Vedic sacrifices, the recitation of Vedic texts, and the attainment of *mokṣa.* It would have been a mistake, however, to believe that the lordship of the Brahman was less than that of the Kshatriya, or that he did not possess lordship of the earth and its inhabitants. In the same way that the Kshatriyas did not themselves directly cultivate the fields, herd cattle, or tend market stalls, so the Brahman ritualists and savants did not directly govern the land and people of the kingdom in which they dwelt. But lords of them and their Kshatriya lords they certainly were (*V.Dh.P.* 2. 32–39a):

> Brahmans expert in the Veda support the whole cosmos (*jagat-sarvam*). O son of Bhrigu, the Brahmans please the gods here on earth and, themselves satisfied (*tṛp*), the gods cause the entire universe to be satisfied. The oblation is offered into the fire, o scion of Bhrigu, by the Brahman; it reaches the sun and from the sun turns into rain [that falls] on the earth's surface. In this way, food originates, and from food, the living being has its origin, thus it is remembered. And so it is that the three worlds are supported in their entirety by the Brahmans. The earth (*bhūmi*) belongs to/originates from (*prabhū*) the Brahman, the sky belongs to the Brahman, and this world as well as the other world belong to the Brahmans. Since it would interrupt their sacrifices (*ijya*), Vedic recitation (*svādhyāya*), and austerities (*tapas*), the Twice-born do not take possession of (*vid*) lordship (*svāmya*) on earth; for this the Kshatriyas were made. The pronouncements of Brahmans are always to be heeded by kings, for the cosmo-moral order (*dharma*), the acquisition of wealth (*artha*), and pleasurable enjoyment (*kāma*) are grounded (*pratiṣṭhita*) on their words. The king (*bhū-bhṛt*, lord of the land) desirous of prosperity is ever to restrain (*nigraha*) people and show them favour (*anugraha*) on the advice of Brahmans.

Not all Brahmans, however, lived as sacrificialists intent on release. Some Brahmans, as the quotation shows, even though learned, took up service with a king and became his ministers. The *mantra* they imparted to their king consisted not of Vedic formulae, but of practical advice for rulers (*rāja-nīti*). Similarly, Brahmans skilled in *dharmaśāstra* and reasoning (*ānvīkṣikī*) were appointed as officers of justice (*dharmādhikārin*) and judges in the courts of kings (*V.Dh.P.* 2. 24. 24b–25a). The Brahman who posessed, among other qualifications, knowledge of the science of weaponry, Dhanurveda, the science of portents, and of medicine, was considered especially competent to be appointed by a king as a *senāpati*, commander of the armed forces, though a Kshatriya who had acquired this knowledge from a Brahman could also be appointed to this post (*V.Dh.P.* 2. 24. 8–11).

Still other Brahmans, even though they were learned in the Veda to at least some extent, were unable to live from the income of those occupations enjoined on Brahmans. Such men, however, were able to follow the 'orders [for those] in distress' (*āpad-dharma*),[6] which permitted the Brahman, according to the *V.Dh. P.*, to adopt the livelihood of the Kshatriya or even the Vaishya, which were latent in the Brahman because of his hierarchic encompassment of these two *varṇa*. Moreover, these Brahmans continued to be Brahmans by caste. As such, they still embodied the Veda, however minimally; hence, they were not to be insulted or harmed. The penalties for insulting, assaulting, or killing a Brahman were apparently the same whether he was living by trade or agriculture or as a master of the Veda.

Brahmans who served a king or lived as Kshatriyas or Vaishyas were distinguished from the three Brahmans who, in the *V.Dh.P.*, performed the royal rituals. One was the Brahman appointed by the king as royal physician (*vaidya*); the second, the one selected as the royal priest (*purohita*); and the third was the royal astrologer (*sāṃvatsara*).

All of these Brahmans were, in turn, sharply distinguished from the Brahman sacrificialist and savant who avoided these involvements in the lower affairs of the world. Generally, these were designated by the terms *veda-snātaka* and *śrotriya*. The latter term means 'one who is concerned with listening', that is, 'a man who is devoted to the study of the Veda' (*Manu* 4. 31 with Medatithi). The former term means 'the one who has bathed after learning the

Veda', referring to the bathing rite (*snāna*) a Brahman underwent when he had completed the acquisition of a branch (*śākhā*) of the Veda. Some of these Brahmans, like their predecessors who had officiated at the Vedic sacrifices of kings that required three fires in the period before ours, might have been officiants at the sacrifices (*ijyā*) performed in connection with a Vaishnava or Shaiva temple for which the king was the sacrificer (*yajamāna*).

Other Brahmans, however, would have hesitated even to perform royal sacrifices, avoiding thereby the relation of dependency on the king implied by the acceptance of the sacrificial fees (*dakṣiṇā*). Living not in a royal capital, but in Brahman villages carefully separated from the other villages of the countryside, these Brahmans spent their entire time engaged in rituals and Vedic recitations, preparing themselves for release. These Brahmans, unlike the others, did not depend on the king for their livelihood. They, or their ancestors, had accepted donations of land from a king, at his request, not theirs, and obtained their subsistence from these lands. Since these Brahmans *par excellence* were by definition not only the masters of the Veda but also lords of the land itself, these gifts should not be considered gifts that placed them in their royal donor's debt, but rather as the 'return' of a portion of their lands to them for the highest human purpose.

There were, of course, many bodies of knowledge that a Brahman could master beyond the Veda (which, one presumes, normally meant one of the Vedas and its attendant texts), and when it came to those texts that were soteriological in their orientation, there were disputes about their relative validity among and between Vaishnavas and Shaivas, Purva-mimamsakas and Uttara-mimamsakas, never mind the Jainas and Buddhists, who did not accept the validity of the Veda. And these disputes were translated into disputes about who should be accorded which precedence in a kingdom. The highest precedence was accorded in the *Viṣṇudharmottara Purāṇa* to those Brahmans who were not only masters of the Veda, but also of the Vaishnava Purana. These men, one of whom would have been appointed as the king's preceptor (*guru*), were knowers of the Pancaratra and observed the five-old rite (*pañca-kāla*) of this Vaishnava sect. Also referred to as Satvatas, these were the highest devotees of Vishnu, the Brahmans closest to the attainment of release, the highest goal in the Vaishnavite kingdom envisaged in the *V.Dh.P.*, those who most resembled Vishnu, the Cosmic

Overlord in his highest aspect, asleep on the Cosmic Ocean. These high Brahmans, both the Srotriyas and the even more complete Pancaratras, were to the ordinary Brahmans as the king or king of kings was, in Hindu discourse, to the ordinary Kshatriya.

Conclusion

It is certainly true that the Indian ideas of mastery, lordship, and overlordship that I have tried to outline here in relation to caste are in some sense about 'property' understood in terms of hierarchic, inclusive mastery over things, animals, and persons. In his thought-provoking essay on the concept of property (*svatva*) in India, Derrett (1977:86) concludes at one point that, 'the distinctive feature of the Indian concept of property, therefore, is the capacity of *svatva* to exist in favour of several persons simultaneously . . . ' What he sees as characteristic of India's narrower, more technically precise and logically sophisticated idea of 'property' is, in my opinion, due to its participation in a discourse which presupposes the broader, more indeterminate concepts of mastery, lordship, and overlordship as the fundamental categories of what we might refer to as Hindu social thought.

I have tried to show here how these ideas were constitutive of the system of four *varṇa* in the *dharmaśāstra.* The building block of the caste system of a kingdom was the householder, the master of a wife, sons, movable wealth, house, and, typically, fields. To a significant extent, the distinction between the three Twice-born *varṇa* and the once-born Shudra was the distinction between those men who were masters and those who were not. Another way to put it is that those men who had the competence to become masters of the Vedic fire and Vedic *mantra* were complete householders in relation to those who lacked this competence, the Shudra. The lesser Shudra was himself not even, or just barely, the master of a household. Higher Shudras (such as the Vellalas or Kayasthas, sometimes referred to as *sat*, or 'pure', Shudras), in so far as they resembled the Twice-born, were also classed as more complete householders, having the competence to become masters of wealth, like the Vaishya, or of arms and of land, like the Kshatriya, and to have a Vedic fire (though they were to pronounce *namo*, meaning 'obeisance,' in place of the Vedic *mantra* a Twice-born would have recited).

All three of the Twice-born *varṇa* had the same competencies as the lowest of them the Vaishya, namely, the competence to be master of wealth acquired by trade, agriculture, and cowherding, and to make that wealth increase. And they could in difficult times take up these livelihoods. But the Kshatriyas and Brahmans were not simply masters of wealth, they were also lords. Kshatriyas, by virtue of their power to fight, were lords of the land and the people (the Vaishya and Shudras) on it. The Brahmans, by virtue of their competency with respect to the privileged knowledge of the Veda and of Vedic sacrifice, complete in relation to the other Twice-born, were lords of the entire cosmos in relation to the Kshatriya, making pronouncements to the Kshatriya that had the force of commands or injuctions that were to be obeyed. Note that it is not the purity of the renunciatory Brahman that contrasts with the secular power of the Kshatriya. Both are lords. Knowledge and its manifestation in words and statements constituted the domain of the Brahman and they were his power, just as much as the lands, people, war-animals, and weapons of the Kshatriya were his domain and also his power. Nonetheless it is true that the masters with their respective powers and domains that made up these *varṇa* were adamantly hierarchic. The lordships (or masteries) of the higher castes included those of the lower. Thus, the lordships and masteries of the four *varṇa* were not simply 'simultaneous' (Derrett), but they were also hierarchically ordered (Dumont).

This picture of the hierarchy of lordships and masteries that constituted the set of four *varṇa* is in itself incomplete. It remains to draw the king, the king of kings, the Srotriya Brahaman, the temple, and especially the gods themselves into the net of this discourse on lordship.

NOTES

This essay has greatly benefited from the criticisms of Michael Dalby and Jean-Claude Galey and, as always, of Bernard S. Cohn. It builds on, but also departs from, an earlier essay on caste by McKim Marriott and myself, 'Caste Systems', *Encyclopaedia Britannica* (1974, 15th ed.), III, pp. 928–991.

1 Consult Damodar Dharmanand Kosambi, *An Introduction to the Study of Indian History*, pp. 285–372; Ram Sharan Sharma, *Indian Feudalism: c. 300–1200;* and Dinesh Chandra Sarkar, *Landlordism and Tenancy in Ancient and Medieval India as Revealed by Epigraphical Records*. For the problem of 'sovereignty' see the essays in *In Defense of Sovereignty* edited by W. J. Stankiewicz, especially that of F. H. Hinsley, pp. 275–288. The study of H. N. Sinha, *Sovereignty in Ancient Indian Polity*, too much concerned with the European construct, does not take the Indian evidence seriously enough.

2 The relationship of encompassment and confinement is not formal or figurative in Purusha Vaishnava and Shaiva cosmologies. Unitistic and emanationist, they maintain that material nature was an emanation of a single all-powerful Purusha, designated as either Shiva or Vishnu. This Purusha, infinite and unchanging, emitted Prakriti from himself and entered her with a portion of himself, while at the same time, he continued to surrounded her, remaining himself undiminished in power, substance, or activity.

3 This term, also translatable in certain contexts as right, authority, or eligibility, is used in specific senses in the technical commentaries on Vedic sacrifice, for which, see Kane, *History of Dharmasastra*, 5, pp. 1317–1318, and on property, for which consult Derrett, *Essays in Classical and Modern Hindu Law*, pp. 21–3.

4 I have tried to keep the number of notes here to a minimum. Virtually all of the evidence on which this essay is based is to be found in the *Viṣṇudharmottara Purāna*, 2.32, 80–2, 85–7, 95, 130–31. For Manu see chapters 2–4, 9, and 10 with the commentaries of Medhatithi and Bharuci, the former edited by Ganganth Jha and the latter by J. Duncan M. Derrett. The *Viṣṇu Smṛiti*, chapters 2, 27, 29, and 88–96, with its only commentary, the *Kesavavaijayantī* of Nandapandita is pertinent as this is the *dharmaśāstra* to which the *Viṣṇudharmottara Purāṇa* attaches itself. Valuable also is Robert Lingat, *The Classical Law of India*. For a brilliant essay on property see J. D. M. Derrett's 'The Development of the Concept of Property in India c. A. D. 800–1800,' in his *Essays in Classical and Modern Hindu Law*. Also to be mined is P. V. Kane, *History of Dharmasastra*, 2, pp. 105–64.

5 See for example, *Mahabharata*. Dronaparva. Critical Edition, Appendix I, no. 8, line 766, p. 1144.

6 The *V.Dh.P.*, 2. 83–84, devotes considerable attention to this problem, expanding on earlier rules in *Manu*, 10. 83–94.

REFERENCES

Derrett, J. D. M. 1977. *Essays in classical and modern Hindu law*. Leiden: E. J. Brill.

Dumont, L. 1970. *Homo hierarchicus: an essay on the caste system*. Translated by Mark Sainsbury. Chicago: Univ. Press.

Hocart, A. M. 1950. *Caste: a comparative study*. London: Methuen.

Kane, P. V. 1941. *History of dharmasastra*. Vol. 2. Poona: Bhandarkar Oriental Research Institute.

Kosambi, D. D. 1956. *An introduction to the study of Indian history*. Bombay: Popular Book Depot.

Lingat, R. 1973. *The classical law of India*. Translated by J. Duncan M. Derrett. Berkeley & Los Angeles: Univ. of California Press.

Manu Smriti 1932–1939. Ed. Ganganath Jha. Calcutta: Asiatic Society of Bengal.

—— 1975. Ed. J. Duncan M. Derrett. Wiesbaden: Franz Steiner Verlag.

Sewell, W. H. 1980. *Work and revolution in France*. Cambridge: Univ. Press.

Sharma, R. S. 1965. *Indian feudalism: c. 300–1200*. Calcutta: Univ. of Calcutta.

Sinha, H. N. 1938. *Sovereignty in ancient Indian polity*. London: Luzac.

Sircar, D. C. 1969. *Landlordism and tenancy in ancient and medieval India as revealed by epigraphical records*. Lucknow: Univ. of Lucknow.

Stankiewicz, W. J. (ed.) 1969. *In defense of sovereignty*. New York: Oxford Univ. Press.

Tribe, K. 1978. *Land, labour, and economic discourse*. London: Routledge & Kegal Paul.

Vishnudharmottara Purana 1912. Bombay: Srivenkatesvara Steam Press.

Vishnu Smriti 1964. Ed. Pandit V. Krishnamacharya. Madras: Adyar Library & Research Centre.

PARADIGMS OF BODY SYMBOLISM:

AN ANALYSIS OF SELECTED THEMES IN HINDU CULTURE

Veena Das

Introduction

Recent work in symbolic anthropology has emphasized the importance of the body as a central symbol in various systems of classification. This paper attempts to discuss some of the issues which have been raised and to interpret anew the evidence on the representation of the body in selected Hindu contexts.

In a recent survey on symbolic anthropology, Turner (1975) contends that the semantic field of symbols is polarized round two clusters of nuclei. One cluster, according to him, refers to bodily experiences and phenomena and the second refers to ethical principles and values. Turner calls the first the orectic pole and the second the ideological or normative pole.

The term 'orectic' is derived from *orexis* and refers to conative and affective aspects of experience—relating to impulse, appetite, desire, and emotion. Turner states that on this cluster (the orectic pole) there is a closer associative link between *signans* or vehicle and *signata* or meaning,[1] since the body's experiences are more concrete and universally shared by members of the species. He also associates the orectic pole with iconophilic religions which develop complex and elaborate systems of ritual, where symbols tend to be visual and exegesis is bound up with the ritual round.

Turner's argument echoes the earlier arguments of Mary Douglas (1970) about group and grid modes of behaviour. Underlying all these arguments are the assumptions that the body is something given in nature and its experience is universally shared; that the experiences of the body are concrete rather than abstract; and that the body in consequence can only be described and made the subject of conative and affective aspects of experience. It is these experiences which are given priority over the body as a culturally cognizable object. It is for this reason that many authors have shown such hesitation in describing the role of the body in Christian thought, both as a means of continuity between this-world and the other-world, and as a means of providing substantive links between the devotee and god.

It is my contention here, that the moment we look at the body as a system of meanings rather than as biological substance, it ceases to be merely given. It is, then, culturally created. Further, the notion of the body as representing a mode of being that is essentially ambiguous seems to be used in ritual and cosmology to evoke and define the various modes of man's existence. Thirdly, the body as represented in ritual and myth is a cognitive vehicle of cosmological ideas. One suspects that the implicit cosmology behind the rituals in which the body has a central place is simply not examined, since it assumes at the outset that the body cannot convey ethical principles, values, and cognitive understandings regarding man's being.

In this essay I shall try to show the cognitive and abstract values which are sought to be conveyed through the symbolism of the body. I shall be using several textual and ethnographic accounts, but a word of caution about the use of these sources may not be out of place here. The data presented here have been used primarily for purposes of illustration. Clearly each of the following sections is capable of considerable futher expansion, both in terms of interpretation and in terms of examination of sources. I am particularly conscious of the fact that the sources used here do not form a cohesive set in terms of their spatial and temporal origin. I offer the following materials, nevertheless, to show the cognitive use of the body as a model. In the following sections, I shall first examine the modes by which the body is sought to be ritually constructed in some rites of transition. Next I shall show that the presentation of the body in everyday life has strong ritual connotations, and that the ritual prescriptions regarding the presentation of the body convey abstract ideas about the structuring of existence. I shall then argue that even the 'concrete' experiences of the body, such as that of sexuality, are interpreted through a comprehensive cultural understanding of the cosmos. Far from ritual drawing its symbolism from universal, human, organic experience as Turner and many other authors contend, the organic experiences are conceptualized through means of ritual imagery. I hope to show that the metaphor for the perfect sex act, for example, comes from outside the act itself and therefore needs the common reservoir of societal symbols to be itself conceptualized as a *human* act.

The Ritual Construction of the Body

There are many theories about the body which are postulated in the context of the different philosophical systems of the Hindus. For the moment, I wish to ignore the highly verbalized accounts of the body as, for instance, the theory about the many sheaths of the body, the theories about *sthūla śarīra* (gross body) and *sūkṣma śarīra* (subtle body),[2] or the theories about the *liṅga śarīra*, i.e. the body as a mould which provides the continuity between the different births of a man. I do not, for one moment, wish to deny the importance of these theories or their applicability for understanding the everyday reality of the Hindus, but I wish to focus the discussion on *implicit* theories about the relation between the human body and the cosmos as contained in certain rituals.

In a recent article on the symbolic merger of the body, space and cosmos, Brenda Beck (1976) has argued that there are a variety of specialized Hindu rituals in which a symbolic merger of the body and the cosmos takes place. She gives an account of the highly esoteric rituals of the cosmic recharging of the images in a temple, which is expected to take place once every twelve years. It is clear that in this cosmic recharging, the body of the god is seen as recreated by the priest. He does this by means of several *mantra* (sacred formulae) connecting—or perhaps giving—parts of his own body to that of the god. While Beck's argument remains true to the general intent of the ritual, the specificities of the ritual are given very little attention. In fact, this particular mode of calling the body into existence and bringing it into a relationship with the cosmos is quite common and figures in other rituals as well. It is not clear, however, whether the relation between the body and the cosmos remains the same in every case. In this section, I should like to concentrate on the details of one such ritual. The ritual I refer to is the consecration of the Hindu king, which has been discussed in a recent article by Inden (1977). The details of the ritual were taken by Inden from the *Viṣṇudharmottara Purāṇa*.[3] I have added some further details which were necessary for the interpretation, using the same source.

As Inden shows, as soon as a king dies, the 'law of the fishes' is said to prevail, implying a condition in which the social order has eroded and chaos has ensued. Therefore, when the new king emerges after his consecration, it is not only the king, but in a sense the whole social order which emerges. This is symbolized by the emergence of the king as a new *person*, simultaneously with ministers of all four *varṇa*, who stand at the four sides of the king's seat.

The consecration itself has three parts. First the king has to take his ordinary bath. This is followed by what is called a clay bath in which various parts of the king's body are daubed with clay brought from different parts of the earth. Finally the king is bathed with water in which different kinds of substances and herbs have been immersed. After the three baths he emerges in a dry condition with all his ministers. I intend to give an interpretation of the second part of the ritual, the clay bath of the king. I use a different method of interpretation from Inden's but my conclusion does not invalidate the other parts of Inden's analysis. It is, in fact, consistent with them.

Table 1 shows the parts of the king's body which are touched, and the parts of the earth from which clay is brought. Inden's interpretation is given in the third column. The table has been taken from Inden's paper.

It is clear from Inden's interpretation, given in the third column, that he tries to interpret the symbolism of the king's clay bath by a term-to-term correspondence in which each part of the king's body is seen to be associated with a part of the cosmos through a relation of external analogy. It seems to me that this interpretation commits the atomistic fallacy in which neither of the two series is seen as a totality constituting a *system* of relations. I suggest that instead of looking for external analogy, we look for the relationship between the two series in terms of internal homology.

First, let us call the series associated with parts of the king's body, series A, and the series relating to parts of the earth, series B. Now, before attempting to relate these two series to each other, let us try to see the relation between different parts of the same series. Only after these relations have been established may we attempt to find the internal homology between the two series.

Table 1. *King's Clay Bath*

Part of King's body	*Part of Earth*	*Inden's Interpretation*
Head	Mountain top	Head/top of earth
Ears	Anthill	Ears of earth
Face/hair	Vishnu/Shiva temple	?
Back of neck/ shoulders	Indra/Chandra temple	Strong-shouldered warrior god
Heart/mind	Royal palace	Control centre of earth's body
Right arm	Earth dug up by elephant's tusk	Where earth's body is marked by aggressive virility
Left arm	Earth dug up by bull's horn	do.
Back	Tank	Contains liquids of earth's birth
Stomach	Confluence of two rivers	Where liquids combine
Sides	Two banks of a river	Contains liquids
Loins	Courtesan's doorway	Locus of concentrated sexual potency
Upper leg	Elephant's stall	Site of strong and/or swift legs
Knees	Cattle pen	do.
Lower legs	Horse stable	do.
Feet/hands	Earth dug up by chariot's wheels	When earth's body is marked by speed and strength of warrior's vehicle

I should add that since the description of the king's clay bath has been taken from the *Viṣṅudharmottara Purāṅa*, it may become necessary to look at other parts of the Purana in order to establish the meaning of specific ritual acts. In particular, I draw attention to chapters 97–116 on the installation of the image of Vishnu, one chapter (100) of which concerns the purification of the image with clay and other elements. The verse used for the consecration of Vishnu's image makes it quite clear that while the earth is absorbing the impurities of the image, the ritual also defines the properties of the earth so that it is in a harmonious relation with the newly-installed image of god. A free translation of the verse would be:

> O earth, being trodden by chariots, horses and Vishnu. O clay, take away my sin and whatever wickedness I have committed. You are supported by Vishnu in the Form of a boar, by Krishna, and by Indra. O clay, please grant the desired and become one who grants all desires.

The above passage shows that the ritual not only cleanses the image but also prepares the earth to be in a harmonious relation with the image that is going to be animated by Vishnu. It seems to me that similarly the touching with clay not only cleanses the king but prepares the earth to be in a benevolent frame of existence, for we must remember that, in the Hindu theory of kingship, the fate and deeds of the king are irretrievably bound up with the fortunes of the earth whose lord and husband he is deemed to be.

Keeping this point in mind, we now look at the second series and try the following mode of groupings:

(1) Mountain top.
(2) Anthill, Vishnu/Shiva temple, temple of Indra/Chandra, royal temple, courtesan's doorway.
(3) Earth dug up by elephant's tusk, earth dug up by bull's horns, earth dug up by chariot's wheels.
(4) Tank, confluence of two rivers, bank of two rivers.
(5) Elephant's stall, cattle pen, horse's stall.

The first, mountain top, refers to staticity. In the second case, the use of clay from an anthill is similarly prescribed and is accompanied with the formula, 'O earth, you are Kusmanda and are the Devi Durga'. Kusmanda itself is a name of Durga and refers to the practice of worshipping her by sacrifically severing a pumpkin (*kuṣmāṇḍa*). In the sociological literature on Hinduism much has been written about the difference between vegetarian and meat offerings to deities. But as Meena Kaushik (1979) has recently argued, the substitution of a vegetarian offering for a meat offering need not alter the structure of the offerings. For instance, in the propitiation of various mother-goddesses the earlier practice was to sacrifice a beast in such a manner that its blood fell on the representation of the goddess. In some communities, the traditional sacrificial beast has been replaced by a coconut but care is taken to see that red water is sprinkled on the coconut which is hacked in a manner that its water falls on the representation of the goddess (Belliappa 1980). While it is understandable that a late Vaishnava Purana like the *Viṣṇudharmottara* should prefer to emphasize the severing of a pumpkin rather than the blood sacrifice that the goddess Durga demands in many regions, it still refers to the propitiation of Durga as a mother-goddess through sacrificial offerings.

The propitiation of the mother-goddesses, I contend, has a covert reference to their uncontained sexuality. When Durga is represented with her husband Shiva, she is benevolent, life-giving, and can be offered only vegetarian offerings. When she is alone and represented as fighting the demons, which incidentally she would be unable to do as Parvati, she reveals her terrible form. In this form she has to be placated with sacrificial offerings (as opposed to *pūjā*, the mode of offering in which no victim is designated), otherwise she would let loose forces of destruction and death. Thus the use of mud from the anthills, and the accompanying formula, 'You who are pleased with the hacking of the pumpkin', point to forces of uncontained sexuality at the cosmic level.

The clay from the anthill thus becomes associated with the clay from the courtesan's doorway and establishes a relation between uncontained sexuality at the social (courtesan) and the cosmic (Durga) level which has to be constantly kept in check.[4] Similarly, power at the cosmic level and the social level is sought to be contained by binding it in temples and royal palaces.

In the third grouping, a relation is again established between riotous movement and contained movement. Elephants and bulls are represented here as wild, while the movement of the chariot is controlled by the charioteer.

In the fourth group again, we have reference to the free intermingling of water in which boundaries are obliterated. But two different modes of containing the waters are discussed simultaneously, the natural mode by the banks of the river and the cultural mode by the construction of a tank.

In the fifth series, the wild animals appear as completely domesticated not in the jungle, not in wild movement, but in socially constructed 'homes'. If we contrast the top and the bottom of the series, there is a clear opposition between untrampled mountain tops, incapable of 'domestication', to wild animals as they have become domesticated and controlled. In between we get a series of mediations where cosmic and social forces of power, sexuality and movement are sought to be contained.

It seems to me that the contrast between the staticity of mountains and wild movement, as also its mediation through containment of movement, evokes *in absentia* the association with the three *guṇa*. In the Hindu theory of *guṇa* a distinction is made between *sattva* standing for the principle of *stasis*, *rajas* or the principle of controlled movement, and *tamas* which may simultaneously stand for inertia and riotous movement.[5] As concepts expressing the relation between being, becoming and non-being, *sattva* stands in a relation to *rajas* as motion transcended stands to motion, while *rajas* stands in a relation to *tamas* as motion achieved is to inertia and meaningless motion. It would also seem that the two meanings of *tamas*, as inertia and riotous movements, allow it to be contrasted with *sattva* as transcendence on the one hand, and *rajas* as controlled movement on the other.

I would not suggest for a moment that the meaning given to the *guṇa* here exhausts all their possible meanings. The important terms in a symbolic space are capable of being woven into different matrices. The *guṇa* are no exception to this rule and are used in several domains, to classify foods, distinguish gods from demons, and also to inform the organization of philosophical discourse. What is relevant for my purpose here is that at the level of Puranic mythology, a relationship between *stasis* and controlled movement on the one hand, and inertia and riotous movement on the other, is often articulated through the three *guṇa*.

Coming back to the ritual of the clay bath itself, the sequence of touching the different parts of the king's body proceeds from head downwards to the feet. I have argued earlier that this is a mode by which the body is seen as constituted of parts that are hierarchically related (see Das 1977a). It now becomes clear why the head is related to the mountain top. As embodying the principle of *sattva* or *stasis*, it encompasses the subsequent investing of the king's body with *rajas*, movement that is controlled, power that is encompassed. The king as a symbol of the entire system has to be invested with purity and power and, as we shall show, also divested of his evil. Hindu mythology has already made us familiar with the notion that the king contains both good and evil and the earth will prosper only if the king's evil can be banished.[6] The clay bath invests the king with *sattva* and *rajas*, while divesting him of his *tāmasik* properties by the containment of movements. It further defines the body in a hierarchical mode encompassed by the sequence in which the bath proceeds. Just as the head encompasses the other parts of the body, the king's *rajas* or power is sought to be contained within his *sattva*, or his orderly pure being.

It is clear that I am proposing a theory of *guṇa* here which posits that each *guṇa* embodies a relation at different levels between purity, power and the cosmic order, between being, becoming and non-being, and that the *guṇa* are not attributes.[7] In some contexts, it is clear that *sattva*, *rajas* and *tamas* form a series in which each previous term encompasses the subsequent ones. For instance, the *sāttvik* goddess Parvati may in times of danger send forth a *rājasik* emanation such as Durga, who may send forth a *tāmasik* emanation such as Kali. It should not, however, be forgotten that this relationship obtains within the cosmic order. When this order is threatened as by the *tāmasik* demons, the threat can only be met by a *tāmasik* goddess and not by a *sāttvik* one.[8]

The second major point that I have tried to make is that Hindu ritual requires the investing of the body with appropriate moral qualities. I owe this insight to the recent work of Inden and Nicholas (1977) on Bengali kinship where they stress the importance of the body as a central symbol of Bengali kinship. They have shown how rituals of transition have, as a major aim, the generation of the right kind of body. This is true not only for the child, the bride and the groom, but also for the dead man. Along with Marriott, they have formulated the notion of the non-dualistic conception of substance and code within Hindu thought.

To the important insights contributed by these authors, I would only add that in Hindu thought the body may be regarded both as a substance and as a *system of moral relations*. In the ritual of the clay bath of the king the body generated through ritual constitutes a system of moral relations and is analytically separated from the body as a thing-in-itself or from the body as biological substance. This contention is supported by the idea of generating a body for the *preta* (ghost) or *pitṛ* (ancestor) through the various rituals of *śrāddha*. The body of the ghost or the ancestor is not considered to be a substantial body.

The difference between the body as *substance* and the body as a *system of moral relations* is also reflected in various contradictory statements about the body which are found in Hindu texts. Thus the body is sometimes said to be like a temple, a means of acquiring *dharma* on the one hand, and a disgusting object, something which gets destroyed in a moment (*kṣaṇa bhaṇgura*) and hence not worthy of being made the subject of any deep emotions, on the other. The former kind of statement seems to refer to the body as a system or moral relations and the latter to biological substance. It seems to me, therefore, that ritual seeks to redefine the body away from biological substance to a system of moral relations. It is in its latter form that the body has to be matched to the moral conduct or the moral position of a person. While supporting the important insight of Inden, Marriott and Nicholas, that the generation of the right body is a central concern of ritual and of everyday transactions, I should like to stress that the body which is called into existence in the course of a ritual is not a biological substance defined in sensory experience. Through the imposition of a hierarchical difference between different parts of the body, it comes to be redefined as morally appropriate for the incumbent of a particular status.

The Body in Everyday Life

In the preceding section I examined the manner in which the body is ritually constructed in one kind of rite of transition. However, it is not only in ritually circumscribed events that the generation of the morally correct body becomes important but also in the everyday life of the Hindus. In some of my earlier work, I have briefly alluded to the use of body-symbolism in defining impurity (see Das 1976b and 1977a). As I noted, great care is taken in everyday life to see that the body is presented as a bounded and contained system. Women are expected to keep their hair well oiled and groomed. Loose and flowing hair may not only subject them to dangers from witches and ghosts, but may also lead others to accuse them of the practice of magic and sorcery. In their normal state, women are also expected to see that body-extremities are properly bound by the use of bangles, anklets, etc. I suggested that this mode of presentation corresponds to the containment of categories in the social system.

The normal mode of presenting the body is reversed during periods of impurity, the paradigmatic case of which is provided during mourning. During this period women keep their hair uncombed and unkempt. They do not resort to the normal parting of the hair which is filled with vermilion. Bangles and anklets are not used for this period. Men are required to abstain from shaving, from paring their nails and from the use of footwear. I suggested that the presentation of the body in its natural unbounded form, like that of the ascetic, corresponds to the liminal state. Other authors have also pointed to the belief that women in their natural state (i.e. with uncombed hair and unadorned bodies) are considered inauspicious. Thus the presentation of the body in everyday life has strong ritual connotations. It is like a concrete and condensed statement of abstract ideas. I should now like to show that not only is the mode of presentation of the body different as between different ritual states but also that a variety of groups express their structural differences through the presentation of the body in everyday life.

The study of religion in a pluralist context has rarely considered the question of how groups conceptualize and express their differences while sharing the same semantic domain. The recognition that relations of opposition and inversion are as important as relations of similarity and parallelism opens up the means to explore the ways in which different kinds of groups express their differences. I contend that different modes of presenting the body in everyday life are utilized in a significant manner for presenting the different structural positions of groups.[9] I shall try to show this with the example of rules relating to the Buddhist monk in the Vinaya texts of the Buddhists.

The Vinaya texts which were compiled in the period fifth to third century B.C. are the earliest attempts to organize the Buddhist monks within a monastic order. There are different kinds of rules described but those which interest me here relate to the types of robes that a monk may wear and the physical bearing of a proper monk. In the Vinaya texts, the Buddhist monk appears in a series of oppositions with other social categories the chief of which are the lay householder, the Brahman, and the members of other wandering sects.

At the most general level, the Buddhist monk is distinguished from the householder in a variety of ways. As Tambiah has pointed out, there are many rules which eloquently express this contrast. The resources of the *bhikkhu* according to these texts are 'mendicancy, clothing in cast-off rags, forest life, and using urine as medicine'. The contrast between the 'homeless wanderer' and the stable householder is clear in the early rule that except in the rainy season, the monk was not to stay in a place for more than three days. As Uma Chakravarti (1978) points out, the worst insult to a monk was to call him a shaven householder.

The rules regarding possession of robes by monks make it clear that a monk was not allowed to have more than three robes at a time. When a householder wished to gift a robe to a monk, he could only do so when one of the robes which the monk already had in possession was stolen or otherwise became unwearable. In such cases, however, the monk was not allowed to ask for the robe; he could only go and stand silently and hope that the householder would understand the purpose of his visit. Even when a monk was aware that a householder was having a robe woven for him, he was not permitted to indicate his preferences in any manner. The *Suttavibhaṅga* of *Vinaya-Pittaka* lays out the following rule:

> A man or a woman householder who is not a relation may cause robe-material to be woven by weavers for a monk. Then if that monk, before being invited, going up to the weavers should put forward a consideration with regard to the robe-material saying, 'Now sirs, this robe material is being specially woven for me. Make it long and wide and rough, and make it evenly woven and well scraped and well combed. If you do so, we could give the venerable ones [a polite, even cajoling, way of address] something or other in addition'. And if the monk speaking this, should give something or other in addition, even as little as the contents of a begging-bowl, there is an offence of expiation involving forfeiture.

On the one hand, the monks were to be dressed in robes which would not indicate their personal preferences for material texture or shape. On the other hand, they were also not allowed to appear dishevelled like members of other sects. One of the instances discussed in the same text gives the following account:

> Now at that time monks thought: 'It is allowed by the lord when staying in lodgings in the jungles to lay aside one of the three robes inside a house.' These, laying one of the three robes inside a house, were

> away for more than six nights. These robes were lost and destroyed, and burnt and eaten by the rats. The monks became badly dressed, wearing shabby robes. Other monks spoke thus: 'How is it that your reverences are badly dressed, wearing shabby robes?'

Thus a large body of the Vinaya texts affirms the contrast between the *bhikkhu* and the householder in terms of the materials they were allowed to use for personal wear and the rugs that they could use. The colour of the border on the rugs and the manner of acquisition pointed to an ascetic mode of existence. There is very little room for doubt that the contrast between the *bhikkhu* and the householder is expressed through clothing and supported by rules which describe how a *bhikkhu* should walk, laugh, talk and eat so that his distinction from the householder is maintained.

The contrast between the Buddhist monk and the Brahman is more problematic. Tambiah states that in the matter of acceptance of food, the rules which emphasize his acceptance of *cooked* food without any discrimination from any devotee constitute a rejection of the orthodox rules of commensality. There are many rules in which the Buddhist monk is contrasted with the Brahman but there are other rules which lump him categorically with the Brahman. To work out this contrast it would be necessary to consider the context of each appearance of the term Brahman, for the latter category itself appears as one which is sometimes opposed to the householder and at other times lumped with it. This is again a feature which the later Sanskrit texts share with the Buddhist texts, as is shown in my analysis of the categories Brahman, king and *saṃnyāsin* from a later caste Purana (see Das 1977a). In any case, the idiom through which the relation between the monk and the Brahman is discussed is more that of food and gifts than of the presentation of the body.

This brings me to my last question. Does the contrast between the householder and the monk imply that the monk provides a model for the ascetic or *vice versa*? The text leaves us in no doubt that while the monk is opposed to the householder at one level, at another level the Buddhist monk is further opposed to other ascetics. We have already referred to the scolding of the monks who appeared shabbily dressed. Another rule makes this contrast explicit:

> Now at that time several monks were going along the high road from Saketa to Savatthi. Midway on the road, thieves issuing forth plundered these monks. Then these monks said:
>
> 'It is forbidden by the lord to ask a man or woman householder who is not a relation for a robe.'
>
> And being scrupulous, they did not ask, [but] going naked as they were to Savatthi, they saluted the monks respectfully. The monks said:
>
> 'Your reverences, these Naked Ascetics are very good because they respectfully salute these monks.
>
> They said, 'Your reverences, we are not Naked Ascetics, we are monks.'
>
> Those who were modest monks spread it about, saying, 'How can monks come naked? Should they not come covered up with grass or leaves?' (Horner 1949: 45–46).

On hearing this, the Buddha allowed monks to ask for robes in such periods of crisis and if the monk was unable to obtain any kind of covering, he was to come covered in grass or leaves, but not naked like members of other sects.

Apart from this explicit contrast, an implicit contrast is also being made through the rules about food and dress. The Hindu texts define a *saṃnyāsin* essentially as a man of nature. He goes around naked or dresses himself with products of nature such as bark, leaves, skins of wild animals. Fasting, living on fruits and leaves, he is, in cultural terms, an asocial being.

The Buddhist monk is also a wanderer but stands in a different relationship to the social world. He is earlier enjoined to collect rags from garbage and graveyards and sew up these rags together for his robes. Even when later, he is allowed to accept new robes, this is done on condition that the cloth is cut into small pieces and then these are sewn together so that the monk's robe should resemble 'a ploughed field'. Similarly, in the case of food, he is not allowed to accept raw rice, probably the traditional gift to the priest, which could be stored for varying lengths of time, but neither is he encouraged to live off the products of nature. The daily alms-round enjoined on the Buddhist monk, in the course of which he is to accept whatever food was cooked in the household without indicating any preferences, without getting an invitation to a meal on the exhortation of another monk or nun, without ever accepting any money in lieu of the food and, above all, without ever verbally asking for alms but silently standing with his begging bowl, ensures a regular relationship with the householder. But he is simultanously required to eat his food in a manner different from the householder for he is not to make it into a ball and, unlike the householder, he is not required to refrain from touching his lips with his hands. He is also enjoined not to smack his lips in appreciation—in short, his way of eating is to indicate that food is accepted but not enjoyed. Incidentally the monk cannot be offered left-over food, separating him conceptually from those who received such left-overs and are perhaps in positions like that of domestic servants often mentioned in the Vinaya texts.

Now it seems to me that all these rules differentiate the monk from the householder, which may create the impression that he is parallel to the *saṃnyāsin*. His mode of renunciation, however, is not similar to that of the *saṃnyāsin*, for he is neither in a back-to-back relation with society, nor is he the threatening *saṃnyāsin* who demands obeisance from the householder, as the rules about silence indicate.[10] It is because this subtle play of symbols has been overlooked that an impression of *similarity* between the Buddhist monk and the Hindu ascetic has been created at the cost of the significant relations of inversion.

The above discussion also throws light on the manner in which the public manipulation of symbols can be used to express different cognitive values. Manipulation of symbols does not imply an idiosyncratic construction of meaning but implies the existence of a commonly-shared code *within* which the manipulation of symbols can be interpreted and communicated. In an earlier work, I have illustrated this process of manipulation with reference to Uberoi's (1967) excellent paper on the five symbols of Sikhism (see Das 1977a). I argued that by means of the five symbols (long groomed hair, comb, sword, steel bracelet, and loin and thigh garment), the Sikh *guru* tried to define a new structure of existence for the Sikhs by *neutralizing* the categorical oppositions obtaining in the medieval Hindu world. This neutralization becomes possible through two processes. First, a certain symbol is taken which has a sedimented meaning, and by combining it with a new symbol, a new meaning is bestowed upon it. For example, the steel bracelet which already had the meaning of constraint, is combined with a sword, and together these become a symbol of the honour of every Sikh rather than that of kings or warriors alone. Further, the whole syntagmatic chain, by representing in simultaneity the long hair constrained by a comb, the sword constrained by a bracelet, and the uncircumcized male member constrained by a loin-and-thigh garment, form a metonymic chain, linking the previous terms of each pair in relations of contiguity with the latter ones. However, each term of the chain also evokes by association certain oppositions *in absentia*. For instance, the long groomed hair of the Sikh is opposed to the *jaṭā*, the matted hair of the astetic, the sword of the citizen to the sword of the soldier and so on. It is the combination of oppositions *in praesentia* with oppositions *in absentia* which succeeds in obliterating the categorical partitions between renunciation, kingship and householdership which obtained in the Hindu world.

The analysis of the particular rules about clothing in the Vinaya texts further supports the insights of Barthes (1967) about the garment system. Every time the Buddha is confronted with a new situation, he modifies the existing rule in a manner that the generalized code is not violated. For example, the earlier rule was that the monks were to collect rags from graveyards and stitch them together to make a robe. However, when the householders complained that this amounted to an injunction against the acceptance of robes as gifts from householders, the Buddha modified the rule. He allowed them to accept robes from devout householders provided that the material was cut into small pieces and then stitched together. Thus the norm is derived from what Schneider would call the generalized culture, in the sense of conceptions regarding man and his place in the scheme of the universe. In other words, the particular norm is generated from general conceptions about the structuring of human existence (see Schneider 1976).

Organic Experiences and their Cultural Construction

I have tried to argue in the earlier sections that the body serves as a symbolic vehicle for the organization and expression of cognitive beliefs about the nature of man and his place in the social and cosmic order. In this section I wish to show that the body itself is as much an object of thought as a seat of instincts. It has been assumed by many anthropologists that universal, human, organic experiences provide the model for a primordial classification of reality. I shall argue, on the contrary, that bodily experiences are themselves culturally defined and derive their meaning as *human* experiences from the cultural definition given to them. In this sense one may say that, at least for some purposes, nature is itself a construct of culture.

Victor Turner (1966) has argued for the primacy of organic experience in the primoridal classification of reality in his justly famous paper on colour classification among the Ndembu. Arguing that the basic colour triad—black, white, and red—occurs across many cultures and plays a significant role in ritual, Turner (1966:81) says:

> Not only do these three colours stand for the basic human experiences of the body (associated with the gratification of libido, hunger, aggressive and excretory drives, and with fear, anxiety, and submissiveness), they also provide a kind of primordial classification of reality.

In the initiation ceremony among the Ndembu all three colours receive equal emphasis because, according to Turner (1966:80):

> . . . [the colours red, black, and white] epitomize the main kinds of universal human organic experience. . . Each of the colours in all societies is multivocal, having a wide fan of connotations, but nevertheless the human physiological component is seldom absent wherever reliable native exegesis is available. *Initiation rites often draw their symbolism from the situation of parturition and first lactation, where, in nature, blood, water, faeces, and milk are present* (emphasis supplied).

When we take the body as being biologically given and then try to see how systems of ritual incorporate the biologically given, we assume that the body provides the fundamental imagery for ritual systems. I shall argue, contrary to Turner, that bodily experiences are themselves culturally defined and derive their meaning as *human* experiences from the cultural definition given to them. In this sense one may say that at least for some purposes, nature is itself a construct of culture. Indeed, even a branch of knowledge as purportedly natural as medicine may take the comprehensive understanding of the cosmos for granted and define the body in terms of this comprehensive understanding of symbols. In the final section of this paper I shall take the example of the medical definitions of semen from certain texts on medicine and show how metaphoric and metonymic devices are used to give a definition to body fluids and to the act of sexual intercourse.

Some of the recent work on sacrificial and fertility rituals among the Hindus has shown that the symbolism of milk and semen occurs frequently in these rituals. A few examples will suffice here.

Inden and Nicholas describe the ritual of *sādha* in Bengal which is performed for pregnant women. This is similar to the ritual of *sīmantonnayana*, described in the *Gṛhya Sūtras*. One important part of the ritual is the feeding of thickened milk to the expectant mother by her husband. It is popularly believed in Bengal—and support for this may be found in popular medical texts like the *Prasuti Tantra* compiled in the beginning of this century—that thickened milk increases the proportion of semen to uterine blood in the woman resulting in the birth of a son. Inden and Nicholas interpret this custom as the feeding of symbolic semen to the woman.

Many stories in Hindu mythology may be drawn upon to support this interpretation. In the famous epic *Ramayana*, King Dasratha performs a *yajña* (fire sacrifice) in order to get valorous sons. Pleased with him, the Lord of Fire, Agni Devata, himself appears and gives to Dasratha ritually consecrated food which he is to feed to his queens.

This food, which makes the queens pregnant, is described in Kalidasa's *Raghuvaṃśam* as *payasam saram annam*, and in the commentary of Tekachand as *haviṣyannam.* The first expression means food which has the essence of milk, and the latter expression means sacrificially consecrated food. Thus there is here a symbolic equation between thickened milk, sacrificially consecrated food, and semen.

Thus it seems clear that a symbolic equation is made between semen and ritually consecrated food which happens in most cases to be thickened milk. I would stress the last point since all the references to semen as thickened milk are in the context of the performance of rituals. In other contexts, semen is described as *payas* (liquid, milk) in the *Suśruta Saṃhita*, in the earlier Vedic texts, and in some references in the Puranas. In other places, however, it is described as *apas* (water), making a simple equation between milk and semen difficult to sustain.

According to the medical texts, *Suśruta Saṃhita* by Susrusa and *Bhāva Prakāśa* of Bhava Mishra (1958), semen should be creamy, fluid, and of the consistency of molten silver. It should be thick and not as liquid as water. It should smell of lotuses. Bad semen is said to be tinged with colour, thin, and foul-smelling like a corpse. It also smells of urine and faeces. Bad semen, say these texts, is incapable of impregnating a woman.

In view of the fact that good semen is said to be of a thicker consistency than water, its description as *apas* (water) seems puzzling. A few examples from the Atharva Veda (16.1.1–4), which describe semen as *apas*, water, may be worth quoting here:

> I have abandoned the desire which leads to the shedding of water-like semen, which is spread throughout the body. That desire makes one ill, kills one. It makes one take the crooked path, destroys the power of the mind, destroys virtue, burns one out, spoils the soul, and makes the body impure. I throw away that desire. I wash myself clean of it.

Thus when semen is used in the service of erotic desire and shed often, it drains man of all his vitality. When embodied with erotic desire, semen is said to be a terrible fluid—*yó va āpo-agnírāvivéśa śa eṣá ýadvo ghorám̩ tádetát*, which, freely translated, is 'O semen, when desire enters you, it makes your form terrible'.

The same semen which, when embodied with desire (*kāma*), becomes so terrible is described in different terms in the context of sexual relations for rightful procreation. The Atharva Veda itself says, 'May our semen become without sins', and in the Yajur Veda it is said, 'Let this *havi*, sacrificial offering, bestow on me the power to procreate ten sons'.

The evidence seems reasonably clear that the use of semen for fulfillment of erotic desires is considered to be improper and fraught with many risks. But when used for procreation, according to *dharma*, semen is described poetically as having the qualities of molten silver and the smell of lotuses. The Atharva Veda is explicit that a man should not use his genitals for fulfillment of erotic desire but according to *dharma*, for carrying on the creation of God (Atharva Veda 16).

On the basis of the materials discussed above I should now like to suggest that the equation between *payas* (thickened milk), *havi* (sacrificially-consecrated food), and semen is made in order to stress the redefinition of semen as a 'ritually consecrated fluid' rather than as a biological one. The body fluids are linked to sacrificial rituals, not because sexuality provides the model for sacrifice but in order that sexuality itself should be defined away from its erotic associations to become a supreme religious duty on the model of sacrifice.

The ritual rules governing the act of sexual intercourse in various Hindu manuals, seem to stress the fact that the performance of the sex act is not merely a bodily function, instinctive and unguided by rules.[11] On the contrary, it is guided by the greatest ritual sanctions and is, indeed, itself a ritual act. Texts like the *Gṛhya Sūtras* (manuals for performance of domestic rituals) set out the rules about the exact movements of the body during intercourse, and also give the appropriate verses which a husband and wife should recite just before penetration of the vagina.

The medical texts themselves give rules which are to be observed during intercourse for the conception of a 'good' offspring. According to *Bhāva Prakāśa* and *Suśruta Saṃhita*, intercourse should take place on the fourth day after the onset of menstruation. A man who does not have intercourse with his wife on this day is guilty of *bhrūṇa hatya*—killing of the foetus. On this day, the girl should bathe, rub sandal-paste all over her body, wear a garland of sweet-smelling flowers, and adorn herself with beautiful clothes and jewellery. The husband, who has been observing celibacy during his wife's menstruation, is required similarly to prepare himself. According to *Suśruta* the man should have drunk *ghī* (clarified butter) and *payas* (thickened milk) while the girl should have only light food.

Both texts emphasize that intercourse must take place in the straight, lying position, otherwise either conception will not take place, or the child born will have a contrary disposition so that, if a boy, he will be effeminate and, if a girl, she will behave like a boy.

It is my contention here that the whole act of intercourse and the depositing of semen in a woman is conceived on the analogy of the process of creation through the sacrificial act. It is well known that the original paradigm of sacrifice is provided by the sacrifice of Purusha, through which the world is created. Purusha sacrificed the different parts of his body from which were created different objects of the natural and the social world. The sacrificer who repeats the sacrifice of Purusha sets in motion a whole new cycle of regeneration. What is dispersed in the sacrifice never goes to waste and returns many-fold to the sacrificer. It is in this sense that the Atharva Veda says that man should think of the genital organ as an organ of Indra. Through it he should carry God's creation further.

When the medical texts assert that semen is comparable to molten silver, or smells of lotuses, it is clear that these are metaphors and not mechanical substitutes for original 'natural' meanings. Neither the resemblance between semen and molten silver, nor the resemblance between the smell of semen and the smell of lotuses exists in a cultureless, objective world. It is not a resemblance that is somehow felt. Rather, it is the whole function of metaphor here to redefine reality and to call attention to other levels of existence. By comparing semen to molten silver, lotuses, and the purest of ritually consecrated foods, a transcendence is being made to a new level of reality in which sexual intercourse becomes invested with deep religious meaning. Simultaneously, the resemblance between semen and other bodily products is destroyed. It becomes instead an offering comparable to the offering in a sacrifice, setting in motion a rejuvenating process. At the cosmic level, if a resemblance is perceived between the waters of a cloud and semen, it is because the cloud sheds its water to rejuvenate the barren earth, just as man's semen makes fertile the woman, herself conceptualized on the analogy of earth. The Pandit informants of Madan who told him that a Pandit was the fruit of *dharma* (duty), and not of *kāma* (erotic desire), spoke from just this religious tradition (Madan 1978). Without entering into a debate about primacy of religious interpretations of biological facts, I shall only reiterate that the biological facts are pretransformed in culture before they enter *human* consciousness. In so much as the processes of the body are thought about, endowed with meaning, the cultureless reality, whatever its nature, would hardly remain for a human being.

Simultaneously, as the metaphors for good semen define it positively, the characteristics of bad semen which is incapable of producing children serve to separate it from its physical associations. The texts tell us that semen is bad and unproductive if it smells of urine or faeces. It is because of its association with life that its contrary, 'bad' semen, is said to smell of a corpse and thus of death. Only when semen becomes an embodiment of *kāma*, uncontrolled eroticism, is it fatal to the well-being of man. Dumont's (1970) important formulation that *kāma* is encompassed by *dharma* is fully validated here.

And yet, once we have understood the respective places assigned to *dharma* and *kāma* in the ideology, we must not forget that the social world constructed on the basis of this ideology is considered to be extremely fragile, for code is constantly threatened by ties of substance. I have described in earlier papers how the social construction of the world (*duniyādārī* in Punjabi and Hindi, *saṃsāra* in Bengali) is constantly threatened by what society describes as 'biological realities' on the one hand, and the values of the *saṃnyāsin* (renouncer) on the other (see Das 1976a and 1977b). The very same Pandits of Madan (1978), who say that they are fruits of *dharma* and not of *kāma*, also have a proverb, 'Legitimate or illegitimate, the nine months of my womb', showing that the ties created by the womb are stronger than the ties of morality. The *Prasuti Tantra*, a popular Bengali text on sexuality and procreation, says that when the soul arrives to form a foetus in the woman's womb, it lets its nature be known through the pregnant woman's cravings for food. The text enjoins that these cravings for particular foods must be fulfilled even if they are for highly sacriligeous food like beef. For the foetus arrives with its own *karma*, the code it followed in its last birth, and the type of food it demands is consistent with its nature which has already been formed by past actions. The foetus cannot alter its nature. The Hindu world is caught between the monist position, that past *karma* determine the kind of body a person acquires as also the kind of food he eats and these, in turn, will determine his future *karma;* and the contrary position, that performance of a higher code of conduct (including contracting hypergamous marriage alliances or *sanskritizing*) will ultimately alter the substance of a person. The implications of the former may be found in Marriott (1976), Inden and Nicholas (1977), and of the latter in Tambiah (1973) and Inden (1976).

Conclusion

It will be clear that this paper has treated the reality of the body as identical with its cognizability. It seems to me to be a position to which symbolic anthropology is led for it is only when singular experiences of emotion or private sensations enter into symbolically-mediated inferences and become parts of interpretations that are inter-subjective that they come to constitute a reality that is social. While individual ritual actions have pragmatic rather than logical ends, it is mistaken to suppose that the internal logic of symbolic systems is not relevant to their understanding. Individuals are aware of the sense of the symbolic code available for their use, even though this code remains virtual until actualized in individual acts. It is this code which provides individuals with categories of description that distinguish them as members of one culture as opposed to another culture. It is also the code which provides a guide to action. It does not, however, follow that the relationship between collective code and individual use is linear in the sense that from code we can deduce use. It seems to me that the two belong to two different levels of reality corresponding to first-level propositions and second-level propositions. Progress from understanding the code to individual use of the code requires the setting up of new structures and new descriptions which assume the understanding of the code rather than preclude it. I hope to have contributed to the understanding of body symbolism in Hinduism only to the limited extent of having delineated some components at the level of the first order. In future work I hope to be able to proceed to the second order and to integrate code with use.

NOTES

I would like to thank Professor Ralph Nicholas for many lively discussions on this subject in the spring of 1977 which helped me to formulate many of the ideas expressed here. Subsequently Professor T. N. Madan read earlier drafts of this paper and I am grateful for his thoughtful comments which helped to clarify many obscure points. Extensive comments on parts of the paper were made in seminars given at the Centre for the Study of Developing Societies, Delhi; the School of Oriental and African Studies, London; and the Department of Anthropology at the University of Harvard. I thank the members of those seminars who commented on the paper. I am fully responsible for the shortcomings that remain due to my inability to make better use of their comments.

1 There is a vast literature on terminology in symbolic anthropology, with no two authors using the same term with the same meaning. One set of authors uses different terms such as sign, symbol, index and icon to bring out the different types of relations between any two *relata*. As Barthes (1967) showed by his analysis of the terms, signal, index, icon, sign, and allegory, as these occur in different authors (Hegel, Wallon, Peirce and Jung), the contradictions encountered in the use of a term by different authors disappear by transfers of meaning from one term to another *in the same* author. As he said, '. . . the words in the field derive their meaning only from their opposition to one another. . . and that if these oppositions are preserved, the meaning is unambigous'. Therefore, it is not very useful to keep producing new definitions, especially if the *total set* of terms is ignored.

The above definitions rely on a term-to-term relation between the signifier and the signified, but we may also derive a classification of signs on the basis of the organization of the signs into a system, e.g. on the basis of whether the signs are metonymically or metaphorically related as Lévi-Strauss (1964) did in *Totemism*, distinguishing the cult of guardian spirit from totemism on the basis of metonymic and metaphoric relations. It must be remembered that the distinction between metonymy and metaphor in Lévi-Strauss is equivalent to the distinction between syntagmatic and paradigmatic, though its relation to association *in praesentia* and association *in absentia* is not at all clear. Turner (1975) also uses the distinction between metaphor and metonymy but derives their definitions from rhetoric, and not from the two axes of a language as in Saussure (1960).

2 Inden and Nicholas (1977) point out that in Bengali culture the body is not contrasted with the mind as in Western culture. Instead, we get a contrast between gross body and subtle body which they say is a contrast in 'more' or 'less' terms. In actual use, it seems to me that the contrast between gross and subtle is formulated in terms of relative pervasiveness. It is in this sense that liquids are said to be more subtle than solids, and

air is more subtle than liquids. It is because a person takes on his subtle body after his death that he may be in several places whereas in life he is bound by space and time.

3 It is notoriously difficult to give any reliable date for the authorship of the Puranas. Indologists place the *Viṣṇudharmottara* before A.D. 1030 since Alberuni mentions a text of this name. Its date, according to some indologists, may be pushed back to the period between the second half of the fifth century A.D. and the first half of the seventh century A.D. For details of this Purana, see Shah (1958), Hazra (1958), and Kramrich (1946).

4 At least in one region of India, viz. Bengal, the association between the goddess Durga, courtesans, and uncontained sexuality is quite explicit. Chattopadhaya (1974:377), writing on the social history of Bengal, has described the norms for the public worship of Durga. He says that on the ninth day of the worship, many sacrificial offerings were made to the goddess. On the tenth day the image was immersed in the Ganges. The procession carrying the image, according to him, had to include courtesans, dancing and singing girls. It was also customary to indulge in vulgar banter in which frequent reference to the genitals was made. The author goes on to say that it was commonly believed that those who did not participate in the exchange of obscenities or who took offence, would be cursed by the goddess.

I am grateful to Abhijit Sarkar for bringing this book to my notice.

5 Following the Samkhya tradition, one tends to associate *tamas* with inertia and darkness. The Puranic mythology, however, points to the element of riotous movement. For instance, Shri Aurobindo's book on 'The Mother' has this to say about Mahakali, the *tāmasika* goddess: 'The impulses that are swift and straight, and frank, the *movements that are unreserved and absolute* . . . are hers' (emphasis supplied, quoted in Shankarayanan 1968). The *tāmasika* goddess is created to fight the demons and she has to use the very properties of *tamas*, which she is fighting in the demons.

6 See in this connection the well-known story of King Vena, whose evil results in prolonged suffering for his people. It is only after he is killed that the evil in him is churned out by the sages and comes out from his left side in the form of a dark evil being. Then the good part of him is born as the righteous King Prithu, who then brings prosperity to the people. In other stories the good and evil are invested, not in the same person, but in brothers, as in the famous story of the Ramayana where Ravana is eminently evil but his brother Vibhishna is not. Significantly Rama, the hero, kills Ravana but does not appropriate his kingdom, which is restored to the 'good' brother Vibhishna. It seems to me that the ritual of the clay bath performs the same function as the twirling of Vena in the story given above.

7 The scheme of the three *guṇa* has not received much attention in the anthropological literature on India. The reason for this according to Béteille (1977) is that the scheme of *guṇa*, 'unlike that of *varṇas* does not lend itself easily to analysis in terms of simple binary oppositions; a practice much in vogue among those anthropologists who are described as

structuralists'. We do not have to go along with Béteille on the rather simplistic assumption that structural analysis consists of finding simple binary opposites. If it were so, three terms would pose no further problems than two terms, for instead of one binary relation we may simply find three binary relations, making the basis of comparison a multilateral one. The literature on triadic classifications is extensive and ranges from the lesser known work of writers in the Russian folklorist tradition to well-known papers like that of Turner (1966) on colour classification among the Ndembu.

Béteille seems to share this view with Goody (1973) who also thinks that structural analysis consists of the setting up of tables of binary opposites. If one could rise above what seems like narrow sectarian quarrels, one can easily see that most work in structuralism and in the field of symbolic anthropology shows that a particular element may enter into several oppositions, one opposition may *include* another opposition. The *guṇa* share in these characteristics of symbolic space and the basis of comparison in the case we are discussing is the *type* of movement posited in each *guṇa*.

In passing, I may note that Béteille's (1977) contention about the *varṇa* system that 'the same account [for the *varṇa*] is repeated again and again in *hundreds of texts* in both Sanskrit and the regional languages' (emphasis supplied) and that 'despite all these variations the texts seem to present the same basic structure' is open to doubt. In fact the statement may be true only if we restrict ourselves to the legal tests. Studies of other kinds of texts are few but two recent studies show that the conceptualization of the four *varṇa* differs according to region, period, and the social group within which the text is composed (see Inden 1976 and Das 1977a). It is precisely this complacency about categories of thought in Sanskrit and regional texts, which has prevented anthropologists from making serious and detailed studies of these texts.

8 The *Viṣṇudharmottara Purāna* mentions that after the demons had been killed by the mother-goddesses, they appealed to Vishnu to allow them to receive blood sacrifices as they had become used to eating meat and drinking blood and liquor. Vishnu then ordained that they might be offered blood sacrifices at certain specified periods.

9 In general there has been a tendency to emphasize the similarities between different groups of ascetics rather than their differences. Tambiah (1970) is impressed by the initial similarities between the Buddhist monk and the Hindu *saṃnyāsin*, although he recognizes that later developments within Hinduism and Buddhism led to different conceptualizations of the two. Müller contended that the Brahmanical 'ascetic' was the model for the Buddhist and Jain counterparts. Dutt (1960) argues, on the contrary, that the ancient *parivrājaka* (wanderer) tradition provided the seed-bed which gave rise to all the wandering sects. It seems to me that Müller, Dutt, and to some extent Tambiah, have not paid attention to the attempts in the Vinaya texts to distinguish the Buddhist monk from the other types of ascetics through manipulation of the modes of presenting the body in everyday life.

10 In theory the renouncer has nothing to do with the social world. But in

some ways the renouncer is a person who can demand respect from every person in the social world since he speaks in the name of the whole of humanity, and not just in the name of the social group to which he belongs. Also because of his accumulation of *tapas*, the power of asceticism, he has the power to curse anyone and even forces the gods to fall in with his wishes. The stories of ascetics who were quick to be angered and demanded obeisance are frequent even in the epics.

11 To writers like Turner, as for many others, the body and its experiences like sexuality represent the ultimate in spontaneity, *communitas* and the ever elusive search for pure being. This spontaneous, playful sexuality is an illusion, for if Hinduism seeks to bind it by ritual rules, the modern West achieves the same through the notion of 'correct technique' as any modern manual on love-making would testify.

REFERENCES

Barthes, R. 1967. *Elements of semiology*. London: Jonathan Cape.

Beck, B. 1976. The symbolic merger of body, space and cosmos. *Contributions to Indian Sociology* N. S. 10, 213–244.

Belliappa, J. 1980. The religious ideology of the Coorgs. Unpublished Ph.D. thesis, Univ. of Delhi.

Béteille, A. 1977 *Inequality among men*. Oxford: Blackwell.

Bhava Mishra 1958. *Bhāva Prakāśa* with the Hindi commentary of Pandit Lalachandreji Vaidya. 2 vols. Delhi: Motilal Banarsidass.

Chakravarti, U. 1978. The structure of categories in the Vinaya texts of the early Buddhists. Paper presented to the Research Seminar in the Department of History, Univ. of Delhi.

Chattopadhyaya, S. 1974. *Banglar samajik itihaser bhumika*. Calcutta: Calcutta Sahitya Samsad.

Das. V. 1976a. Masks and faces: an analysis of Punjabi kinship. *Contributions to Indian Sociology* N. S. 10, 1–30.

—— 1976b. The uses of liminality: society and cosmos in Hinduism. *Contributions to Indian Sociology* N. S. 10, 245–263.

—— 1977a. *Structure and cognition: aspects of Hindu caste and ritual.* Delhi: Oxford Univ. Press.

—— 1977b. The social construction of adulthood. Paper presented to the ICSSR seminar on Identity and Adulthood in India. Forthcoming in Sudhir Kakkar (ed.) *Identity and adulthood in India*. Delhi: Oxford Univ. Press.

Douglas, M. 1970. *Natural symbols*. London: Cresset.

Dumont, L. 1970. *Homo hierarchicus: the caste system and its implications*. London: Weidenfeld and Nicolson.

Dutt, S. 1960. *Early Buddhist monachism*. Bombay: Asia Publishing House.

Goody, J. 1973. Introduction. In Jack Goody (ed.) *The character of kinship*. Cambridge: Univ. Press.

Hazra, R. C. 1958. *Studies in the Upa-Puranas*. Calcutta: Sanskrit College.

Horner, I. B. 1949. *The book of the discipline:* translation of *Vinyapitaka*, vol. 111. London: Luzac.

Inden, R. 1976. *Marriage and rank in Bengali culture.* Berkeley: Univ. of California Press.

—— 1977. Ritual authority and cyclical time in Hindu kingship (mimeo.).

Inden, R. & Nicholas, R. 1977. *Kinship in Bengali culture.* Chicago: Univ. Press.

Kaushik, M. 1979. Religion and social structure of the Doms of Banaras. Unpublished Ph.D. thesis, Univ. of Delhi.

Kramrisch, S. 1946. *The Hindu temple.* Calcutta: Univ. of Calcutta.

Lévi-Strauss, C. 1964. *Totemism.* London: Merlin Press.

Madan, T. N. 1978. Person, purpose, and procedure: the ideology of the householder (mimeo.).

Marriott, McKim 1976. Hindu transactions: diversity without dualism. In Bruce Kapferer (ed.) *Transactions and meaning: directions in the anthropology of exchange and symbolic behaviour.* Philadelphia: ISHI Publications.

Schneider, D. N. 1976. Notes towards a theory of culture. In K. Basso and N. Selby (eds.) *Meaning in anthropology.* Albuquerque: Univ. of New Mexico Press.

Shah, P. 1958. *Visnudharmottara Purana.* Baroda: Oriental Institute.

Shankarayanan, S. 1968. *The glory of the divine mother.* Madras: Sri Ramakrishna Math.

Tambiah, S. J. 1970. *Buddhism and the spirit cults in north-east Thailand.* Cambridge: Univ. Press.

—— 1973. From *varna* to caste through mixed unions. In Jack Goody (ed.) *The character of kinship.* Cambridge: Univ. Press.

Turner, V. 1966. Colour classification in Ndembu ritual. In M. Banton (ed.) *Anthropological approaches to the study of religion.* London: Tavistock.

—— 1975. Symbolic studies. In B. J. Seigel et al. (eds.) *Annual Review of Anthropology* 4, 145–159.

Uberoi, J. P. S. 1967. On being unshorn. *Transactions of the Indian Institute of Advanced Study*, Simla 4, 87–100.

SOME PHENOMENOLOGICAL OBSERVATIONS ON THE STUDY OF INDIAN RELIGION

A. Piatigorsky

0. *Introductory Remarks on an Understanding of the Phenomenology of Religion.*

0.0. Phenomenology has a natural affinity with both the anthropology of religion and religion itself, in that each can be taken as a different case of self-awareness. The outward direction of anthropological work to the study of other religions and cultures is accompanied by an inner understanding of our own culture, either by silent comparison with what we are not (when customs are seen in their cultural specificity), or by subsuming features of both our customs and theirs as two instances under a more general principle (in which case some kind of common denominator is thereby assumed). The anthropological approach therefore always entails some degree of reflexive understanding, even when this is not expressed. Religion is also, in general, characterized by a speculative tendency to consider the very nature of religion and thus to develop theoretical terms for its own self-description. But whereas religion contains within its theory much that is not related to an understanding of itself, phenomenology as such can in principle be entirely reduced to self-awareness, which features as the core of its theory and the only practical result of its methods of investigation.

0.1.0. In phenomenology, if taken apart from its specifically Husserlean interpretation, consciousness figures as the category which comprises both thinking and its contents. In other words, consciousness is thought of in phenomenology as that to which all objects of thinking are related as contents (including thinking itself when it has become such an object). The contents of consciousness are therefore relative to consciousness and, equally, consciousness itself is relative in its reverse relatedness to its contents. What is postulated here, are not two consciousnesses, one related and the other unrelated to its contents, but only one consciousness wherein such a relatedness is already presupposed. All contents of consciousness imply a differentiation of consciousness. For example, the category 'ordinary language' implies its conscious differentiation from other kinds of language, say the theoretical language in terms of which it is described. It follows that the category of consciousness not only contains differentiation (as a necessary characteristic of its content), but can be conceived as itself being such a differentiation, because we can conceive of no other procedure by means of which differentiation could have been produced. In any phenomenological approach, therefore, it can be asserted that consciousness is taken as the principle of differentiation.[1]

Each time we refer to 'the phenomenon of . . .', this means that the principle of differentiation of consciousness has already assumed its concretization in this particular case. Speaking terminologically, what we call 'a phenomenon' is nothing but the fact of establishing difference and ascertaining its examples. Correspondingly, a phenomenological investigation is concerned not only to establish differences (i.e. to identify the features by virtue of which a particular phenomenon is distinguished from other phenomena) but, more importantly, to chase after the cases where such a differentiation exists, for we cannot tell in advance where it will be found. For example, we differentiate God from man in our own consciousness: that is already something. But there is no certainty that a similar distinction is to be found in all religions: it has to be pursued, it cannot be axiomatized. And, indeed, in Hinduism this distinction is blurred rather than absolute, men being distinguished from rishis in more fundamental ways than from some gods.

0.1.1. Two points appear to be central to a phenomenological investigation of religion. Firstly, given the principle of differentiating consciousness, we may assume that consciousness itself can be variously directed (i.e. can be thematic in Husserl's terminology). In other words, we do not chase after all differentiation, we choose an inner line of direction according to our individual preference, which becomes the theme of our investigation. Suppose, for example, our consciousness, in studying others' consciousness, is directed to the liberation from physical existence as an object of study. This quest is not found in all religions, so we are directed to those religious situations where this is present as a structure of consciousness. From the initial selection of a theme it does not, however, follow that we have captured the distinction in a given case: we have to travel, not only to identify the incidence of the phenomenon, but also to explore it in its cultural specificity.

0.1.2. Secondly, each religious consciousness implies, and already includes in itself, a certain potentiality of interpretation in the sense of which certain facts, not yet acquired, will be interpreted and to which these facts will be reduced. Another structure of religious consciousness does not necessarily possess the same potentiality, in which case facts of this category cannot be included within it. For example, Christian consciousness has always been ready to appropriate the very fact of war as a fact of religion (either positive or negative) in the sense of holy wars against the infidel or in terms of Christian eschatology (each war bringing nearer the total destruction of the world), or in some other way. Hindu self-awareness, on the other hand, because of its cyclical and ahistorical character, has for a long time not included any structure of consciousness wherein war could find an interpretation. War in Hinduism remained religiously neutral until in Gandhi's time it became incorporated as part of the struggle for freedom associated with a 'reformed' Hinduism.[2]

0.1.3. The application of criteria of differentiating consciousness is thus the corner-stone of a phenomenological investigation. From whatever point of view a religion is studied—be it that of psychology, anthropology, philosophy, or even that of another religion—the task of the phenomenologist is to apply these criteria to two sets of concepts indifferently: the concepts of the religion studied and the concepts used by the investigator in his analysis of the religion. The point of view of the phenomenologist will therefore always be more general than the most general postulations of a religion and the most general rules of investigation itself. Thus, in considering these two sets of concepts, I try to mark out a neutral approach which will include both as objects detached from their cultural framework. Similarly, in considering a given philosophy, I try to work out a third position, wherein both this philosophy and mine are seen as two particular cases of a more general principle. Ultimately, in turn, elements of this third position may be encompassed by a still wider view. The effect of the inclusive generality of a phenomenological approach is that each particular orientation becomes manifest in its specificity. For the very fact of admitting the possibility of a third position, from the point of view of which my consciousness will be seen as other than that of the third position, divests my own theory of its finality. It is seen as one among others and the particular features of its orientation become open to objective study. When the third position is not admitted, the investigator runs the risk of approaching his object of investigation in a theoretically naive manner. This may not be apparent to him when he analyses another religion in his own terms but it becomes apparent when the investigated uses his terms to interpret the investigator's own religion. A Tantric scholar, a man of shrewd intelligence and wide-ranging knowledge, made the following observations on the passion and resurrection of Christ. He explained the first by the evident fact that Christ, like many ascetics, had obtained *siddhi* (instanced both in his 'knowledge' and in his miracles), in consequence of which he suffered no pain on the Cross; and the second as a typical example of the burial and later disinterrment of an ascetic in meditative trance, a phenomenon of common occurrence throughout the subcontinent. Are many Western interpretations of Indian phenomena, *mutatis mutandis*, more pertinent?

0.2.1. The nature of a phenomenological approach and, more particularly, its ability to reveal the specific character of the religion studied, can be shown by a methodological contrast with the universalist approaches of philosophy and, at times, of anthropology. The philosophy of religion interprets religious phenomena in terms of a number of 'universal' categories such as god, rite, myth, belief, essence, cult, sacrifice, worship and so forth. As a result, wherever it goes, it tends to find variations of the same thing. Zaehner, from a philosophical position, characterizes the religious teaching of the Upanishads as follows: 'The basic doctrine of the Upanishads is the identification of Brahman with Atman, that is to say, of the changeless *essence* that upholds the universe ... with the same changeless *essence* that indwells the human spirit' (Zaehner 1972:viii, my emphasis). Zaehner's 'essence' is that of Aristotelian logic and Christian theology. In a similar way, Renou characterizes ancient Indian religion in terms of 'divine entity': 'Comme Bergaigne l'a montré autrefois ... toute entité divine vient aboutir ... à l'image du feu (Agni sous ses diverses manifestations) ou à celle du Soma ... tout se ramène (dans le Rigveda) à des combinations entre les divers modalités d'Agni et de Soma . . .' (Renou 1956:8–9) As in Zaehner's case with essence, the category of entity is used here as if it were taken for granted that 'divine entity' is universal and common to all religions, or to Religion. The term 'cult' is also used in the philosophy of religion as an absolute category, i.e. as a category not related to any particular culture or related to all of them indiscriminately. Phenomenology, on the other hand, distinguishes between the notion of cult as related to a culture, and the notion of cult as used by the investigator as a meta-concept of his own approach. Thus sacrifice (*yajña*) as described in the Rig Veda can be put under the rubric of cult in the second sense, but only provided that oppositions such as cult/myth or cult as objective rite/mysticism as subjective communion (cf. Leuba) are understood as irrelevant, because Rig Vedic sacrifice included in itself both the objective and subjective aspects of religion as they are culturally understood by us. Thought (e.g. internal repetition of the *mantra*) was not here opposed to action but itself conceived as a type of sacrificial action on a level with doing, organizing, chanting and so forth. The subjective/objective distinction does not arise within the framework of Vedic terminology at all: it arises only in our work of rendering.

0.2.2. Anthropological studies also have their received categories including, these days, classification and analysis in terms of dualistic oppositions. 'What principle governs the formation of the original myth?' asks Leach, '. . . Binary oppositions are intrinsic to the process of human thought. Any description of the world must discriminate categories in the form "p is what not-p is not" ' (Leach 1969:9). Human thought, in Leach, is something which obviously encompasses the thought of the mythologist and that of 'receivers of the message of Genesis'. This is demonstrated by the fact that both are governed by one and the same principle—that of binary opposition, albeit the former knows it and knows how to describe it in a meta-language of his science, whereas the latter do not. If, however, the concepts of the theory of information are as binary as those within mythic structures of thought, then awareness of their use seems to be the only distinction between the meta-language of science and the Word of God. In which case, we can suggest a slightly blasphemous, though phenomenologically quite possible, explanation: that God (whom Leach calls 'supernatural sender') plays *within* the framework of the myth of Genesis and with respect to receivers, the very same role that Leach plays *outside* this myth and with respect to this myth as a whole. He comes to myth only to discover that which has already been revealed in his own thinking (or culture)—binarity. Or, to adopt a Jakobsonean position, it is myth, or any other text not possessing its own meta-language, through which binarity as an intrinsic feature of his own thinking is revealed to him.

Binary oppositions, according to Leach, are intrinsic only to the process of human thought, not to its contents. In order, therefore, to move from method of investigation to contents of investigated thought, Leach introduces the category of mediation, which at the theoretical level seems to play a role similar to transformation or re-integration in Eliade, and to transference in psychoanalysis. In relation to the role of myth in religion, he writes: 'The central "problem" of religion is . . . to re-establish some kind of bridge between Man and God' (Leach 1969:10). The bridging function of myth serves to make the myth as a whole comprehensible, serving as an intermediary link between 'receiver' and 'sender' within a myth and also between the inner situation of myth and the external situation of the mythologist. In modern mythological analysis this situation is taken as absolute and non-reversible because the mythologist interprets his data as the work of a consciousness which is not his, which is 'other' consciousness and, as such, incapable of exchanging positions with the consciousness of the mythologist. This approach also excludes the possibility of a third position from the standpoint of which the consciousness of the mythologist is seen as other than that of the third position. I am reminded here of the main mythological standpoint of Jung that the very structure of our own personality is necessarily mythic. (The role of the analyst is thus to participate in the mythological situation of the patient, knowing at the same time that the analyst's access to this situation is necessarily limited by the framework of his own 'myth'.) If, however, the third position is admitted, it seems that whenever an anthropologist applies the principle of binary opposition, he invariably ends up with a tristructurality of myth. Can we then say that tristructurality is a universal phenomenon of consciousness which becomes available to an anthropologist only through the principle of binary opposition?

In the end one cannot help feeling that the current fashion for dichotomies such as cult/myth (all too easily reducible to form/content or even expression/content) or praxis/theory are becoming more and more obsolete and uninteresting. This is due not only to the cultural character of these dichotomies—a fact of which we are becoming increasingly aware—but to the more important limitation that binary oppositions in such spheres of 'modern knowledge' as structural anthropology, structural linguistics and semantics no longer satisfy the requirements of meta-language in the observation of religious phenomena today. Furthermore, notions such as sacred/profane, pure/impure cannot be used in phenomenology as they are used in anthropology and philosophy, for they were coined in the context of a universal religion which remains their natural sphere of application. When applied outside this context, they tend unconsciously to assume the status of meta-concepts of science, rather than of religion, and thus to over-lay or disguise the fundamental categories of the religion investigated. This can be illustrated by an anecdote.

0.2.3. When a friend of mine, a *smārta* Brahman from Madura, was told that if he left India to study theoretical physics at Cambridge, he would lose his caste (Aiyar in this case), his situation invited a number of comments from his friends. One of them, a philosopher from Boston, said that the whole situation derived from the purely traditional and thereby sacred character of his culture, in the sense that the interdiction was a logical transposition of temporal limitations, as exemplified by a Brahman's cycle of rites, on those connected with movements in space. The second opinion, that of an Indian historian, was that this was a banal case of prohibition connected with the ritual purity of brahmanical status (he had not read Dumont yet, but had already read some Dharmashastras). But the young man himself, being a born phenomenologist, considered his situation from an entirely different angle. He said to us that 'a Brahman of my family (*kuṭi*) is a person living in India (*paratakaṇṭam*) and there are no Brahmans among those living outside'. In other words, according to his phenomenology of his own religion, the brahmanical purity of Dharmashastras is itself a derivative from brahmanical status as an ontological entity, not the other way round. Thus a Brahman, as a 'naturally' dharmic being, is not one who conforms to brahmanical ethics; on the contrary, so-called brahmanical ethics are a secondary description of what a Brahman is and what he does. From this point of view it makes no sense to talk of the *dharma* of Brahmans, and still less to subordinate brahmanhood to purity or ethics, for brahmanhood in itself is *dharma*.

0.3. Phenomenology has a dual aim: to explain religion in terms, wherever possible, that the religion has developed for its own self-description, and simultaneously to explain the religion to the external observer in his terms. Without this there is no phenomenology. It is therefore of great importance to identify the main conditions under which terms corresponding to 'religion', or 'ritual', or 'cult'—where such exist—are used in a religion investigated as meta-concepts for its objective understanding of itself. This task requires an investigation of concrete situations and texts where analogous terms were used both in the description of facts and, at the same time, as the means of interpretation of these facts. In the Indian case these terms of reflexive understanding developed within speculative structures of consciousness which neither codified the religion (as in theology) nor existed separately from it (as in philosophy) but analysed the religion from within the religion itself. To this case I now turn.

1. A Phenomenological Approach to Indian Religion

1.0. The application of a phenomenological approach to the study of Indian religion entails two quite different methodological procedures. The first consists in identifying the terms and notions of Indian religion with the terms and notions used in our investigation of Indian religion, that is, used as meta-terms of our investigation. The second consists in identifying the various phenomena of Indian religion in terms of the concepts, the meaning of which has been established in the first procedure. In this way the meaning of the concept in question is made manifest in the observable phenomena of religious experience. These two procedures are elaborated below.

1.1. The first procedure identifies the terms to be used in our analysis and establishes their meaning. This is not simply a problem of appropriate translation. It involves an investigation of the relation between the language in which Indian religion describes itself—from an inner point of view, so to speak—and the language of an external observer of Indian religion. This procedure is particularly difficult when the terms used by the external observer in his observation of a religion other than his own are the very terms used in the inner description of his own religion, as is commonly the case both in anthropology and indology. The existence of anthropology as a science can be connected historically with a widespread cultural rejection of religious belief, but even when atheistic (as in Soviet anthropology), or theistic (as in Frazer's case), or entirely agnostic (as in the case of Lévi-Strauss), anthropology remains, from the point of view of an external observer, an epiphenomenon of Christian culture, evident in the culturally given meanings of 'religion', 'magic', 'god', 'myth' and other such terms that the anthropologist brings to his work. This is also true of indology. For instance, when Zaehner (1966:49) writes of the development within Hinduism of 'strong monotheistic trends', he obviously applies the term 'monotheistic' used in Christianity in its own inner description to his external description of Hinduism (an observation much more accurate in the case of Islam because Islam itself developed an idea of monotheism). This means that the phenomenology of religion cannot begin unless we have started understanding our own understanding of religion (not necessarily our own religion for we may have none). To take an example, analysis of our use of the term 'religion' reveals its inner character as a kind of general denominator. Although we cannot be certain in advance that a term serving an analogous function is to be found in any Indian religion, this need not prevent us from looking for it, provided, however, that we are constantly aware that religion is used here simultaneously in at least three different senses: religion as a term of inner description within the religion (i.e. as a term by which the religion observed describes itself); religion as a meta-term of observation; and religion as a term of inner description within the religion of the external observer.

1.1.1. The task of arriving at an appropriate terminology is sometimes complicated by the fact that the religion studied may have achieved a degree of self-awareness which enables it to view itself (or another religion) as an object and thus to develop terms for its own description. This development, which is equivalent to an external point of view within an inner point of view, I refer to below as an *objective religious situation.* The Rig Veda, as a collection of hymns devoted to ritual procedures, provides no description of its religion or of any other. Vedic religion (although not Upanishadic religion) first finds objective description in the Upanishads where initiation into knowledge (*ātmabrahmavidyā*) was considered more important than all ritual of the post-Vedic period. Vedic ritualism (*yajña*), formerly conceived as the instrument of maintaining the universe in dharmic order, more important than the object of ritual (the god), not to speak of its subject (the worshipper), was reinterpreted as one variety of religious pursuit among others and thus neutralized or given its place without being rejected or criticized.[3] By contrast, *ātman-brahman* is never described objectively in the Upanishads because it is thought of as broader than any religion and as such outside description. We thus have the specifically Indian phenomenon of one religion finding its description within the framework of another which encompasses it as *a* religion, an object, compared with *the* religion which is indescribable.

1.2. The second procedure of a phenomenological approach consists in reducting the meaning of the concepts, established in the first procedure, to the observable phenomena of religious experience. Here, however, we must recognize that religion cannot be observed as *one* phenomenon and all its elements analysed simultaneously, so that it needs initially to be broken down into the varying phenomena which constitute it. These are considered here not in terms of objects such as rite, symbol and so forth, but rather in terms of complex categories of consciousness postulated at the outset. Three such categories are assumed in our methodology: (a) the structure of religious consciousness, (b) the religious situation, and (c) tradition.

1.3.1. A structure of religious consciousness can be defined as a complex whole, the related elements of which reproduce in their totality a complete model of religious behaviour, i.e. of the religion. Although this concept is introduced as part of the theory of the investigator, a particular structure of consciousness can be empirically identified through the extant material of a concrete religion. So, for instance, the main Upanishadic principle of *ātman-brahman* can be considered as a structure of religious consciousness finding its exposition in certain passages of the early prose Upanishads. From these the following elements in its composition emerge:

(a) the subject and object of religion are not present as two different entities, but as two instances of one and the same entity;

(b) the objective realization of this can be achieved through a special knowledge (*ātmabrahmavidyā*) which figures as a transformation of Vedic ritual (*yajña*) such that knowledge of the ritual is substituted for its performance;

(c) all phenomena of the universe, be they of physical, mental or supernatural character, taken in their atmanic being as bearers of self, are related to *ātman-brahman* through this type of knowledge, for knowledge is the only principle by virtue of which this atmanic being can be realized or, indeed, can be said to exist al all;[4]

(d) a certain type or class of ascetic meditator exists as the human manifestation of both *ātman-brahman* and its relatedness to all phenomena.

1.3.2. Each structure of religious consciousness in a given religion may represent in its turn a facet of what can be called the world outlook of the religion. In the various early Hindu movements and schools *ātman-brahman* figures side by side with other structures, such as *mārga* (path), *bhakti* (devotion), *bhagavān* (lord), and so forth. Some of these were reinterpreted in the context of other structures, although persisting as a self-sufficient source of identification and interpretation. So, for example, *karma*, which remained unchanged in the case of Buddhism and Jainism, was reinterpreted in the Shaiva-Siddhanta in the sense of *pāśa* (linkage between soul and matter) and finally, in the latest developments of the school, was connected with the grace (*aruḷ*) of Shiva. In all these cases, however, *karma* remained the same in respect of the elements constituting it and the mode of their interrelation.

1.3.3. As a structure of religious consciousness, the Hindu concept of god (*deva*) implies a specific kind of differentiation fundamentally different from the concept of God (and from that of pagan gods) in Mosaic religion. Modern indologists come near to it when they view gods in terms of various gradations of beings which occupy a place in the classification of the universe, particular natural and non-natural objects being seen as the manifestation of particular gods. The main elements of this structure can be presented, in summary form, as follows:

(a) A god is, more often than not, identified not as a single being in time and space taken in his uniqueness, but as a class of beings, such as Shiva as all *mūrti* of the Trimurti, or Vishnu as all his *avatāra*, or Krishna (in the Bhagavad Gita) as all Rudras.

(b) Taken at a given time and in a given place (at a point of his time-and-space singularity, so to speak), a god is present as an *iṣṭadevatā* (chosen deity), that is, as a phenomenon in which the idea of the god momentarily present coincides in time and space with that of his devotee and is merged with him in the context of this particular subjective religious situation. As in the case of *ātman-brahman*, the subject and object of worship are not here opposed to one another but seen as two instances or manifestations of the same entity.

(c) All gods (*deva* or *īśvara*)—leaving aside their internal classification into groups such as *rudra*, *aditya*, etc.—constitute a single class of beings which figure in Hindu 'cosmology' as one among others, such as men, animals, ghosts, ancestors, great ascetics and sages, *guru*, etc. (their number varies). Gods are not opposed to any of these classes, including that of men, in a binary way. The rishis were considered like gods, although in human form, and by *tapas* (austerities) they could become more powerful than gods. In the post-Vedic period it was held that a man, by accumulating good *karma*, could be born as a god so that diachronically there was no distinction between them. The categories of god and man also overlap synchronically in the case of the *guru* and the Brahman.

(d) When, however, considered as 'one God', a given god often partakes of the nature of the impersonal and indescribable *ātman-brahman*, a tendency which reflects both the sectarian wish to elevate the *iṣṭadevatā* above the gods of other sects and discern the universe through him and the fact that in Hinduism all primary symbols are universal symbols in that the whole can be attained through apprehension of any of them indifferently. Here two structures of religious consciousness, that of *deva* and that of *ātman-brahman*, overlap.

(e) In some cases the phenomenon of god, taken in his relation to an adept, is both mediated by and manifested in the figure of the teacher of tradition (*guru*).

It is apparent that the Hindu concept of god differs markedly from that of God in Judaeo-Christian tradition, notably in the absence of a notion of the absolute personality of God and of the opposition between God and man, so that categories developed in the latter, such as 'theism', 'polytheism', and sometimes 'god' himself, prove extremely awkward when applied in the Hindu context.

1.4. Now we pass to the category of a religious situation. A religious situation can be understood as an event or fact of any order, nature, or character described or referred to from the point of view of the distinctions established in a structure of religious consciousness.

1.4.1. We can illustrate this category with reference to the principle of self (*ātman*), taken as a structure of religious consciousness, and such well-trodden classical episodes of the Upanishadic repertoire as 'cattle, men and gods' and 'Mithila in flames'. With regard to Upanishadic religion the principle of self can be seen as structuring all other elements of religion and making them into a series of hierarchical configurations. I would even go so far as to assert that *ātman*, taken as a structure of religious consciousness, can be described as possessing the dual capacity of including all religious situations in its religion and of changing all situations into religious ones. In the episode, 'cattle, men and gods', it is stated that cattle are to men what men are to gods. When cattle become aware of what they are, they are thereby lost to men. Likewise, when men become aware of what they are, they are lost to the gods. That is, when one becomes aware of one's self (*ātman*), one is lost to one's master (god, man). But *ātman* is no master, for it is one's self; that is, it is neither a god who is always other than a man nor a man who is always other than his cattle. Thereby the distinction between gods, men and cattle, pertaining to one structure of religious consciousness, is superseded from the standpoint of *ātman*. This simile shows how a religion formally descibed in terms of mastery and subjugation finds its place in the structure of religious consciousness named *ātman* and becomes, therewith, an objective religious situation—objective in the sense that it ceases to be self-sufficient and closed to external observation and evaluation and becomes open to objective treatment by a religion of a higher order, namely the religion of *ātman-brahman*.

1.4.2. The second episode recounts how King Janaka, on learning that his capital Mithila was ablaze, said: 'Mithila is burning, but nothing is burning that is mine'. 'That is mine' here means that which is, or is related to, *ātman*. We have, as it were, two steps of interpretation made objectively from the standpoint of *ātman*. The first establishes the distinction: one thing is an object named Mithila and quite another thing is 'mine', namely *ātman*. The second establishes a positive relation of everything which is not *ātman*, including the city of Mithila, to *ātman*. This occurs by means of and through Janaka himself as the chief mediating agency in this situation. Janaka knows the *ātman*, he knows what is not *ātman* too, and what is intermediary between them in his own knowledge. For the atmanic being of all phenomena, which relates them to *ātman*, exists in the knowledge of this relatedness.[5]

1.5. The category of tradition is particularly important to a phenomenological approach for, in spite of its cultural universality, tradition is usually given to us as a concrete historical fact. It is precisely this temporal character of religious tradition which often leads its investigator to overlook its equally important spatial dimension. The transmission of tradition by a teacher to his pupil can be said to be temporal in that the pupil will in turn become a teacher, but it can also be viewed synchronically as the dissemination of the tradition in space. And, indeed, it is in its latter aspect that tradition is usually encountered by the anthropologist in the field and analysed by him, not only historically, but chiefly in terms of current sectarian organization.

1.5.1. The content of a religious tradition can be termed knowledge. Traditional knowledge can be classified into three types, all three of which are found in all religious traditions although one may be predominant:

(a) Personal knowledge, connected with a given instructor and unique to his personality. Such knowledge is irrepeatable: if manifested in another instructor, it becomes another knowledge. This view of knowledge is typical of Mediterranean religion.

(b) Impersonal knowledge, held to exist even if no one knows it. Only because it exists, can it be given as knowledge by an instructor. Culturally speaking, this knowledge is usually connected with an idea of a sacred text, the existence of which is independent of those to whom it was revealed (*śruti*).

(c) Knowledge as recognition of the fact of belonging to a tradition. This is usually connected with initiation and related to the formal status of teacher and pupil as such, even if they know nothing. For example, in some varieties of Tibetan Tantrism it is enough that one is initiated into one or other Tantra in order to be considered the receptacle of some knowledge; or, again, on being given permission to read a *sūtra*, the initiate is treated as if already in possession of the knowledge which the *sūtra* contains.

1.5.2. The specific characteristic of Indian tradition is its subjective awareness of itself as a continuing religious experience, in which knowledge of its content is secondary to the perpetuation of the tradition itself. Its special knowledge relates not to the content of religion which is continued through the tradition, but to the means, ways and agents of its transmission. These became fixed in particular types of instruction and a particular type of instructor.

1.5.2.1. Among the varieties of religious instruction found in the Upanishads and the Mahabharata as well as in the Puranas there can be identified an absolutely impersonal type of instruction. In this case, the knowledge of tradition is held to exist apart from and irrespective of both the instruction and the instructed. At the same time each actual act of instruction is uniquely individual and personal because the impersonal knowledge produced in the *guru* is seen as his *own* knowledge. The role of the *guru* is crucial for admission into a tradition, even when this admission takes the form of imparting the knowledge or content of the tradition through texts (written, oral or figurative), for recourse to the texts themselves does not in itself constitute knowledge (in the same way as a '*mantra*' is not a *mantra* unless bestowed by the *guru*). One becomes a pupil in order to obtain connection with knowledge through the instructor and in some cases knowledge is no more than recognition of the very fact of being initiated into a tradition (he who has taken initiation has the knowledge by definition, irrespective of whether he is aware of it). It follows that the phenomenon of the text is to be regarded as secondary to or derivative from tradition and not the other way round.[6]

1.5.2.2. To define the specifically Indian type of instructor it is necessary to identify two cases: an instructor in the context of a tradition and an instructor in the context of a religious situation. In the first case the act of instruction is conceived by both the instructor (*guru*) and the adept as formally related to a certain succession of instructors. The existence of pupils is of no significance here. A *guru* is not a person who has pupils, but one who has himself had a *guru* in a particular line of sucession and has been so named by him. Here tradition assumes its phenomenal meaning because the temporal aspect of instruction prevails over the transmission of instruction in space. In the context of a religious situation, on the other hand, an instructor is a person who knows the meaning of a given situation and the instruction is given to all comers irrespective of their belonging to a particular tradition.[7] What matters here is the knowledge of the master, which is imparted outside the situation of initiation, so that dissemination in space prevails over transmission in time. In certain circumstances, however, such knowledge may be incorporated into a tradition as when the sayings of the master, given in the context of a religious situation, later become part of tradition.

1.5.3. The content of religious tradition is often largely cultural, in which case religion becomes a shell through which cultural phenomena are carried through time and its function is mainly conservative.[8] This is true of early and mediaeval Japan, mediaeval Rabbinic tradition and Muslim tradition. In relation to Indian tradition, on the other hand, it may be useful to introduce the notion of a 'specifically religious tradition', often in hidden or open opposition to culture, which contains within itself the means or possibility, not only to preserve its culture, but also to separate from it and pursue its own development independently. Here religious postulates do not play an important cultural role and the tradition provides its own dynamism. In the first millenium B.C., for example, all knowledge was held to be the privilege of Brahmans. In the Upanishads there was a reinterpretation of the idea of brahmanhood as 'having the knowledge' which was not necessarily possessed by Brahmans (a change which coincided with the change from the Brahman as teacher to the teacher as teacher irrespective of being a Brahman). They gave tradition another meaning by reinterpreting it. In this case one can say that because the content changed, the tradition was different. But if one allows for the internal dynamism of tradition, it is possible to conclude that the change was within the same tradition and, indeed, characteristic both of its self-awareness and of its development. Religious tradition in India was not meant to perpetuate anything but itself and its cultural functions seem to have been very limited, if indeed they existed at all.

2. *Commentary on the Papers*

2.1. *Religious Identification in some of its Aspects.*

2.1.0. Religious identification is the procedure whereby a person is identified, by himself or by a second person, as included within a particular religion. This procedure can be realized by means of or as manifested in any of the three methodological categories proposed above, namely, structure of religious consciousness, religious situation, and tradition. Identification through a structure of religious consciousness alone is not, however, possible for an external observer, because it is an inner state which cannot be directly observed. He has therefore either to resort to a tradition, to which a person or group of persons formally belong, or to pass to inner identification. In the first case a person is identified—or identifies himself—as, say, a Vaishnava, not because he believes that Narayana whom he worships is the chief manifestation of Vishnu, but by virtue of the fact that he or his family belong to a particular Vaishnava tradition, irrespective of the structures of consciousness which this implies. The second case is based exclusively on criteria and postulates brought about within the religion itself, so that the observer identifies a person through his own self-identification and not through the external criteria of the observer, which may or may not be the same. For example, on the basis of early Tamil texts the ethnographer may say that the *bhakta* behaved like madmen. Sundarar also said: 'I am a madman because Shiva called me so.' Here inner and external identification coincide (although the ethnographer's criteria of madness are likely to be different from Shiva's). But this is not always the case. Certain shamanistic behaviour may be seen by the ethnographer, using his criteria of madness, as hysterical or disordered, but by the shaman himself they are seen as trance and never as madness. Anthropological writing in general is weak in combining inner with external identification, and sometimes even in distinguishing the two.

2.1.0.1. The problem of inner identification is of exceptional methodological importance in any phenomenological study of religion. In using this notion we mean, on the one hand, that certain basic distinctions of a specifically religious character have already been made. And, on the other, that these distinctions can be presented as related to at least two aspects of the religion investigated—the objective aspect, when the object of cult is identified, and the subjective aspect, when the subject of cult is identified. These two aspects imply a third, consisting of the link or active connection (*religio*) between the two. When this identification is termed 'inner', it means that this twofold distinction (at the very least, for in most cases religious distinctions cannot be reduced to this opposition) was established within the religion itself and does not necessarily follow from a chosen methodology of investigation. The distinction between the subject and object of cult, often found in the form worshipper worshipped, can be taken as the minimum criterion for the existence of a religious situation.

2.1.0.2. Thus, for example, we may assert, though without much conviction, that in Vedic religion it is the 'sacrificer' who can be identified as the subject and the 'god', to whom this sacrifice is directed, as the object.[9] In the religion of the Upanishads it would be the 'knower of *ātman-brahman*' figuring as the subject and *ātman-brahman* itself as the object. For nowhere in the prose Upanishads does one find *ātman* in the sense of a subject, functioning as if it were a worshipper, or least of all, a sacrificer.[10] It is interesting to note, in connection with the problem of inner identification, that the fundamental formula of the Upanishads—'Thou art that'—neither reflects the primary distinction between an individual self and the self of the universe, nor establishes the identification of a subject of religion with its object because both 'thou' and 'that' figure here in a purely objective sense ('thou' being used to refer not to the individual but to the self of which he is the bearer). In other words, they belong to a wholly objective structure of religious consciousness.

2.1.0.3. This last structure was translated in the Bhagavad Gita (and later in Shankara's commentary thereon) into the whole system of the object of religion, although this was not followed by all subsequent sections, schools and branches of Hinduism. So, for instance, in the context of the Shaiva-Siddhanta, the threefold distinction between *paśu* (cattle in the sense of selves), *pāśa* (fetters) and *pati* (herdsman, master) definitely presupposes the identification of the first as the subject and of the last as the object of the religion of Shaivism. It seems to be even more complicated in Buddhism where inner identification followed a quite different pattern and, in the final analysis, led almost to the entire dismissal of the duality subject/object in religion and to the formation of an exceedingly complicated system of object. It is within this system that some transitional or intermediary structures of consciousness figure now as subjective, now as objective ones, given that the latter always prevail.

Comments on Southwold's paper

2.1.1. The notion of a religious situation can be used in our attempt not only to identify anything concretely observed as a religion, but also to identify a religion in terms of its own authenticity. This may well be a dangerous methodological trap for the anthropologist, because to define a religion as 'true' or 'untrue', 'authentic' or 'spurious', 'pure' or 'corrupt' and, perhaps most of all, 'archaic' or 'modernistic' invariably implies not only hierarchical but also ethical connotations. This applies also to what Leach (1969) calls 'practical religion', for, alas, our criteria of 'practicality' are invariably theoretical. And indeed, when Southwold was attempting to classify contemporary Buddhism in Sri Lanka and his middle-class friends urged him to resort to texts with which he had been familiar long before he thought of studying Buddhism as an anthropologist, they were entirely right in doing so, for their only criterion was 'the text'. That is, not a real text of, say, the Pali Canon, but 'the text' understood as the point of departure for any actual, potential, or ideal religious identification in all Buddhist contexts. Southwold's argument that 'both village Buddhism and middle-class Buddhist modernism are forms of ... practical religion ... and must be distinguished from what Leach would call philosophical Buddhism ... that is, what Western scholars have made of Buddhism', seems to be a case of sheer anthropological overconfidence. For what both Southwold and Leach call 'philosophical Buddhism' is, in fact, a *normal* (in the Buddhist sense) apprehension and interpretation of the classical apprehension and interpretation of Buddhist texts by Buddhaghosa's School and the Theravadin scholarly tradition in general. Given, of course, that Buddhaghosa's School included a vast amount of contemporary religious material which was reinterpreted, not philosophically, but in a manner which *now* seems to be philosophical to Leach and Southwold from the point of view of modern philosophical apperception. What Southwold describes as his own and other anthropologists' foreknowledge of Buddhism, he fails to recognize as a phenomenon lying in the background of all 'practical Buddhism'. To see the matter in this way, he would have to understand this phenomenon as the potentiality of interpretation of a structure of religious consciousness empirically given in the actuality of a religious situation.[11] One cannot conceive of a real distinction between 'philosophical' and 'practical' kinds of Buddhism, unless it has been made in Buddhism itself. The simplest phenomenological analysis shows that if in the context of Buddhadhamma (the teaching of Buddha, in the sense of the classical commentaries on the Pali Canon) this distinction was hard to make, it has become much harder in the context of any 'living' Buddhism in Sinhalese society. Because even the most conservative Bhikkhu-scholars have assumed the Western mode of apperception of philosophy in general, losing sight of the fact that, strictly speaking, there has been no *darśana* in the Theravadin tradition. It cannot be otherwise, for *darśana*, if taken in the classical Hindu sense (as, for example, one of the six *darśana* or one of their derivations), means the final fixation of the content in a philosophical tradition and also implies a considerable degree of objectification, for it is meant to be used outside a tradition as well as within it. While in Buddhism, by virtue of being a universal religion by definition, such a distinction is completely irrelevant and superfluous.

2.1.2. Now we come to what is probably the most interesting problem in Southwold's paper. In what way can one identify a religion (in this case Sinhalese village Buddhism) through its inner aim? Can it be done, as Southwold suggests in referring to Ling, by the identification of Nirvana with the 'sacred'? What is particularly interesting about this problem is that to be solved it requires a very concrete definition of a given religious situation in Buddhism. When Southwold says that 'Nirvana ... is rarely heard outside of distinctively religious contexts', it is not enough simply to say this, or even to refer to all the contexts. For there are in Buddhism ('practical' as well as 'theoretical') at least three levels of religious situation respecting the use and meaning of this term. First, there is the level on which Nirvana figures as the most general term of religious discourse and the most abstract object in a religious situation. It is usually referred to by the people interviewed as a state not immediately connected with their actual religious experience or with their present religious aspirations and aims. Second, there is the level on which Nirvana is said to be the actual aim of a novice or Bhikkhu, or an immediate object of their religious experience. On this level Nirvana is often mentioned by the Buddha with reference to one or other of his disciples as ensuing from or identified with cessation of suffering.[12] The third level of Nirvana is that which is referred to by the Buddha as the highest objectivity of consciousness (*asaṅkhata dhamma*) and is discussed in an absolutely impersonal way: that is, without any reference either to suffering or to those who are to get rid of it.[13]

2.1.3. It is in the last case only that we can say that Nirvana is the object (or rather one object) in the religious situation formed by the two poles of the Buddha, as subject, and Nirvana, as object. In the second case Nirvana is given as a structure of consciousness through which—or more exactly, through the symbolism of which—one's situation is identified as 'Buddhist'. In the first case we deal with a series of situations where Nirvana figures almost exclusively in discursive contexts and where the actual object of religious experiencing is the Buddha with his symbols and substitutes. One cannot reduce the first level of Nirvana to the third level as one cannot reduce a term to a syntagmatically complex construction. The interpretations of the Four Noble Truths made by Smart and Ling (quoted by Southwold) entirely miss the point, for all levels are confused. The Four Noble Truths cannot be viewed either as proto-science or as proto-medicine because, as such, they cannot be viewed at all on the pragmatic level (which corresponds approximately to the first level). When they can be so viewed, one has to shift to the second level, where they form an extremely complex structure of consciousness totally irreducible to any pragmatic situation. Moreover, it is clearly shown by Southwold that the very notion *āgama* is equivalent to the notion 'religion' in the sense in which the notion *lokottara* (supramandane) is opposed to that of *laukika* (mundane), though by no means in the sense in which this opposition is interpreted by Gombrich (as quoted by Southwold) or by Southwold himself. The point is that the mundane in Buddhism covers practically all pragmatic situations including all pragmatic religious situations.[14] The supramundane cannot be conceived as the 'sacred' and opposed to the 'profane', for it includes several structures of religious consciousness not common to all Buddhist situations, that is, to situations as contexts of religious discourse. I cannot help suspecting that there is no sacred as opposed to profane in Buddhism at all. What we have instead is a series of gradations of movement from less sacred to more sacred, some of which coincide in their direction, some overlap one another, and others diverge from the very start. This multi-directedness of hierarchies is characteristic of almost all Indian religions.[15]

2.2. *Asceticism and renunciation.*

2.2.0. In the following section I shall try to show that the notion of asceticism is used as a meta-term to which correspond several quite different phenomena of Indian religion or, to formulate it in a purely phenomenological way, we can say that what we call asceticism is present in Indian religion as a very complex structure of consciousness covering several different phenomena which figure as its different dimensions or parameters. It does not, of course, follow that the different Indian terms denoting asceticism must directly correspond to those different dimensions, though some of them undoubtedly reflect certain basic distinctions within Indian asceticism understood as a separate structure of religious consciousness. In considering Indian asceticism from this point of view, it appears that the character of a system of asceticism is largely determined by the character of the things and facts which are to be got rid of, renounced, or otherwise dismissed (either in a negative or a neutral way) by those practising this kind of asceticism.

2.2.0.1. The first phenomenon to be considered here is *tapas*, which can be rendered as the heat or energy resulting from asceticism. In the context of the late Vedic and epic literature it meant, first of all, self-exertion, that is, an unusual display of one's inner energy by means of which another supernatural energy was accumulated. Abstinence from social activity and sexual relations, fasting, self-imposed silence, etc. were regarded as negative means by which a natural energy was reworked or transformed into the undifferentiated supernatural energy of *tapas*. We may also conjecture that abstaining from socio-cultural activity (including sacrificial actions) was not marked or singled out from other purely individual forms of abstinence (sex, diet, dress, etc.) so that *tapas* cannot be regarded as the phenomenon of renunciation of the outer world. At the same time, the character of the individual abstention of a *tapasvin* clearly shows the absence of purposeful self-mortification. On the contrary, the process and aims of *tapas* can be seen as the positive heightening of the life-potentiality of the *tapasvin*. The problem of the reality (or unreality) of the world or of the things from which the *tapasvin* abstained was largely irrelevant in this kind of asceticism.

2.2.0.2. If we pass to Jaina asceticism, we can see its self-mortifying character as a direct derivation of the Jainist picture of the world. The material world, which is to be got rid of both on its macrocosmic and microcosmic (that is, its bodily and mental) levels, is absolutely real. It is as real as the living soul (*jīva*) which strives by means of self-mortification to get rid of this matter. Slightly simplifying the problem, we can say that the uncompromising negative attitude of the *dīgambara* Jaina ascetic to his body is determined far more by the absolute reality of his body (fixed as a fact of consciousness) than by the final aim of ascetic self-mortification, namely, the state of liberated living soul (*jīvan mukta*).[16]

2.2.0.3. In the case of so-called classical Brahmanism, in which asceticism figures, at least ideally, in the framework of *varṇāśrama-dharma*, the ascetic (*saṃnyāsin*) does not renounce the whole system of socio-cultural relations, but only three sections of this quadruple framework. Strictly speaking, he renounces only the stage of life (*āśrama*) and socio-cultural status (*varṇa*) from which he passes on to the stage and status of complete asceticism (*saṃnyāsa*), and nothing more. Looking at the matter from the angle of sheer brahmanical dogmatism, one can argue that he renounces nothing, for the rest of the Hindu universe remains as and what it had been before he became a *saṃnyāsin*, an act which was not meant to annul it or even to change it. To sum this up, we can say that from the purely objective standpoint (i.e. not belonging to the context of the *varṇāśramadharma*), the process of brahmanical ascetic renunciation remained integrated in the whole of the dharmic universe and was not opposed to it.

2.2.0.4. In early historical Buddhism, asceticism—if considered in connection with the basic structure of religious consciousness underlying it—appears to be an exceedingly complex phenomenon in some ways opposed to brahmanical asceticism. First of all, the Buddhist ascetic excludes himself, both practically and theoretically (i.e. in his self-awareness) from the cultural universe by the mere fact of forsaking it. Secondly, although forsaken, the material universe, as well as his own material body, remains relatively real. The townsfolk, deities, and horses pictured in the low-and-high reliefs of Buddhist stupas clearly show the relative reality of the world left behind. And, in an analogous way, the body of an ascetic, even of those who became *arhat*, remained naturally and really functioning, though their mentalities trained by *yoga* and *dhyāna* seem to have been long ago divorced from all bodily function.

2.2.0.5. Mahayana asceticism presents a quite different picture. The asceticism itself changes into a purely Bodhisattvic practice of physical self-renunciation (*ātma-parityāga*) for the sake of some other living beings (*sattva*). But the main thing in this entirely new type of asceticism is that, as a structure of religious consciousness, it implies that neither the world of things forsaken by a Bodhisattva, nor those beings for whose sake he gives up his life, nor even his life itself, are regarded as real. The whole picture of the Bodhisattvic universe seems to be so illusory, mind-made (*manomaya*) that the very act of asceticism loses its actuality; and that is probably why it is usually referred to in the *sūtra* as belonging either to the past or to the future.

Comments on Parry's paper

2.2.1.0. A new aspect of the ascetic structure of consciousness is revealed in Parry's description of the Aghoris. The Aghoris differ from the majority of other ascetic groups and movements in their attitude to death. Returning to what has already been said in 2.2.0 about the character of the world which is to be renounced or got rid of, we can say that in the case of the Aghoris it is mainly death itself with its essentials and accessories which is the focus of their religious consciousness, and at the same time constitutes the basis of all their religious situations. Death, one may surmise, is what their universe is to be reduced to, not in order that the universe be transformed, but that it disappear with the totality of its elements and dimensions (such as time, space, materiality, etc.).

2.2.1.1. Hence two types of death are implicitly postulated as two distinctly different elements of the central structure of religious consciousness: (1) the death of 'other people' which the Aghori ascetics attend and with which they are specifically concerned; and (2) death as the chief factor of their own final release from the phenomenal world of death and transformation. The ritual of cremation makes manifest both these meanings of death. To an Aghori ascetic (as well as to children, smallpox victims, lepers, and some other categories of people) this ritual is irrelevant because it implies the natural way of things in the cosmos that is, transformation as repetition and return symbolized by 'birth' (the corpse as an embryo) or 'marriage' (the corpse in the pose of copulation). However, the Eliadean scheme of *retour éternel* does not apply here, for the universe of the Aghoris, as seen in Parry's description, is not based upon an opposition sacred/profane or pure/impure or natural/unnatural, or any other binary construction of consciousness. Theirs is a triple world, not dual.

2.2.1.2. Their main structure of religious consciousness can be reduced to a basic distinction between three components of the universe: (a) that which dies naturally (by way of *kālamaraṇa*, or 'timely death') and is thereby natural; (b) that which dies unnaturally (by way of *akālamaraṇa*, or 'untimely death') and is thereby unnatural; and (c) that which has always been, as it were, already dead, which is within death, and not 'before' or 'after', being thereby supernatural. This structure is obviously a synchronic one because at any given moment the Aghori's universe reproduces itself in this triple way.

This structure easily transforms itself into another quasi-temporal structure of consciousness where the very process of death assumes its triple meaning: (1) the transformation of the soul into a disembodied ghost (*preta*); (2) the transformation of the soul into an incorporated ancestor (*pitṛ*) through its previous transformation into a ghost; (3) the suspended *status quo* of death, which neither presupposes nor entails any further transformation whatsoever and which is not to be changed by any ritual or other religious action *external* to this state (such as a ritual intended to transform a disembodied ghost into an incorporated ancestor). So, speaking of the Aghoris in terms of renunciation as such (see 2.2.0 above), we can say that it is the normal death, or death as transformation, that the Aghoris renounce, and not the normal life.

The last point, however, poses a difficult problem for, as we have already seen, death itself is not an elementary fact or event, but an entire system of meaning: a, b, c, 1, 2, 3. These meanings not only constitute two structures of religious consciousness—a etc. and 1 etc.—but they also serve as basic elements in some other structures which I take up now.

2.2.1.3. The whole cult of ancestors (*pitṛ*) can be seen as a particular religious situation included in the far more general Aghori religious situation, analogous to the way in which a, b and 1, 2 can be regarded as particular and subordinated instances of c and 3 in 2.2.1.2. This cult contains two essential ritualistic phases: the transformation proper of the soul of a deceased and the regeneration (or reconstitution) of a deceased, symbolized by fire and rice balls (*piṇḍa*) respectively. The third phase, connected specifically with Aghoris, is symbolized by the skull.

2.2.1.3.1. Here we are faced with what Parry qualifies as 'a rather different link between death and regeneration', which requires a more detailed explanation. Parry writes: 'If the chief mourner's wife is barren, then in order to conceive a son, she should consume the *piṇḍa* used in the ritual to represent his father's father. Though the notion is clearly inconsistent with the theory of reincarnation postulated by the doctrine of *karma*, the idea is that the great-grandfather comes back as his own great-grandson...' The second statement in this quotation shows that Parry considers reincarnation and *karma* as two aspects of one and the same principle of transformation of self or soul in Hinduism. With this we cannot agree. What is more, they do not even belong to or constitute the same structure of religious consciousness for, as a general principle, reincarnation consists in identifying one person with another on the basis of one and the same personal principle (soul, self, etc.), provided that they are separated from one another by no more than one death or such-like transformation. This identification, if regarded temporally (which is by no means always the case), is made in both projective, as in the example above, and retrospective ways. By retrospective we mean in the sense that the chief mourner's son will be retrospectively identified after his birth as his great-grandfather, whereas the principle of *karma* consists in identifying one action (fact, event, circumstance, word, thought, etc.) with another on the basis of a certain force which reproduces one action as the effect of another action understood as its cause, provided that they are separated from one another by at least one death (although theoretically the number of deaths or suchlike transformations may be infinite or indefinite). Furthermore, in the case of *karma*, the identification is usually made in a retrospective way, that is, by establishing the karmic link as a *fait accompli* rather than in the form of a prediction. Therefore, the principle of heredity which dominates the cult of ancestors in India, as elsewhere, can be considered, theoretically at least, as a particular case of concretization of the theory of reincarnation. That is, the chief mourner's grandfather may be reborn as the mourner's son, and his own great-grandson, provided, of course, that at the time of begetting he was in the state between (*antarābhava*) two rebirths (*punarjanma*). This theory contains no limitations in respect of rituals prompting or preventing one from being reborn in one way or the other (as *piṇḍa-dān* in this case). In the case of *karma*, however, such limitations are quite definitely laid down so that, in principle at least, no ritual or other external action can influence its course. This, however, does not prevent one being reborn as one's great-grandson as a result of one's own *karma* though quite independently of the effect achieved by any ritual performed by a person *other* than oneself.

2.2.1.3.2. In our case, the rebirth induced by a ritual connected with *piṇḍa* is not inconsistent with either reincarnation or *karma*, though it is not inconsistent with them in two different ways. In the context of Hinduism this ritual, in common with almost all rituals directly or indirectly associated with death, can find its interpretation in the theory of reincarnation. Because, apart from being a religious phenomenon (i.e. manifesting in an abstract way a certain structure of religious consciousness), it bears an explanatory function with respect to the whole class of religious situations. That is, if looked at from within, the ritual in question does not need any explanation other than that already provided by the very pragmatism of the religious situation itself—in this case, as determined by the object of begetting a son. It is the theory of reincarnation —and not the ritual—which established a sort of reverse correlation between itself and this ritual. (And, indeed, in many other Indo-European cults of ancestors there was no idea of reincarnation.[17]) The doctrine of *karma*, on the other hand, operates with reincarnation as an already postulated *datum*, although it does not follow that reincarnation is postulated by *karma* or is implicitly included in it. Reincarnation seems to have existed in Indian religion (not only in Hinduism) in a self-sufficient manner and there are some reasons for supposing that its postulation occurred before and/or outside any structure of religious consciousness which included *karma* (or even *ātman* or *jīva* for that matter). In concrete Hindu contexts, however, where both reincarnation and *karma* are present, the very fact of reincarnation can be interpreted karmically, whereas a fact of karmic character does not entail any further interpretation. If considered in its possible relation to the *karma* of the chief mourner's grandfather before his reincarnation, the whole religious situation with *piṇḍa-dān* may not be attributed to his *karma:* such an attribution is possible only if there exists a much broader religious situation which includes *karma* as an essential structure of religious consciousness.[18]

Thus, when observed by an outside onlooker, the cult of ancestors, reincarnation, and *karma* can be regarded as three separate postulates which now coexist, now overlap, now neutralize, but never contradict or deny, each other. This holds true unless we leave the ground of religion and pass into the realm of religious philosophy (*darśana*).

2.2.1.4. The 'striking similarity of the regime of mourning to the code of the ascetic', described by Parry, seems to us to be a far more complex phenomenon than appears on the surface. The chief mourner's temporary abstinence, the optional abstinence of pilgrim-mourners, and the ascetic regime of the Aghoris can indeed be seen as three variants of a certain (though still highly hypothetical) invariant of 'death-asceticism'. This is also complemented by the symbolism of *tapas* figuring as the positive gain and objective in all three ascetic situations. What, however, can be discerned within this variant is again the death transformation which, in the case of the

Aghoris, is their *constant* regime and not an act (as in the second case) or a series of acts (as in the first). Unlike the other two cases of abstinence, their renunciation has an aim which lies beyond the sphere of transformation and the transformable and, therewith, beyond reincarnation and *karma.* This aim can be achieved not by abstinence peculiar to mourning and similar rituals, but by a certain type of positive asceticism which complements the negative asceticism of abstinence and constitutes the core of practically all the essential religious situations of the Aghoris. This type of positive asceticism is manifested in eating the flesh of those who died an unnatural death.

It is far too simple to put this practice under the rubric of Eleadean 'reverse ritualism', or to make of it an example of a ritualistic anti-Hinduism. For the very meaning of reversal, as well as of the oft-noted 'all the sameness', leaves uninvestigated the phenomenon of *siddhi* (supernatural attainment) as such, quite apart from its opposition to 'normal' Hindu ritualism.[19] Eating the flesh of corpses can be seen as a religious situation wherein three different aims are pursued:

First, an external aim: those who died an untimely death are restored by the Aghoris to their normality or 'naturality' (i.e. from an untimely death to a timely death, from a disembodied ghost to an incorporated ancestor, or from b to a and from 1 to 2 in 2.2.1.2).

Second, an internal aim: the Aghoris themselves remain in the state of 'suspended death' (in the sense of 3 in 2.2.1.2).

Third, an infinite aim: by means of the *siddhi* accumulated through this 'eating', the Aghoris escape immediately from their supernatural death into the realm of timelessness.

We can surmise that, as in the case of the 'fifth M' of ritual sexual intercourse (*maithuna*), this 'eating' possesses a certain extra-ritualistic property which, being itself on the verge of ritualism, carries an experienced Aghori out of the sphere of 'natural' religion into that of supernatural being. This resembles closely the heroic practice (*vīra-sādhanā*) in Shaiva Tantricism and it is also reminiscent of far stranger methods of 'material nirvanization' traceable in the corpus of legends connected with the eighty-four Buddhist *siddha* (see Chattopadhyaya 1978:29). The problem is of considerable theoretical importance. It seems that an Aghori *siddha* by eating and digesting dead flesh transforms, as it were, its matter into an attentuated form which can be transferred to or reincarnated in another existence, whereas some of the Buddhist *siddha* ate fishes and through gullet, alimentary canal, and anus sent them straight away to Nirvana. The difference between these two cases is clear. In the Aghori case, the infinite is for the Aghori himself and the finite for his deceased client; while in the Buddhist case, a *siddha* is an infinite (nirvanic) being *par excellence* 'materializing' Nirvana for others.

2.2.1.5. This leads us to another interesting question: can we infer from the flesh-eating of the Aghoris that, underlying this practice, there exists a structure of religious consciousness which implies that matter (flesh) can transmit some traces, signs, or energies of non-matter (self, person, soul, etc.)? In spite of reservations concerning the relation of matter to non-matter in Indian religion,[20] we can say that human flesh is regarded by the Aghoris as the chief agency of transmission of supernatural energies not only in time, but in space. As Cantlie (personal communication) writes: 'If a man repeats innumerable *japa* of a particular *mantra*, the *mantra*, it is believed, becomes engraved on his bones.' This finds its direct analogy in the early Buddhist cult of relics, where the elements of the body (*śarīra-dhatu*) were regarded as transmitting the elements of Nirvana (*nirvaṇa-dhatu*) or even as identical with the latter (see, for example, Bailey 1980:23–8). In both cases we have, approximately speaking, the same structure of religious consciousness in which the direct opposition of matter/non-matter is absent. This, we suggest, can be seen as the structure essential to the cult of relics as distinct from the cult of ancestors.

Comments on Bradford's paper

2.2.2.0. We pass now to quite different material which reveals the positive aspect of Hindu renunciation and, what is more, the aspect where the 'eternalist' scheme of renunciation reveals its eternal duality. The brilliant analysis of this phenomenon by Bradford shows that the Lingayats not only preserved the ancient scheme in the context of late classical Hinduism but also redeveloped some of its most archaic features found in early historical Buddhism and late Vedic Brahmanism.

2.2.2.1. This pristine duality, which is present in practically every variety of asceticism, seems to derive from the fact that it is more a structure of religious consciousness than a type of tradition or pattern of religious situation. The well-trodden opposition sacred/profane (or even less sacred/more sacred) does not apply here, for what we are dealing with in this material is a certain initial distinction between two functions of the divine (rather than the sacred): reproduction and transformation. An essential difference between Pattadevaru and Virakta kinds of Lingayat *jaṅgama* is based on a primary difference between continuation and change in the very process of religion. In the former case the stress is laid on the diachronic aspect. Thus, speaking metaphorically, for a born *jaṅgama* his *guru* is like a father because his father is also a *guru*, whereas the latter manifests itself in a synchronic, or even achronic, aspect. For an initiated *jaṅgama* his *guru* can only be conceived as a father in a symbolic way as, for instance, the wielder of magical knowledge or power in a moment of experience.

2.2.2.2. The dual character of renunciation is complemented by the dual character of space. The distinction between temporal sequence (e.g. life-cycle)/moment of strength or power is complemented by the basic opposition inside/outside. In terms of the religious situation it is the dual character of space in Lingayat religion which is emphasized by Bradford. He classifies the whole *jaṅgama* situation into outside and inside sections of religious topography (comprising also their respective cult objects or, as he puts it, 'both humans and deities'). This division suggests that we are dealing with a kind of duality of open/closed or infinite/finite types of universe. Another interesting feature of this case is that the burial ground definitely constitutes the third section of space—today apparently intermediary or transitional, but in the past functioning as the second part of the tripartite universe. The very distribution of godheads and their functions between outside and inside of the Lingayat universe hints at this primarily triple structure of the 'space of religion'.[21]*

*_Note by N. J. Bradford:_ Piatigorsky writes that 'the burial ground definitely constitutes the third section of space'. If there is a 'third section of space'—and I have *not* argued for this in my paper—then it would not, on the evidence I have, be constituted simply by the burial grounds

A different, and in my view more accurate representation of the ritual organization of space involved here, would be that which is reflected in my Figure 3: what we find is the reformulation and perhaps intensification of structured opposites, not a tripartite scheme incorporating a transitional category. This thesis, for which I claim no originality, may have a more general application in the analysis of South Indian ritual (see my recent report to the SSRC entitled 'Calendrical ritual and village guardian deities in Karnataka, South India'). In short, the Lingayat system of classification appears to be dualistic, not tripartite.

2.3. *Tradition*

Comments on Fuller's paper

2.3.1.0. When Fuller states that there is a wider discrepancy between text and ritual than between different texts, this, in our opinion, amounts to the restatement that no ritual can be entirely theological and, indeed, speaking historically, the Shaiva Agamic tradition in Tamil Nadu seems to be one of the earliest examples of theology proper in the context of classical Hinduism. (One could, of course, argue that classical Hinduism ends where theology begins, and one would be right in doing so.[22]) The most interesting point here is the complex and intricate method by which the tradition of Shaiva Agamas establishes a correlation between the texts (*āgama* and the whole body of commentaries and treatises), rituals, and ideas (aims, values and meanings) in the context of Shaivite temple worship.[23] The general scheme is simple. The rituals (*dīkṣa*) are meant explicitly to bring about an 'actual transformation [of an adept] into Shiva . . . because only Shiva can worship Shiva'. This 'worshipping' constitutes an ideal religious situation which cannot be reduced to or included in the initiatory complex of *dīkṣa* rituals. Sticking to our terminology, we can say that the latter remains, as it were, with the tradition as its mechanism of self-perpetuation, while the former finds itself within a state of religious consciousness (such as the transformation into Shiva) not deducible from the most detailed description of *dīkṣa*. Certain specifically temple rituals, the reduction or absence of which is not noted by the author, clearly show this tendency to isolate from each other various elements of the cult, a feature characteristic of Agamic Shaivism. It can be suggested that it is this relative automatization of texts, within one and the same tradition, that is responsible for reduction in rituals. This, however, requires a further explanation of the Agamic tradition.

2.3.1.1 Taken as a whole, the Agamic tradition, that is the tradition based on the twenty-eight *śaivāgama*, serves as a classical example of the multi-functional role of primary texts in Hinduism. Two points are relevant here. First, the Agamas contain some important ideas concerning the ultimate truth of transformation, but they do not contain anything concerning either the methodology of religious knowledge or the concrete symbology of rituals. Therefore, in this function, they are like the *sūtra* of the six systems of classical Hindu philosophy. Second, two other sorts of texts derived from this agamic core: (a) the texts explaining the general meaning of agamic concepts and categories (quite comparable with, if not equivalent to, the six classical Hindu *darśana*); and (b) the commentaries on the texts containing a general interpretation of rituals in the sense of the above-mentioned transformation and/or some concrete instruction concerning basic rituals. But all this does not mean that these texts constructed the basic rituals or projected them into the future of the tradition. There was never a time when they agreed in all particulars with the corresponding rituals, having always been related to these rituals in the actual religious situations only. Strictly speaking, this relation of the context of texts to ritual in Hinduism is that of relative agreement and not of physical coincidence, for the idea of instruction (as the main content of tradition) has been realized also in the sense of extra-textual instruction, instruction going outside of or side by side with textual instruction.[24]

Comments on Cantlie's paper

2.3.2.0. Our own picture of an observed tradition is dependent on the relation of the methodology of investigation to the mechanisms by means of which tradition perpetuates itself in time and identifies itself in achronic religious situations. As the article by Cantlie shows, even such an external historical notion as 'reform movement' can be used as an important term in the inner analysis of a tradition. This raises the question: why is the Assamese Vaishnavism founded by Shankaradeva (and based on the *Bhagavata Purāṇa*) a 'reformed' tradition, while the non-dualistic religious teaching deriving from the great Vedantist Shankara is not?

The answer seems to be obvious: because the first, as an *avatāra* of Vishnu, established direct contact between his followers and the object of the cult (Vishnu) through himself (and the descendency of successive *guru*), while the latter, formally at least, continued the tradition of the Brahma-sutras, Bhagavad Gita and Upanishads. In the first case we have the appearance of a new type of religious situation, and the perpetuation of this type by means of more or less institutionalized and stationary *guru*ship and initiatory rites, given that the role of the sacred texts remains comparatively insignificant. Whereas in the second case, it is the texts themselves, together with the method of their understanding, realization and reinterpretation, that constitute the main content of traditional instruction. (This in spite of the fact that in the first case, unlike the second, the very reading and understanding of texts remained obviously unreformed.)

2.3.2.1. As against this, it must be noted that the term 'reform' remains methodologically vague unless historically concretized. The founder Shankaradeva did not feel himself to be a reformer, while his followers of the thirties felt themselves to be reforming, not only the current version of *his* ideas and practices, but those of Hinduism as a whole. In the second case one can say that the anthropologist's external observation coincides with the subjective self-awareness of the believer, whereas in the first case the application of the term 'reform' encounters the fact that Shankaradeva regarded himself as a 'traditionalist'. Similarly, although Gandhi never considered himself as a reformer subjectively, he can objectively (and from an external point of view) be put under this rubric. The Lingayata movement, to take another case, regarded itself as reformist from the beginning, but the anthropologist today is quite within his rights when he treats it as a branch of Shaivite tradition. It seems that we possess here only some relative criteria of 'reformism' which require correction in the context of concrete historical situations. Both the idea of 'path' and the attitude to sacred texts can be taken as no more than partial indications of whether a particular movement is reformist or traditional in character. Similarly the identification of the founder as an *avatāra* cannot be assumed to be decisive, for it assumes different meanings in different situations. What then, one may ask, is reformed in this Assamese movement? To answer this question we must return to the two main tendencies underlying almost all bhaktic movements at the time of their origin or at the initial stages of their development.

2.3.2.2. The first and earlier tendency can be formulated in the following way. The whole of Hinduism, if understood as a sum of religious situations, tends to preserve a certain proportion or balance between brahmanhood and the body of ascetics and, thereby, between brahmanical (i.e. in a general sense, not necessarily performed by Brahmans) and non-brahmanical varieties of practical religious experiences. In this sense the 'observance of thirty days after death' is as brahmanical as that of 'eleven days', for the criterion of purity is brahmanical as like as not. When this proportion is threatened or absent, we have the appearance of 'quasi-brahmans' or even 'quasi-ascetics' (as is the context of Vaishnava movements of the eighteenth and nineteenth centuries).[25] The fact is, however, that they have never been directly opposed to one another. The whole situation suggests that the very system of the four *varṇa* has functioned to prevent such an opposition. In Hindu Tantrism this imbalance has been avoided by the establishment of a series of specifically tantrist rituals within religious situations, totally neutral or indifferent to the opposition Brahmans/ascetics.[26] In the context of Shankaradeva's movement the opposition Brahmans/non-Brahmans has become unmediated, which was never the situation in any bhaktic movement of classical Hinduism.

2.3.2.3. The second and comparatively late tendency is monotheism. That is, no longer a kind of Shankarean non-duality (*advaita*), but an unambiguous uniqueness of one god (*ekavāda*), which seems to be the central point in the theology of the modern adepts of Shankaradeva, and which makes the whole movement overtly reformist. The fact that some rites are rejected as brahmanical, while some specifically brahmanical rituals are performed by non-Brahmans as non-brahmanical, shows that we are dealing with a religious attitude which could have developed only given the decline or disappearance of such particularly Hindu structures of religious consciousness as both duality and non-duality. Monotheism of the reformed Assamese Vaishnavas is not a structure of religious consciousness terminologically speaking, but merely a theological postulate entirely alien to the very spirit of Hinduism before the eighteenth century.

2.3.2.4. Another interesting moment in Cantlie's description of this movement is that the category of holy (as opposed to unholy) seems to be totally irreducible here either to pure or, least of all, to sacred. This category evokes certain puritanical associations. As the whole body of Hindu texts is reduced to the *Bhāgavata Purāṇa*, so the whole variety of Hindu paths is reduced to *one* kind of Vaishnava *bhakti*. The contexts in which term 'holiness' figures indicate that its use is markedly inner, i.e. within their own path only. The classical relativism of the term 'path' (*patha*, *mārga*) therefore disappears and certain Vedic rituals also disappear or become irrelevant.[27] This reduction of Hinduism to reformed and impoverished bhagavatism is only one side of the religious situation in this movement. The other is that it obviously failed (unlike all varieties of Tantrism and some other *bhakti* movements) to develop in any significant degree religious practices and symbolism of its own.

2.4. *Symbolism and Symbolic Representation*

Comments on Inden's paper

2.4.1.0. Inden states that in Vaishnava and Shaiva ritual discourse from the eighth to the twelfth centuries 'every conceivable category of thing, place, animal, and person had its lord'. From the point of view of the phenomenology of religion, this statement is tantamount to saying that in Hinduism 'lordship' is one of the universal symbols in the sense that, though used in the context of a certain discourse (in this case a ritual one), these symbols have meaning that exceeds the limits of this, as well as any other, discourse. (It should be noted that the sphere of usability, or the pragmatic aspect of symbols, does not and cannot coincide with their sphere of meaning, i.e. the semantic aspect of symbols.) Inden's term 'ritual discourse' can be understood, with some reservations, as equivalent to the interpretation of ritual or—if we revert to the terminology proposed at the beginning of these remarks—as the interpretation of a religious situation in the sense of a structure of religious consciousness.

2.4.1.1. In his investigation of various religious ideas and practices connected with the symbolism of lordship, Inden singles out a series of qualities, properties and functions which can, as it were, be equated with lord. On some of these equations we are now going to concentrate.

The first proposition of this kind can be formulated as follows: the greatest of lords, such as Vishnu and Shiva, are invisible and thereby endowed with an ontological status. Here we face a major methodological difficulty: what in fact is invisible or imperceptible? Is it the concrete god Shiva as the object of a cult and the focus and target of a religious situation? Or is it his symbolic overlordship? It can be asserted that in the context of any Hindu ritual (not philosophic discourse) a god is an ontological entity—either as such or through some other ontological entity (such as *ātman-brahman*). But this alone does not determine the ontological status of a symbolic representation of the god in question, especially as there are often two or more symbols combined together within one ritual context. The Bodhi-tree and empty throne in Buddhism or the dancing and skulls in Shiva-Nataraja are cases in point. It would be impossible for anyone to define which of them is of a higher ontological status.[28] What therefore we are dealing with is the ontology of symbolic representations of gods, and not with the ontology of gods themselves. Or, more exactly, we can say that we are dealing with the symbolic representations of gods, and not with the ontology of gods themselves. Or, more exactly, we can say that we are dealing with the symbolic representation of certain ontological entities manifested as gods.

2.4.1.2. We can now return to the question of imperceptibility and answer it in the following way: lordship as the symbol of worldly or spiritual power can figure as an imperceptible symbol or even be physically absent. The frontier between worldly (*laukika*) and spiritual (*dharma*) is extremely thin, if indeed it exists at all, in the context of a symbolic discourse. In saying this, we are aware of the differences between the Buddha and Yudhishthira, though both were called King of Dharma. The latter was the best of the actual kings of the world whereas the former, having been the potential ruler of the universe (a fact stressed by his kingly origin), became the spiritual emperor. The Buddha's lordship is by no means metaphoric, for the symbol of the empty throne itself clearly shows the concrete absence of worldly power and its substitution by dharmic power: the throne is, at one and the same time, the imperceptible symbol of the latter and a perceptible symbol of the former.[29] The very emptiness of the throne is not a negation of worldly powers, but a totally independent symbolic representation.[30]

2.4.1.3. Following the general scheme proposed by Daniélou (1964), Inden tries to establish what can be called a universal correlation of overlordship with practically all elements of Hindu cosmology and primarily with *dharma*. It is in this connection that the main difficulty arises for, if considered as correlated, these two notions seem to be highly ambivalent and their correlation assumes different meanings in the context of different structures of religious consciousness. In the context of classical Southern Shaivism, for example, Shiva Nataraja, whose domain is the arena of the universe (to which he is related as male to female), rules over *dharma* which practically figures as a secondary and subordinated entity (i.e. one of the elements constituting the socio-cultural subsystem of the universe). Whereas in the Mahabharata, when Krishna-Vasudeva figures as the 'highest person' (*puruṣottama*) of the universe, he has *dharma* as his immediate domain. In other words, he is bigger than *dharma*, for it is his *dharma*, while in the previous example of Shiva Nataraja it is the *dharma* of the social macrocosm only. In the case of Buddhism, however, the term *dharmarāja*, when applied to the Buddha, means his identification with *buddha-dharma*. And finally, in the case of King Yudhishthira it is no more than an epithet denoting his subordination to *dharma*. On the whole it can be said that *dharma* and overlordship each possesses its own symbolism. (One could illustrate this further with reference to the empty throne, the wheel, and the Bodhi-tree which in the early Buddhist context symbolized overlordship, *dharma* and awakening respectively.)

2.4.1.4. The world of Hindu symbolism is present to an external observer as a class of correlations and correspondences which are achronic *par excellence*. Here temporal successions are substituted merely by structural sequences and everything is repeated and repeatable, given that all symbols retain, as it were, their constant *topos* as determined by the structure. It can be said that there is no absolute hierarchy in Hindu symbolism, for each symbol has the capacity of establishing a hierarchy of its own. In this connection Inden's attempt to oppose the 'mastery' of each *varṇa* to the 'lordship' of the Kshatriyas and Brahmans seems to be beside the point, for they constitute two intersecting hierarchies. What is more, the lordship of the two higher *varṇa* could, in its turn, be interpreted again as dharmic and kingly simultaneously. All this shows that, even when speaking of gods alone, lordship is no more than one of the ways of symbolic universalization in Hinduism.

2.4.2.0. The phenomenon of the parallelism of symbols is one of the most distinctive features of Hinduism and Indian civilization as a whole: the classical Hindu universe is simultaneously represented in several (always more than two) universal symbolisms. By symbolism we mean not only the symbol itself but all its variants: for example, the figure of swastika and the mantric term *svasti* are two variants of one and the same symbol.[31] Such symbolism includes all religious situations in which it is used and all structures of religious consciousness in the sense of which it can be interpreted. In this connection the very concept of semantics becomes extremely vague because if the symbol in question is a primary symbol, then it denotes everything (i.e. its designate is the whole universe) and its semantic field becomes infinite (i.e. the field does not exist for an external observer). In order to acquire its finiteness it must be placed in the context of some definite situation (a ritual, group of rituals, class of rituals) or structure of consciousness (a theory, conception, doctrine) where it realizes its interpretation. This interpretation, however, cannot be made in terms of direct denotation, but in terms of correspondences and correlations between the symbol and universe or between one symbol and another.*

**Note by Ronald Inden:* Piatigorsky treats the category of overlordship as a symbol; in my paper, however, I have avoided this term and have dealt instead with the concepts of mastery, lordship, and overlordship as constituent elements of the Indian world. These concepts also appear in the religious discourses of India, but they are not confined, as Wittgenstein would perhaps have it, to religious discourse. So far as symbol is concerned, the concept of symbol used by anthropologists and historians of religion is largely a creation of European Romanticism and is of very limited use in understanding ancient Indian ideas and institutions. Finally, to treat the concept of lordship as a symbol and, on top of that, to equate it with the emblems of itself (e.g. the empty throne) or of something else (e.g. the Bodhi tree) seems unnecessarily confusing.

Comments on Das's paper

2.4.2.1. Departing from Turner's bipolar scheme in which the semantic field of symbols is conceived in terms of 'human affective experience/socio-cultural norms and values' and in which the body figures as something pre-eminently 'human and natural', Das investigates 'the body as a central symbol in various systems of classification' and establishes another very important binary opposition: the body as a naturally given entity/the body as a culturally cognizable object (or the body as a 'system of meanings'). When the body 'ceases to be merely given', as she puts it, it starts functioning in ritual and myth as a 'cognitive vehicle of cosmo-political ideas'. In its analogy with the cosmos the microcosm of body is invested with the unique mode of construction of the universe. That is, it carries within itself not only all relevant elements of the cosmos but also—and this is far more important—the dynamic principle of its construction and reconstruction.[32] Das also states that the organic experiences of the body (as a symbol) are conceptualized by means of ritual imagery and not the other way round (as Turner contends). Furthermore it is ritual itself which can be read as if it were a 'text' containing the interpretation of body symbolism. Das goes on to argue that it is in ritual alone that the relation between the human body and the cosmos finds its theoretical understanding and explanation. She shows how such a relation can be realized from a series of very aptly analysed rituals, ritualized habits, and attitudes, starting with the consecration of the Hindu king and finishing with some individual rites connected with sexual experience. All these matters are treated by Das with great exactitude and sensitivity. We confine ourselves here to some of the methodological premises underlying the symbolic anthropology used in her article.

2.4.2.2. The symbolism of the body appears as a result of the interpretation of ritual by an external observer. This means—to paraphrase Das's words—that for a Hindu and external observer alike the body exists in its 'natural givenness' and it is its 'cultural meanings' that start to differ from one another. This proposition, in which the body is conceived as a symbol, is very difficult to prove because, if it is true, then the natural and cultural givenness of the body becomes a methodological impossibility—that is to say, the very symbolism of the body prevents us from seeing the body as being really real and changes it into a very complex concept the existence of which we still have to prove. There are additional reasons for being doubtful about this distinction between the naturalness of the body and its existence as a culturally cognizable object. First, the 'natural givenness' of the body is not immediately given to an external observer (be he an ethnographer, sociologist, or psychologist), for nature is as complex a concept as cultural meaning. Second, the very opposition 'nature/culture' is totally inapplicable to, as well as uninferable from, any Hindu interpretational context whatsoever. The latter point is of extreme importance because it is here that we see one of the main cultural differences between Hinduism and Christianity. The concept of *dharma* comprises not only 'all that must be' but also 'all that is'. In other words, *dharma* is the order of things as they are, where prescriptive is not opposed to descriptive. The so-called 'order of fishes' is a case of anarchy, disorder, or *adharma*, but not that of a natural state. That is to say, this order of fishes is opposed to the order of *sanātana-dharma*, but not because it is 'natural', or even more natural for that matter.

In some metaphysical contexts it is *svabhāva* that plays the role of 'individual nature', though it is not opposed here to *svadharma* but rather complements it on the level of maximal cultural individuation. However, it can also be suggested that sexual enjoyment (*kāma*) is not opposed to the sinless and pure desire to beget a child as a natural bodily tendency to the cultural ritualism of *dharma*. On the contrary, what we have here is the wholeness of dharmic interpretation in the context of which each state or status of the body can find its own place.[33] We entirely agree with Das that body symbolism is derived from the interpretation of certain rituals, but we do not think that any concept of the body as a thing could have existed outside a ritualistic context. We even go so far as to say that *dharma*, if looked at from an external point of view, functions simultaneously in three different ways: (1) it totalizes the ritual; (2) it differentiates or atomizes the ritual; and (3) it neutralizes the ritual. Within the context of one and the same situation, the semen (as part of the body) can be dharmically interpreted as pure (when synchronized with *dharma*), impure (when associated with sexual enjoyment), and neither pure not impure (when it does not belong to either of these two categories or, to use Das's terminology, when it belongs to another binary opposition). But the body as a whole remains, as it were, a potential symbolic field waiting to be differentiated, analysed (as in the ritual of the king's clay bath), and totalized in the 'system of [symbolic] relations'. This, however, leads to a further question: is the body as such (in other words, as a thing) a symbol in the totality of Hinduism?

2.4.2.3. The various different parts and functions of the body do indeed acquire their symbolic meanings in the context of Hindu ritual. The whole body, however, remains a kind of empty structure possessing an entirely abstract meaning of 'the whole' in its relation to the whole macrocosm (as in the case of the clay bath), or in its relation to the whole cosmos (as in the case of the body of Purusha or the sacrificial horse in the *Bṛhadāraṇyaka Upaniṣada*). In all three cases we have a system of universal correspondences (or 'relations' in Das's terms) which might be treated as symbolic ones, but which cannot be regarded as symbols proper, for symbols are concrete things endowed with concrete meanings, however universal these meanings may be.

Thus in the system of correspondences in the King's clay bath, 'loins' correspond to 'courtesan's doorway' (in exactly the same manner as 'hind part' of the sacrificial horse corresponds to 'setting sun') and symbolizes in Inden's interpretation sexual potency in the ritual reconstruction of the king's body. But this does not enable us to infer, even in the context of this ritual alone, that the new body of the king is the symbol of his new person (*puruṣa*). For such a symbolization can only be indirectly deduced from an interpretation of the ritual of the king's clay bath (while the symbolization of the cosmos as sacrificial horse is directly given in the ritual itself of *aśvamedha*).

It is methodologically important to note here that the mere postulation of a system of meanings ascribed to a symbolic object (in this case the body) does not imply that any other object conceived as a part of the former can be interpreted as an element of this system. Das includes sexual intercourse and semen in the 'symbolic system of body' for the merely logical reason that they are related to the body as the parts to the whole, ignoring the fact that they may have a symbolism of their own (which, in fact, they do and not in Tantrism alone). So, neither *yoni* nor *liṅga*, taken as symbols, which indeed they are, belong, symbolically speaking, to the body; rather it is the other way round. The body, on the other hand, is entirely devoid of that concreteness, 'thing-ness', so to speak, that makes an object a symbol.[34]

One last methodological remark. From the point of view of European culture (in so far as this can be ascribed to an external observer), a symbol is a cultural phenomenon. What we now call Hinduism never included or implied this point of view, for it presupposes an epistemological position which did not exist in Hinduism till as late as probably the eighteenth century. What Das had succeeded in doing is to make a 'cultural' analysis of symbolic phenomena which were never, in Hinduism itself, opposed to things (as Hindu Knowledge was never opposed to Truth, contrary to the cultural epistemological position). Even in Plato symbols were pre-cultural, while in Hinduism they remained entirely outside the whole of cultural problematics. That is why to 'reconstruct' their cultural meaning may be culturally justifiable, but it is methodologically superfluous.*

**Note by Veena Das:* For many years now, anthropologists and indologists have contended that the opposition of nature and culture is neither ontologically nor methodologically valid for Hindu thought. It does not come as a great surprise, therefore, when Piatigorsky asserts that this distinction is methodologically superfluous. I think it is obvious from my paper that we are dealing with the body as an imaged object and not as image *versus* object. It is from this perspective that I had explicitly stated that nature may be viewed as a cultural construction, and that the image of the body and its functions derives from the cosmology and not the other way round.

On the specific points made by Piatigorsky, it needs to be emphasized that the clay bath of the king is a *saṃskāra*, which is classified as a *puruṣāratha*, that which is for the sake of the person. It will not do, therefore, to dismiss this by saying that the king does not emerge as a *puruṣa*. What is interesting about the *saṃskāra* which are classified as *puruṣārtha* is that they posit a movement from one kind of body to another kind of body, and not from body to soul, or from nature to culture. In the context of various rituals it is emphasized that the body which emerges after the appropriate *saṃskāra* must not be polluted by the everyday functions (*nitya karma*) to which one is subjected simply because one has a body.

Finally, a remark on the 'methodological' point made by Piatigorsky that symbols are not opposed to things in Hindu epistemology and therefore a 'cultural' analysis of symbolic phenomena is superfluous. It is not clear to me whether he is opposing cultural analysis to phenomenological analysis. At any rate, it seems to me necessary to allow a dialogue to emerge between the epistemological position about the body in Hindu thought, and the body in anthropological discourse, if Indian anthropologists are not to become completely parochial. I am not sure that guidelines for such a dialogue have emerged from Piatigorsky's extremely stimulating comments, but one hopes that a beginning has been made.

3. Conclusion

3.0. The material discussed theoretically in these remarks indicates the highly specific character of Indian religion as a whole and the need for a phenomenological approach designed to reveal this specificity. The application of a universalist methodology, though not totally useless, is necessarily limited by the very character of the Indian context. It would therefore be far more economic to start any phenomenological investigation of Indian religion by working out the categories and terms of description which are, at the least, congruent with its specificity.

The following points seem to be of particular importance in such an investigation. First, from the very 'start' of its history Indian religion was characterized by an enormously developed ritualism so that its subsequent stages are marked by the interpretation of rituals rather than by their functional or technical specialization. Second, any particular religious tradition in ancient and mediaeval India came into existence against the background of an enormous and unparalleled proliferation of religious texts. Third, Indian mythology, however rich and diverse, has never figured as the content element in relation to ritual. On the contrary, it often figures as no more than an outer framework of tradition, autonomous of the theoretical interpretation of the rituals involved (theoretical, that is, in terms of religious philosophy and not of theology). Fourth, the extraordinary vitality and tenacity of religious symbolism in India resulted in a phenomenon, probably unique among the religions of the world, in which symbols and symbolic situations were ritualized (rather than the much commoner phenomenon of the symbolization of rituals). This is especially characteristic of Tantrism, both Hindu and Buddhist, in which the whole system of religious situations is based upon symbolism, in which the rituals exemplify the symbols, and the interpretation of symbols outweighs the mythology. Fifth, Indian religion is probably the only religion in the world which has been able to produce and develop within itself its own objective theoretical awareness of itself. The speculative structures of consciousness whereby religion was analysed did not become separated from or opposed to religion itself. This resulted historically in an almost unique phenomenon of religious philosophy equally distinct and distant from theology as from scientific philosophy based on epistemological premises. This last point makes an investigation of Indian religion particularly difficult, for we are dealing with an object which has, as it were, already been investigated by itself.

NOTES

1 In spite of the position taken above, it should be noted that the differentiation of consciousness is chiefly an empirical matter: we always experience it as such. But, both conceptually and semantically, it is possible to envisage a state of pure consciousness, neither subjective nor objective, which is either without content or, at most, contains a matrix of unmanifested proto-thoughts. *Átman-brahman* appears to correspond to such an undifferentiated state which, in itself, is not opposed to any 'different content' (or 'structure') of consciousness and remains an absolutely positive religious postulate. Speaking generally, it is to be doubted whether it is possible to formulate any structure of religious consciousness, ancient or modern alike, in terms of a negative or oppository statement. Thus, when Kolakovsky (1982:220) reflects that, 'in addition to all needs ... related to ... our aspiration for individual and collective survival, there are needs which cannot be explained ... in such terms', his statement cannot be referred to a concrete structure of consciousness. For this is a typically *secondary* reflection on a *non-religious* idea, made from the position of 'no structure of religious consciousness.'

2 More exactly, it can be said that in Hinduism there is only one war, unique and unrepeatable: that chronicled in the Mahabharata. Each great religion has a kind of historical mythology in which war features as a sacred event where the destinies of men are not only mixed with those of the gods but where they find a certain common ground. Thus the Great War described in the Mahabharata, like the Trojan War, required the participation of all important gods. But while the Trojan War—as well as war in the Celtic epics, the Edda, and the holy and unholy wars in the Bible—was regarded as a repeatable event which shaped the pattern of all future wars, the Great War of the Mahabharata was deemed unique and unrepeatable so that by comparison with it all other wars became superfluous and meaningless. This view is connected both with the degeneration associated with patterning in Hindu mythology and with its cyclical nature. In the context of a given Yuga the very reality of the Great War meant that all other wars were unreal. War therefore does not exist as a religious phenomenon, in the sense that we can say that it is sacred, just or unjust, because all other wars are without ethical status. That is why Gandhi himself regarded *satyagraha* as a metaphor of war, following the Hindu or Buddhist idea of war as a conflict within the self rather than between one person and another.

The terms 'Hindu' and 'Hinduism' are used in this article in a merely methodological sense. That is to say, only as a common mark of *their own* differentiating self-awareness, given to an external observer of Indian religion (in accordance with a general idea of S.C.R. Weightman; see also W.C. Smith 1964:115).

3 What seems to an external observer to be the central point or core of the religion observed is often no more than the result of an analysis of one

religion by another, produced within an objective religious situation. For instance, when we read of the predominantly ritualistic or sacrificial character of Vedic religion with rite (*yajña*) as its core and 'the principle of rite' (*ṛta*) as its central structure, we usually lose sight of the fact that these concepts are given to us through the objective situations described, not in the Rig Veda, but in the Brahmanas and Upanishads. The detailed reflexive analysis of the Vedic cult as a 'natural' religion made in the Upanishads established the relative values of *yajña* and *ṛta* and gave them their meaning and value as related to *ātman*. Whereas, if observed in itself and investigated in terms of its inner reconstruction, Rig Veda would reveal *ṛta*, not *yajña*, as the nearest equivalent of the term religion (which was suggested by Renou and explicitly stated by Malamoud). In this case *yajña* can be seen as hierarchically subordinated to the level of *ṛta* which comprises the whole ritually organized universe, figuring as the central structure of religious consciousness and opposed to *yajña* as a ritual itself. But, however universal the meaning of *ṛta*, it could never have applied to any situation other than that of Vedic religion; that is why it was never used as the metaconcept of religion, or even of sacrifice or worship. While, if we return to the early prose Upanishads, we find *yajña* functioning as a metaconcept for the description of Vedic religion and not of Upanishadic religion.

4 Three things can be identified in this structure of religious consciousness: (1) *ātman-brahman*—the principle of self; (2) all living beings, which are *ātman-brahman*—the individual self; and (3) knowledge of this relationship (*ātmabrahmavidyā*)—the Universal Operator, called knowledge or self-awareness, which connects the two. Religion can be conceived as a space within which this triple relation (*religio*) is realized. It is a relation in which nothing is left out and thereby universal. Because it is determined at each point of space by knowledge, what we are dealing with here is an ontology of knowledge, and not an ontology of being. The identity of the individual self and the universal self exists in the knowledge of this fact and exists nowhere else, so that the knowledge of *ātman-brahman* is, in a way, *ātman-brahman* itself.

5 See note 4 above on this point. The principle of *ātman*, though implying the essential distinctions of the cosmic order, explicitly figures, at any rate in the Upanishads and Mahabharata, as the central unifying principle. It is the term and concept of *dharma*, however, which denotes the structure of religious consciousness in terms of which *all* religious situations encountered in the Upanishads and Mahabharata find their interpretation. In *dharma* we find, first of all, the explicitly manifested principle of distinction with respect to the whole socio-cultural universe. And second, in *dharma*, understood as a structure of religious consciousness, we deal with the entirety of the universe, comprising all distinctions, rules and exceptions. For, dharmically speaking, it is 'religion' (in the sense of *dharma*) which unites all beings with the universe, and it is *dharma* itself which establishes levels and gradations of all beings in all religious situations in respect of *ātman*. Returning to the procedure of identification in 1.0–1.1, we can see that *dharma* is the nearest possible equivalent to 'religion', at least in the context of the early prose Upanishads.

6 The earliest Buddhist oral tradition cannot be reduced to that which was called *buddha-vācana* (the Buddha's authentic sayings) because a dominant role was played by the complex and complicated methods of remembering, recollecting, and reproducing both the content of instruction and the methods of instruction. This can be seen in the *Abhidhamma* with its special system of mnemonic-eidetic methodology in which acts of instruction, apprehension, and transmission coincide with and are merged into each other. Even in the context of *buddha-vācana* it was the idea of the authenticity of the teaching (*dhamma*) which must have prevailed, not the idea of the text itself (*sāsana*). It is only in the early Mahayana Sutras, not to mention the *Prajñāpāramitā*, that the text of a *sūtra* assumed its universal religious meaning in such notions as *sutrānta* and, particularly, *dharmaparyāya*, and much later that the idea of scripture (*āgama*) became for the Buddhists of Sri Lanka the basis of identification not only of Buddhism but of all other religions as seen from the point of view of Buddhism.

7 Although the master may gather round himself a company of pupils, he does not address them as a company but speaks to only one at a time. The situation of instruction, therefore, whether in the context of a tradition or of a religious situation, is always that of one teacher imparting knowledge to one pupil, and the presence of other listeners does not affect the personalized nature of this dyadic relationship.

8 This is the position taken by Lévi-Strauss when he states that the main meaning of tradition is preservation of the *status quo* in a culture or society, whence his dual classification of civilizations into traditional and modern.

9 Vedic ritualism underwent a development—one might say over-development – to the point that the sacrifice assumed enormous complexity and importance, and all beings were classified by their relation to it. Thus the classical Vedic Brahman was identified in the Rig Veda, and particularly in the Yajur-Vedic tradition, as a sacrificer first of all, there being too many gods to whom sacrifice was directed for any one of them to serve as the primary basis of identification. The distinction between subject and object of cult, however, remains in the background and, in my view, was probably dominant at an earlier period.

10 Even if such a subjective identification as 'a Christian is a soul' is dogmatically justifiable (let us remember the Pascalean 'each soul is a Christian'), to identify a Hindu worshipper with an *ātman* would be nonsense.

11 One has constantly to bear in mind that the frontier between philosophy and religion in Buddhism is far more fragile, vague, and undetectable than in Hinduism. The very term *darśana* – so precisely defined in Hinduism – is in Buddhism no more than an approximate indication of the differences between Sutras and Shastras, and can hardly be applied to the genuine *Abhidamma*.

12 This level is described in detail in the *Thera-and-therī Gāthā*.

13 This is discussed at length in an excellent paper by Pallis (1964:85–87) who regards *asaṅkhata dhamma* as the 'final objectivity' in Buddhism.

14 This is succintly demonstrated by the abhidhammic classification of the *jhāna* and the corresponding states of consciousness (*dhamma*) into form (*rūpa*), formless (*arūpa*), and supramundane (*lokuttara*).

15 In late Vedic literature the hierarchy of 'Brahmanism proper' only partly

coincided with that of 'asceticism', whereas in early historical Buddhism the yogic (dhyanic) hierarchy appeared as almost entirely separated both from the hierarchy of ascetic perfection and from that of perfect knowledge (de la Valée Poussin 1958:7). It is probably the ideal Brahman of the *Dhammapada* who figures as a mere religious abstraction in the multi-directedness of Buddhist hierarchization. The most intriguing thing about this brahmanship is that it can be deemed a structure of consciousness in which the object of religious experience is not opposed to its subject. What is more, they are probably one and the same thing.

16 This ascetic negativism was so strong in early mediaeval Jainism that it seems to account for the comparatively lenient, or even neutral, stand of Jainism with respect to at least some kinds of socio-cultural values and activities.

17 We are strongly inclined to understand the term 'reincarnation' in as literal a sense as possible. For instance, the preservation of the semen of the prophet Zarathustra at the bottom of a mountain lake until the end of the aeon does not fall under this rubric, for as a structure of religious consciousness reincarnation implies, at the very least, one moment of total 'disincarnation' or disembodiment, without which it would lose all its concreteness.

18 Reincarnation is, in our opinion, one of the universals of religious consciousness while *karma* remains a specifically Indian phenomenon.

19 We do not know to what extent, if at all, the Aghoris can be called Tantrists. They do not seem to possess any Shaiva Tantras of their own. Concerning 'all-the-sameness', see Dasgupta 1950:202–3.

20 Conze (1962:73) writes: 'In Buddhism physical and spiritual reality are coterminous, all spiritual experiences have their physical basis and counterpart.'

21 Another extremely interesting point in Bradford's investigation is that the religious symbolism of kingship belonged entirely to the 'outside section'. It evokes some specifically Buddhist associations in the sense of which the World Emperor (*lokacakkavattin*) is seen as the limit of the finite world.

22 See O'Flaherty 1976:5–8, who mistakenly equates theology with religious philosophy. The main formal difference between the two is that the first is based on the rules of inference from initial postulates whereas the second is based on the postulates themselves.

23 It can be conjectured that, when the texts are oral, the discrepancy between them and the related rituals is much smaller. Agamic tradition, however, was almost certainly written from the beginning.

24 One cannot exclude the possibility that in the past some of the basic rituals might have been developed from textual interpretations of religious symbols. That is, that some texts might have contained instructions about how to realize these symbols practically in meditation, yoga, ritual, etc.

25 This is particularly obvious in the case of Swaminarayan's movement (Dave 1974:81–92).

26 In the sense that, when performing these rites a Brahman does not function as a Brahman (Gupta, Hoens and Goudriaan 1979:18–19, 121–143).

27 One may conjecture that Vedic rituals are rejected, not only because of

their 'brahmanism', but also—or even primarily—because of their general (i.e. Hindu) character and function.

28 In the framework of Indian religion as a whole there is always a hierarchy of ontological entities rather than a simple category of the ontological as in modern Christian theology. In this connection see Conze 1962:24–5.

29 We have doubts about the use of the term 'empty', for the throne *is* and its emptiness is a purely logical deduction from a nonexistent premise. The throne as a symbol of power—of practically undifferentiated power—is often complemented by the purely spiritual symbol of the Bodhi-tree, a fact which is very significant for our understanding of the dual symbolism of power.

30 It is, however, uncertain whether or not the empty throne can be regarded as a primary symbol like the lotus or the *liṅga* itself.

31 In this case we can consider the left-hand and right-hand swastikas as two positional subvariants of one and the same figurative variant of a symbol named swastika. By positional we mean that they occupy two different positions in one system of co-ordinates. It follows that their interpretation is confined to one and the same set of meanings.

32 It must be emphasized that reconstruction has nothing to do with cosmogony, which has far less importance in Hindu contexts than cosmology.

33 This idea derives directly from the concept of *ethos* introduced by Stenzler (1865:151–6) in connection with the *Gṛhya Sūtras*. From the point of view of *ethos*, as we understand it, a ritual may include in itself its own interpretation.

34 In the case of *liṅga* we have an extraordinary transformability of its material which shows the direction of symbolization. In contrast with the passage in the *Bṛhadāranyaka Upaniśad* cited above ('The dawn is the head of the sacrificial horse . . .'), we read in a modern Lingayat pamphlet: 'Lord Basava, the founder of Lingayatism, formed the *iṣṭaliṅga* in the shape of the universe' (Swami Lingananda 1973:68–9). In other words, *liṅga* is like the universe, not the other way round. One of the leaders of the modern Lingayats, Her Holiness Mother Mahadevi (who was a student of mine at one time) referred to the concrete thing *liṅga* that she wore as the 'god', and not as an image of the god.

REFERENCES

Bhagavad Gītā 1979. Commentary by R. S. Zaehner. Oxford: Univ. Press.

Chattopadhyaya, S. 1978. *Reflections on the Tantras*. Delhi: Motilal Banarsidass.

Conze, E. 1962. *Buddhist thought in India*. London: Allen & Unwin.

Daniélou, A. 1964. *Hindu polytheism*. London: Routledge & Kegan Paul.

Dasgupta, S. B. 1950. *An introduction to Tantric Buddhism*. Calcutta: Univ. Press.

Dave, H. T. 1974. *Life and philosophy of Shree Swaminarayan (1781–1830)*. Ed. Leslie Shepherd. London: Allen & Unwin.

Dhammapada 1881. Trans. F. Max Muller. Oxford: Clarendon Press.
Gupta, S., Hoens, D. J. & Goudriaan, T. 1979. *Hindu Tantrism*. Leiden: Brill.
Kolakovsky, L. 1982. *Religion*. London: Fontana.
Leach, E. 1969. *Genesis as myth*. London: Jonathan Cape.
Leuba, J. H. 1926. *The psychology of religious mysticism*. New York: Harcourt, Brace.
Lingananda, Swami 1973. *Emblem of God*. Bangalore: J. Akkamahedevi Ashrama.
Malamoud, Ch. 1977. *Le śrādhyāya, récitation personelle du Veda*. Paris: Univ. Press.
O'Flaherty, W. 1976. *The origins of evil in Hindu mythology*. Berkeley & Los Angeles: Univ. of California Press.
Pallis, M. 1964. The veil of the temple. *Tomorrow*, 12.
Renou, L. 1955. *Études vedíques et pāninéennes*, XV. Paris: L'Institut de Civilisation Indienne.
—— 1956. *Hymnes speculatifs du Veda*. Paris: Gallimard.
Smith, W.C. 1964. *The meaning and end of religion*. New York: New American Library.
Stenzler, A. F. 1865. Über die Sitte. *Abhandlunger für die Kunde des Morgenlandes*, 4, 149–163.
Upanishads: The Principal Upanishads 1953. Ed. S. P. Radhakrishnan. London: Allen & Unwin.
Zaehner, R. C. 1966. *Hinduism*. London: Oxford Univ. Press.
—— 1972. *Hindu scriptures*. London: Everyman's Library.